COVERING
AMERICA'S
COURTS

"If a textbook could teach how to report then Toni Locy would write it. Her career both in the newsroom and classroom has taught her how to nail a story on deadline—whether from a trusted source or a document hidden in a government agency. Getting it first and getting it right has been her hallmark as a reporter, and if those gifts can be taught, it's in this book."

—Stephen Kurkjian, a three-time Pulitzer Prize-winning reporter
and editor of the *Boston Globe*'s Spotlight team

"Toni Locy is one of the nation's most gifted, tenacious court reporters. Her ability to track down records, persuade court clerks to release information, cultivate sources, and make a very complicated justice system comprehensible to the public is unrivaled. Her textbook will prepare young journalists to follow in her footsteps. It has a logical format, explains court procedures in plain English, and uses fascinating examples from her own career to illustrate various reporting principles. It will become THE textbook for journalism teachers looking for a way to teach students to cover our complicated justice system."

—Lucy Dalglish, dean of the University of Maryland's
Philip Merrill College of Journalism

"In an era of deep uncertainty about the changing nature of journalism, Toni Locy—widely admired at the top of the profession for so long—provides a critical contribution as to what values need to endure and should be taught to all journalism students. Along with this, the book is a thorough run-through of the practicalities of the craft from an honorable and experienced practitioner."

—Neil Lewis, a former senior correspondent for *The New York Times*

COVERING
AMERICA'S
COURTS

This book is part of the Peter Lang Media and Communication list.
Every volume is peer reviewed and meets
the highest quality standards for content and production.

PETER LANG
New York • Washington, D.C./Baltimore • Bern
Frankfurt • Berlin • Brussels • Vienna • Oxford

Toni Locy

Covering America's Courts

A Clash of Rights

PETER LANG
New York • Washington, D.C./Baltimore • Bern
Frankfurt • Berlin • Brussels • Vienna • Oxford

Library of Congress Cataloging-in-Publication Data
Locy, Toni.
Covering America's courts: a clash of rights / Toni Locy.
p. cm.
Includes bibliographical references and index.
1. Courts—United States.
2. Justice, Administration of—United States. I. Title.
KF8719.L63   347.73'1—dc23   2012041678
ISBN 978-1-4331-1450-2 (hardcover)
ISBN 978-1-4331-1449-6 (paperback)
ISBN 978-1-4539-0975-1 (e-book)

Bibliographic information published by **Die Deutsche Nationalbibliothek.**
Die Deutsche Nationalbibliothek lists this publication in the "Deutsche
Nationalbibliografie"; detailed bibliographic data is available
on the Internet at http://dnb.d-nb.de/.

Author photo by Michael Todd; design by Michael McGuire
Cover photo: Photo of Betty Currie, used with permission from The Associated Press/AP Images

The paper in this book meets the guidelines for permanence and durability
of the Committee on Production Guidelines for Book Longevity
of the Council of Library Resources.

This book is dedicated to my

nephews Bryan, Daniel, Tyler,

Zachary and Dalton,

and my nieces Jordan and Delaney,

and it is in loving memory of

my youngest niece, Cameron,

my hero and my heart.

About the Cover

■ ■ ■

Betty Currie, President Bill Clinton's personal secretary, clutches her purse as she and her attorney, Lawrence Wechsler (left) are mobbed by the media outside the U.S. courthouse in Washington after her testimony before a federal grand jury on Jan. 27, 1998. The image, by Stephan Savoia, was part of a collection of photographs by the Associated Press that won the 1999 Pulitzer Prize for feature photography. The collection chronicled key events in Clinton's affair with White House intern Monica Lewinsky and his impeachment hearings.

Contents

■ ■ ■

Acknowledgments

■ ■ ■

I would like to thank my mother, Priscilla, my late grandmother, Nellie, and my sisters Joni, Tracey and Philimane, and brothers Howard and Ron for believing in me from the time I was eight years old and announced that I wanted to be a journalist when I grew up.

I also want to express my appreciation to my colleagues in Washington and Lee University's Department of Journalism and Mass Communications for their support and encouragement. I owe special thanks to Brian Richardson, the head of the department when I was hired, and Pam Luecke, who succeeded him.

And I am grateful to H.F. "Gerry" Lenfest for his generous gift to Washington and Lee that provides financial support for faculty and enabled me to spend two summers traveling and working on this book.

I, of course, must acknowledge my students at Washington and Lee. Each term, I've learned something new from you all about teaching.

Preface

■ ■ ■

Journalism is hard, intense work, but above everything else, it's supposed to be fun. Working as a reporter is a great job, and covering courts is one of the best beats in the news business.

By no means does this textbook tell you everything you need to know about covering courts in the United States. My goal was to provide you with a basic understanding of the law and journalism that you can use to report stories that tell your readers, viewers and listeners whether their legal system is worthy of respect.

We are a nation of people who are obsessed with crime and the law. We are devoted viewers of *Law and Order*, *CSI* and other cops-and-robbers television shows. We can't help but watch lawyers scream at each other on cable TV, as they argue about the quality of evidence in high-profile trials. When we slip and fall in the grocery store, we sue. When we cannot agree on what society should value, from gay rights to a woman's right to choose whether to have a baby, we turn to the courts to solve our moral conundrums. The law has permeated American life so thoroughly that knowledge of the courts and legal principles is essential for any reporter, whether you cover sports, business, entertainment or politics.

To cover courts, reporters must understand that they serve as a check on the enormous power wielded by the players in the American justice system. This book introduces undergraduate and graduate journalism students, bloggers and citizen journalists to the U.S. court system, its players, its language and its impact on the public. I offer advice on how to find stories in the courts and how to read legal documents and make sense of them to write accurate, fair, clear and compelling stories for mass audiences.

My intention is not to look back at my experiences as the glory days of journalism, but to encourage and challenge future reporters to build on what my generation accomplished and to address our shortcomings, particularly by repairing the relationship the press has with the public. The Internet is not the enemy. In fact, it could save journalism because it provides a worldwide platform for members of the traditional and new news media to reveal injustice and right wrongs. Democracy can benefit from the increasing number of voices in cyberspace, but people who want to be taken seriously as journalists should know what they're talking about. It doesn't matter whether stories appear on newsprint, are broadcast over airwaves or are accessed by a cell phone or tablet. What matters is that good stories are told. Technology will continue to change, but the standards for a good story should not.

The public has always loved trials involving the rich and famous. In response, editors and reporters have treated celebrity trials like sporting events by using so-called experts on the law to oversimplify and exaggerate developments into screaming sound bites. Singer Michael Jackson's molestation case received far more attention than the Bush administration's efforts to create a separate court system for suspected terrorists held at Guantanamo Bay, Cuba.

This isn't new. But reporters must be more than surrogate voyeurs for the public; they also must serve as the people's watchdog on power.

Covering courts isn't for wimps. You cannot be afraid to go nose-to-nose with a federal judge who is trying to kick you out of a courtroom so he can conduct the people's business in secret, or bully you into divulging the names of your sources. I believe journalism—and covering courts, in particular—is a calling to public service. Courthouse beat reporters keep cops, prosecutors and judges on their toes simply by being in the building. If officials know they're being watched—or could be—they tend to behave themselves a little better.

I have divided the textbook into four sections, each of which includes three chapters. The first section, "Breaking the Law and News," introduces students to the courts, the law and the players in the criminal justice system. The second section, "Chasing Paper and People," explains how to find and interpret key documents, and one of the chapters deals with the workhorse of the law, state courts and the cases they handle, including capital murder. The third section, "Pressing the Bench," walks the reader through criminal and civil trials that occur if the parties fail to reach plea bargains or settlements. Section IV, "Balancing the Checks," covers secrecy and terrorism, and culminates with the U.S. Supreme Court, which gets the last word on American law.

In 25 years as a reporter, I learned many valuable lessons that I share with you in this book, and I offer the following pieces of advice:

- Resist the urge to simplify and exaggerate. Choose substance over superficiality by digging deeper and by making one more phone call.
- Stay humble. Don't get cocky, because the journalism gods will sucker punch you if given a chance. Understand that you probably won't know about all of the evidence that police and prosecutors have gathered. You won't know everything a defense attorney knows about his client. And you won't know all of a judge's reasons for making a decision.
- Be curious.
- Dare to be different by refusing to follow the pack's "conventional" wisdom. When other reporters swarm one way, strike out on your own in the opposite direction.
- Make your readers, viewers and listeners laugh. Make them cry. Make them angry. Make them care.
- Seek the truth.
- Change the world.

And, as they say in professional baseball, don't let them throw any cheese by you.

Toni Locy
Lexington, Virginia
July 30, 2012

· *Part* ·

Breaking the Law
and News

Covering Courts in a High-Tech, Celebrity-Obsessed World

■ ■ ■

Of the tens of thousands of cases that pass through American courts every day, most are routine and unremarkable. In the past, only people who lived near the scenes of sensational crimes usually paid attention to what happened in court. They read their hometown paper, watched the local TV news or ventured into the courthouse. Cable TV and the Internet have transformed the way people learn about high-profile crimes and follow trials and how they increasingly interact with information about those cases. Today, millions of people around the world keep track of developments in a case via computers, tablets or cell phones, even though they have no geographic or emotional connection to a crime, its victim or the defendant. Emboldened by their cyber powers, average citizens participate in the news, adding their opinions and, in some cases, personal knowledge about a crime to comments tacked on to stories.

The law is a high-stakes function of government: A person's freedom or life is at stake. That means the police, prosecutors, judges, defense attorneys and reporters have a great deal of power and much in common. Journalists and lawyers love facts and evidence. In both roles, information is marshaled into cohesive, compelling tales: The journalist writes a story. The lawyer writes a lawsuit, brief or court opinion. Yet there is often disagreement between the two groups on what—and when—the public should learn about pending cases.

Judges need to be obeyed, but they don't have armies to enforce their orders. To be effective, they need the public to believe they are above politics and deserve respect as independent guardians of justice. Prosecutors are supposed to protect the public with their power to initiate investigations and hold accountable citizens who break the rules. Defense attorneys are expected to represent their clients zealously but ethically. Jurors are supposed to be impartial as they sit in judgment of members of the community. Journalists need to be unbiased, fair and accurate to make all of it work. They must be relentless in questioning officials about use of the government's wide-ranging power to subpoena Americans to testify against one another, to search citizens' homes and offices, to peek at email and listen to phone conversations. Reporters must remain skeptical of what they are told by police, prosecutors, defense attorneys and judges to avoid being used to smear a target of a misguided investigation for political gain, or pressure a suspect into cooperating.

It is important to remember that the American justice system is not as good as it is on TV. The overwhelming majority of crimes are not solved by good-looking CSIs who work in fancy, high-tech labs, or by police detectives with obsessive-compulsive disorders. Most crimes in America are solved when police extract confessions from the usual suspects. Not all Americans are athletes or actors who misbehave and get into trouble. But, as you will discover in this chapter, the privileged few receive the most attention, and coverage of their cases affects the way the courts deal with journalists and the public in all other matters of lesser interest but equal importance.

Feeding Frenzies: From Jesus to O.J.

> Now the chief priests, the elders, and all the council sought false testimony against Jesus to put Him to death, but found none. Even though many false witnesses came forward, they found none. But at last two false witnesses came forward and said, "This fellow said, 'I am able to destroy the temple of God and to build it in three days.'" And the high priest arose and said to Him, "Do You answer nothing? What is it these men testify against You?" But Jesus kept silent. And the high priest answered and said to Him, "I put You under oath by the living God: Tell us if You are the Christ, the Son of God!" Jesus said to him, "It is as you said. Nevertheless, I say to you, hereafter you will see the Son of Man sitting at the right hand of the Power, and coming on the clouds of heaven." Then the high priest tore his clothes, saying, "He has spoken blasphemy! What further need do we have of witnesses? Look, now you have heard His blasphemy! What do you think?" They answered and said, "He is deserving of death." —Matthew 26: 59–66 (*New King James Version*)

The richer, the more famous, the more reviled the defendant, the more likely the trial is to captivate the public's attention. According to the Bible, the trial of Jesus was a sham, orchestrated by a corrupt church and legal elites to eliminate the threat he posed to their power over the people. The theme is a simple one that repeats itself throughout history: Under the guise of law and order, political and religious leaders whip the public into a frenzy of fear and loathing of the accused.

From the nation's beginning, a trial was a social event that attracted people from miles away. Public hangings were as popular as picnics in certain parts of the country. In 1692, when several young girls accused women and men of witchcraft in Salem, Massachusetts, the crowd that gathered was so large, the hearing had to be relocated from a tavern to the bigger meetinghouse. People crammed into a courtroom to hear evidence against Lizzie Borden, the young Fall River, Massachusetts, woman accused of hacking her parents to death in 1892; and they stood for hours in the sweltering sun in Dayton, Tennessee, in 1925 for the Scopes "Monkey" Trial to witness the showdown over evolution between two titans of the time—political and religious leader William Jennings Bryan and renowned criminal defense attorney Clarence Darrow.

Trials with wealthy defendants have always been sure bets to draw a crowd, especially if their sexual habits were revealed. In 1906, Pittsburgh coal-and-railroad fortune heir Harry K. Thaw shot to death Stanford White, the nation's most famous architect, at the premiere of a musical on the rooftop of the old Madison Square Garden in New York. The murder case revealed the moral excesses of the Gilded Age, with accusations that the victim, a respected member of high society, had preyed on poor teenage chorus girls whom he plied with liquor and gifts in exchange for them taking rides while naked on a red-velvet swing in his penthouse apartment. One of them was Evelyn Nesbit, a poor but beautiful girl from Pittsburgh who became the equivalent of today's supermodel and was raped by Thaw and White. Even President Theodore Roosevelt followed newspaper coverage of the salacious details. The courtroom was packed with reporters who swarmed witnesses before and after they took the stand with the same aggressiveness we see today with paparazzi, and traditional and new media.

"A Roman Holiday"

By the 1950s, radio and TV changed news coverage of trials forever by providing the public with live accounts of dramatic testimony from those who witnessed murder and mayhem as well as spicy sound bites from grandstanding lawyers.

"Murder and mystery, society, sex and suspense were combined…in such a manner as to intrigue and captivate the public fancy to a degree unparalleled in recent annals," wrote the Ohio Supreme Court in 1956, describing the trial of a Cleveland surgeon convicted of killing his pregnant wife. "Special rooms in the Criminal Courts Building were equipped for broadcasters and telecasters. In this atmosphere of a 'Roman holiday' for the news media, Sam Sheppard stood trial for his life."

On July 4, 1954, Marilyn Sheppard was beaten to death in her bed. Her husband said he was asleep on a couch downstairs when it happened. By Christmas of that year, Dr. Sheppard was convicted in a court of law and the court of public opinion. The Sheppard case is one of the most enduring examples of what happens when the police, prosecutor, judge, jurors and journalists behave irresponsibly.

No one was innocent, with the possible exception of the defendant, who spent the next 12 years in prison until the U.S. Supreme Court ruled that he had been the victim of such heinous pretrial publicity that he was entitled to a new trial. The prosecutor was running for a judgeship. The judge was seeking re-election. The coroner was basking in the spotlight—and hugs and kisses from women after his performance in a raucous preliminary hearing.

In the role of responsible handmaiden to justice, reporters in Cleveland failed, as U.S. Supreme Court Justice Tom Clark described it in the high court's decision to order a new trial. Journalists pressured authorities into conducting a fast and flawed investigation. Louis B. Seltzer, editor of the *Cleveland Press,* published front-page editorials that taunted the police until they charged Sheppard with his wife's murder. On July 20, 1954, the editor alleged that "someone was getting away with murder" and accused police of favoritism toward Sheppard because of his wealth and status. The next day, Seltzer turned up the heat on the coroner, writing, "Why No Inquest? Do It Now, Dr. Gerber." In another front-page editorial on July 30, the headline screamed, "Why Isn't Sheppard in Jail?"

Seltzer, like other editors and reporters in Cleveland at the time, ignored several key provisions of the Bill of Rights. The editor attacked Sheppard for exercising his right to remain silent. Seltzer criticized Sheppard for hiring a smart lawyer, which was his prerogative under his right to counsel. The newsman also fumed that police had allowed Sheppard to remain "scot-free" during the investigation, contrary to his right to be considered innocent until proven guilty.

Run, O.J., Run

Forty years later, the trial of ex-football star O.J. Simpson dominated news coverage in newspapers and on network and cable television for 18 months after his estranged wife and a waiter were found stabbed to death outside her Los Angeles home. Simpson's trial in 1995 was broadcast on *Court TV* and marked a major change in news coverage of high-profile cases. The best part of the ubiquitous news coverage was that average Americans became interested in the courts and learned about the law. I remember overhearing two elderly women on the Metro in Washington as they debated the admissibility of various pieces of physical evidence. The downside of the coverage seemed to overwhelm its educational value. Cable television, with its 24-hours-a-day, seven-days-a-week format, needed to fill airtime, and the O.J. trial was a godsend. The case spawned a pack of lawyers-turned-commentators who fed the beast by screeching at one another about the quality of evidence, truthfulness of witnesses, and soundness of the strategies employed by the prosecution and defense.

The Simpson murder trial also exposed another disturbing aspect of American life—the persistent racial divide in this country, one that most reporters failed to notice or ignored until the jury reached its decision. I watched the televised announcement of the verdict with several African American women who worked in the clerk's office at the U.S. courthouse in Washington. Every one of them rejoiced in Simpson's acquittal, a familiar scene played out across the nation. Many white people thought Simpson was guilty, while many blacks believed he wasn't. To some African Americans, Simpson represented every black man who had been accused of doing a white woman wrong. They believed he had beaten the system by playing it, hiring a "dream team" of high-priced lawyers to gain an acquittal, as some whites have done throughout history.

Lady Justice, the famous blindfolded woman holding scales, suggests that justice is oblivious to a defendant's race, gender or ethnicity, but America's jails and prisons are packed with a disproportionate number of blacks, Hispanics and other minorities. Most of them are too poor to pay a bond and meet bail conditions that are set to ensure a defendant will appear at subsequent hearings. That means that a significant number of people are serving time for crimes for which they have not been convicted—or even tried. What's worse is that, unlike Simpson, they cannot afford to hire good lawyers. They will be stuck with the counsel the courts give to them, and that means they can receive less-than-stellar representation by lawyers who may be overworked, outmatched, or incompetent.

Simpson was so beloved by the public that people lined the Los Angeles freeways and shouted their support during the famous slow-speed police chase of the Ford Bronco driven by his friend, Al Cowlings. In Alabama in 1931, a group of young black men received a far different reception when they were hounded by a mob and nearly lynched after they were accused of raping two white women. Fearing the mob would try to storm the jail, the sheriff asked the governor to send armed troops from a nearby National Guard post to ensure the prisoners' safety. Within two weeks the "Scottsboro Boys" went on trial. Eight of the nine were convicted of rape and sentenced to death. While appeals dragged on, large demonstrations were held in New York and other northern cities that criticized southern justice as racist and unfair. In the northern press, the defendants were portrayed as victims, charged with rapes that had not occurred. In the southern press, they were depicted as predators, until years later when a couple of newspaper editors began questioning the quality of the evidence. The cases went up to the U.S. Supreme Court twice, resulting in landmark decisions on the rights of poor defendants to counsel. But nine men spent more than 100 years behind bars.

News coverage of black-on-white crime continues to raise troubling questions. If a black woman goes missing at the same time a pretty white girl disappears, images of the blue-eyed blonde or cute brunette will fill television screens and the front pages of newspapers. Her name—Natalee Holloway, an Alabama teen who disappeared in Aruba in 2005, or Chandra Levy, a Washington intern who vanished in 2001—will become household words.

Few missing or dead black women generate the same kind of publicity. Far too often police make assumptions, as they did in Boston when Kasha Blount, a young pregnant black woman, was found dead in 1990. The medical examiner and homicide detectives assumed she was a crack addict who died of an overdose, despite her robust appearance. After I wrote a front-page story for the *Boston Globe* that questioned those assumptions, police charged her boyfriend, who did not want his mother to know about the pregnancy. By then, opportunities to gather forensic and other evidence had been lost. The boyfriend was acquitted.

Secrecy v. Openness

As much as critics decry "perp walks," where police parade a suspect before TV cameras, the publicity acts as another check on the power of police and prosecutors. If arrests were done in secret, how would the public assess the work of cops and prosecutors? In America's courts, there is a tradition of public access to criminal trials, which means there is a presumption of openness. The U.S. Supreme Court said so in *Richmond Newspapers Inc. v. Virginia* in 1980.

Writing for the majority, Chief Justice Warren Burger said open criminal trials serve a therapeutic function for people in a community who are distraught or frightened by a crime. Open courts also discourage witnesses from lying about evidence, thwart official misconduct and improve the performance of all of the players in a case, the chief justice wrote. Like most aspects of the law, there is an exception to this rule. Judges can seal, or keep from public view, portions of a criminal trial, but they need good reasons and they must consider alternatives to closures before they lock the courtroom doors.

That doesn't mean the war over access to trials has been won. Reporters must remain on high alert because some judges act as if they've never heard of the *Richmond* decision. Judges continue to seal documents and proceedings, particularly if there aren't any reporters in the courtroom. Who will know if a reporter isn't there to remind a judge of his obligations to weigh the pros and cons of secrecy?

People involved in the criminal justice system often joke that "Everyone in prison says he's innocent." The reality is that some of them are, and no one will know unless the courts remain open for public inspection. Dozens of prisoners have been exonerated because of advances in science and the use of DNA to exclude defendants as possible suspects. Most of them spent decades behind bars for crimes they did not commit. Jaded cops and prosecutors might say their imprisonment was justified because the defendants more than likely committed another crime and got away with it. Please don't think that way. It's dangerous for police and prosecutors to believe they can bend or ignore the rules because they suspect a defendant committed *some* crime, if not this one. Reporters need access to the courts to hold cops and prosecutors accountable by determining whether indictments are based on proof, not guesswork.

There are other reasons that courts must remain open to the public: Cops can—and do—make mistakes. Most police officers are honest, but they are human, and they have personal biases and baggage. They can develop tunnel vision, ignoring clues and evidence that lead them to focus on the wrong suspect. In 1996, the FBI zoned in on Richard Jewell, a security guard who noticed a suspicious bag in an Atlanta park during the summer Olympics. Jewell acted quickly but one woman was killed when the package exploded before the area was cleared. FBI profilers thought Jewell was similar to a firefighter who commits arson and then shows up to put out the flames. It turned out that Jewell was a hero, and the bomber was Eric Rudolph, an anti-abortion, anti-gay zealot who hid in the North Carolina woods for years before he was captured.

The public also needs to know that some police officers are not fit to wear a badge. Crooked cops have planted evidence, stolen drugs, and beaten and abused people. Being a cop is not easy, and the power to carry a badge and a gun can have a perverse effect on some people. For all of those reasons, reporters must remain skeptical of the information they receive from police and prosecutors.

▪ Life in the Big Leagues ▪

"Isikoff's got something!" reporter Susan Schmidt hissed into the phone.

It was Friday, January 16, 1998, when Schmidt, a colleague of mine at the *Washington Post*, called my federal courthouse office to ask if I had noticed anything unusual on the third floor, where grand juries, more than a half-dozen at that time, were investigating allegations of corruption in the Clinton administration.

She was referring to Michael Isikoff, a former *Post* reporter, who had gone to work for *Newsweek* a few years earlier after an argument with a *Post* editor over a story about President Bill Clinton's dalliances with women who weren't his wife. Schmidt had been assigned to keep tabs on the grand jury that was investigating Whitewater, an Arkansas real-estate deal involving the Clintons. As the paper's federal courts beat reporter, I helped her by watching the comings and goings of witnesses on the third floor.

Schmidt's fear of being beaten on a story quickly infected me, and we spent several minutes speculating about the "scoop" Isikoff might have landed. We came up empty, and a long holiday weekend was about to begin. I was heading to Pittsburgh to celebrate my nephew Tyler's fifth birthday, but I assured Schmidt that I would be available to call my sources, if she needed me to do so.

I didn't hear from her. I learned later that she spent the weekend trying to nail down that Independent Counsel Kenneth Starr was making an effort to catch President Clinton in a lie about his relationship with a former White House intern, Monica Lewinsky. I also didn't know that blogger Matt Drudge had reported on Saturday that editors at *Newsweek* had killed Isikoff's story about Starr's investigation. Drudge had gathered explosive information about the allegations against the president, but he focused his efforts on criticizing the editors at *Newsweek.* Schmidt and other reporters for "mainstream" publications understood that *Newsweek*'s perceived lack of fortitude wasn't the real story and that Starr's investigation mattered more.

When I returned to work Tuesday, I conducted my usual rounds in the courthouse, checking the clerk's office and making repeated passes through the third floor. All was quiet, and I left work earlier than usual, at about 6 p.m.

A short time later, Bill Hamilton, an assistant national editor at the *Post*, called me at home. He said Schmidt had confirmed that Starr was investigating whether Clinton and people close to him had pressured a White House intern to lie during a deposition about her sexual relationship with the president. Hamilton said we had confirmation from Starr's camp, but the *Washington Post* could not publish a story about the president of the United States based solely on information from prosecutors who had already been accused of playing politics with their investigation. Hamilton asked if I could run it by my sources in the Justice Department.

I told him I'd do my best. I pulled out the phone number of a source I thought would level with me. I had worked hard to earn this source's trust and respect. If this source could tell me, I thought, this source would. When I repeated what Hamilton had told me, the source sighed. It was true—all of it.

Starr had asked Attorney General Janet Reno to support him in his request of a special three-judge panel that oversaw independent counsels to expand his investigative mandate to include the Lewinsky matter. "Starr made it clear he needed this," my source said. "We did not want to look like we were slowing down the process." The source said Reno made her decision "right away" and that Starr's allegations shocked people in the Justice Department. "It was really a situation where people were floored," the source said.

Less than 15 minutes after Hamilton had asked for my help, I called him back. "I got it," I said. I powered up my computer and, using old-fashioned dial-up (what I had back then), sent my notes to Hamilton. I also made another quick call to a second source, leaving a message.

Leonard Downie, the *Post*'s executive editor, called to ask for the name of my source. There are times when editors need to know the names of a reporter's sources, and this was one of them. We were publishing a story that said the president of the United States was under investigation for pressuring a young woman into lying under oath about a sexual relationship she had with him. After I talked to Downie, my second source returned my call and confirmed everything I had been told. I called Hamilton and told him I had confirmation from two sources.

I was flying. The story was a blockbuster, and I knew it. But my excitement turned quickly to suspicion when Schmidt called and tipped me, or let slip (I'm not sure which) that my byline wasn't going to be on the front-page story. There were going to be plenty of opportunities for me to get a front-page byline on follow-ups, she assured me. Like hell, I thought. I had obtained information that Schmidt—and several other reporters in town—had failed to get.

I called my supervisor, Assistant Metro Editor Keith Harriston, at home. I quickly summarized what I had done to help the National Desk. The National Desk and Metro had a history of fighting over the work done by the federal courts reporter, who technically was assigned to the Metro Desk. There was no love lost between editors on both desks. Harriston called Jo-Ann Armao, assistant managing editor for metro news, who turned her car around and went back to the newsroom to make sure my name was on the story.

What a night, right? One of the biggest moments of my career was nearly taken from me. I experienced the high of coming through in the clutch and the satisfaction of knowing that my hard work had paid off. But I also saw the ugly side of journalism—the fierce competition. I survived because I had two editors who had the guts to stick up for me and make sure I received the credit I deserved.

If reporters get pulled into the maelstrom of an unjust high-profile criminal investigation, the suspect doesn't have a chance—nor does the integrity of the legal system and journalists who cover it.

Reporting, Reporting—and More Reporting

When you gather a piece of information, you need to verify it and assess its importance. You need to know that it is true and whether it matters before you disseminate it. You figure that out by running it past someone who knows—a detective, prosecutor, judge, defense attorney or witness—and by reviewing court filings or other public records. For me, the process of verification was constant: I reached out to as many people as I could, given the constraints of a deadline, to check what I had heard. I repeatedly asked myself, who else would know if this were true?

You also need to determine whether your source has an agenda, and if he is providing you with an unvarnished version of what occurred. I would make a phone call if I thought there was even a remote chance someone else could help me. I re-read court records, including footnotes and exhibits, to find confirmation hidden in indictments, motions and plea agreements. More often than not, I uncovered clues that led me to more people and paper. I loved those aha moments. I loved the hunt for details, for facts that would confirm—or refute—what I'd been told. Above all else, I wanted to get it right. But there's more to getting it right: Was I fair? Was I skeptical?

Critics of "mainstream" journalism accuse reporters of bias when they read or hear facts that suggest points of view contrary to their own. Or they automatically blame a journalist's mistake on personal bias. This is true more today than when I started out as a reporter. The nation is bitterly divided and more partisan than in any other period in my lifetime. Unfortunately some people want their beliefs validated, not challenged. When a news story questions strongly held beliefs, readers and viewers often shoot the messenger, a time-honored tradition of human beings everywhere. It is, after all, easier to discredit a reporter and dismiss a story than it is to change your mind or admit you were wrong.

The truth is good reporters make mistakes for many reasons. We get bad information from police. Investigations are fluid; police gather evidence from witnesses who, in the rush of adrenalin, often mistakenly identify suspects and misstate what they heard or saw. When cops and witnesses make a mistake, journalists magnify the error.

The March of Technology

In the digital age, there has been nothing short of a revolution in journalistic productivity. Reporters must do more, and do it faster than ever at news organizations that have shrunk dramatically because of cutbacks in staffing. To succeed, you must work hard. You must hustle. And you must be creative with the traditional news-story model by figuring out which technological tool helps you tell a story in the most compelling and interesting way. Is it audio, video, a slideshow, interactive graphics, original court records, text alone or a combination of those tools? Websites are not static entities; they are living things that require constant updates to stay fresh and attract viewers. At the same time, reporters must give readers more than tick-tock accounts of breaking news; journalists also must develop expertise to provide readers with insight and smart commentary that they cannot get anywhere else.

Social networking sites such as Facebook and Twitter have changed what people care about, and how they want to interact with information and its providers. These tools were used to organize protests over layoffs of high school teachers in 2010 in New Jersey and to provide accounts of police crackdowns on protesters in 2011 with the Occupy Wall Street movement in several cities. For reporters, social networking sites also are great places to find information, tipsters, witnesses to events and other people who want to be interviewed. But a word of caution: Check out these people and their information. The Internet has been a boon for people who enjoy "punking" the unsuspecting among us. Don't let them make a fool out of you. Check them out and verify what they say before you tweet, re-tweet, upload a video to YouTube or quote what someone wrote on a wall on Facebook.

News organizations continue to struggle in developing clear, fair and hip guidelines for social-media use by employees, particularly younger reporters and bloggers who grew up in the Internet's culture of sharing each and every thought with friends and strangers—and doing so now, not later. It's not been any easier for the nation's judges, who are grappling with how to control jurors' use of technology to Google information about defendants, lawyers, legal terms and crime scenes. The problem is serious: Jurors are supposed to consider only evidence they hear or see in the courtroom. If they gather information on their own, some accurate, some not, it could improperly influence their verdicts and deny a defendant a fair trial.

In response, courts are developing policies to control jurors' use of cell phones, tablets and other electronic devices in the courtroom. Judges are going even further, establishing rules for when and where reporters can tweet, blog or capture and post video online. Some judges allow tweeting from the courtroom, while others don't. In other high-profile cases, judges set up "overflow" courtrooms, where reporters can move about freely, tweet and post their stories online while watching closed-circuit feeds of the proceedings. Your ability to tweet or blog in real time will depend on the judge.

The contents and tone of your tweets and posts will depend on the standards set by your website, blog, newspaper or TV station. Many of the nation's largest news organizations urge their employees to avoid expressing personal opinions in emails, tweets, or on their Facebook pages. Purists in cyberspace think such a rule is ridiculous: To them, lacking opinions is a sign of stupidity or apathy, neither of which is desirable in a person who gathers and disseminates information. This debate highlights fundamental differences between new and old media. I came of age as a reporter at a time when objectivity was a lofty goal and a point of pride. In the digital age, the buzzwords are transparency, interactivity and speed. Pull the curtain back, allow readers to respond and put it all out there faster than ever.

When I attended the University of Pittsburgh's School of Law in 2006, I often asked younger fellow students how they got their news—and why they frequented some websites and not others. I remember one student asking me why reporters don't put notes at the end of their stories that revealed the journalists' opinions about the issues. At first I didn't understand what he meant. "Who should we believe?" he asked. Why, he wanted to know, don't reporters tell readers whether they believe the people they quote in their stories? "Do you want me to tell you what to think?" I asked, recoiling in horror. His response was "kind of." These days, I have a better idea about what he might have meant. He wanted transparency: He wanted to know how stories were put together. He wanted interactivity: He wanted to engage in a dialogue with the reporter and other readers. He wanted speed: He wanted the experience to occur immediately.

The Sociable Professional

When using social media and the Internet, reporters need to remember that nothing is private in cyberspace, no matter how many security settings a site offers. Your personal and professional lives are not separated online; they are one, no matter how much you wish they weren't. What you do online will affect your credibility and integrity as a reporter—and it will blow back on your employer. News organizations are businesses, and no business wants to look bad. If that happens, you may be looking for another job.

Here are a few tips to stay off the unemployment rolls:

- *Don't talk trash.* If you want to say something that you know you couldn't get past an editor in a news story or say on the air, don't put it in a tweet, or in a blog or Facebook post.
- *Understand that speed can kill.* In journalism there is constant pressure to be first with the story. Unfortunately mistakes can have a longer shelf life than scoops. To avoid embarrassment, exercise judgment on breaking news by sticking to what you know. Don't get greedy and pontificate about an event's greater meaning until you've had time to report it out and digest what's happened.
- *Learn the meaning of TMI.* Don't tell the world everything there is to know about you, especially your political beliefs, unless it's appropriate. The boundaries are different in the digital age than they were in the print era. Establishing a unique voice online is crucial to a blogger's success, but you need to learn that there are times to turn it on, and off. People will stop listening if you give them too much information about yourself, or if you scream all of the time.
- *Choose your "friends" wisely.* On Facebook, the term is almost meaningless, but in the news business it could be misconstrued. If you "friend" a prosecutor, make sure you "friend" the defense attorney. But be discreet: You don't want to reveal a source's identity by "friending" him or her.
- *Don't beat yourself.* Many news organizations want to break news you've gathered. That is why they pay you, and they sometimes don't want you to reveal your scoops on your personal blog, Twitter feed or Facebook page before it appears on the news organization's website,

in its print version or on the air. Your employer probably can live with it if you post to your work and personal blogs simultaneously. But make sure you ask.

- *Think before you tweet.* We all think we're funnier than we are. Keep in mind that one person's witticism is another person's insult. Strive for the clever turn of phrase; it's called good writing, and it can be done in 140 characters or less.
- *Think before you re-tweet.* The Internet's culture of sharing can be a problem for a reporter who forwards links to stories by competitors, companies, politicians or strangers. By re-tweeting information, especially explosive tidbits, you as a reporter are appearing to vouch for its authenticity, whether you are or not. This is a brave new world for news organizations, and their policies reveal a conflicted industry trying to keep up with technology that threatens its survival. Some reporters are adding "disclaimers" to their Twitter bios. What's next? Disclaimers on news stories? That's silly, not to mention cowardly and lazy. You still need to do the reporting and check out what you see online by making calls, asking questions, and talking to people in a position to know whether it's true. If you do your own reporting, you will establish credibility in social media and make the most of what's happening online.
- *Be proud.* Never, ever lie about being a reporter. Never lie about your employer, or what you're trying to find out.
- *Ask for help.* If you're concerned about what you're saying in a tweet or post, run it by an editor or the social-media folks at your news organization.
- *Be careful.* Read the terms of service for the social-media site. Remember that sites often roll over when FBI agents show up asking for information. That means the site could turn over everything you've posted—and not tell you.
- *Behave.* Conduct yourself online as you would if you were talking to a source in person. Be respectful, courteous and civil.

Don't Bungle the Basics

To cover the criminal justice system well, you must sweat the details. You can't have a comma or a piece of data out of place. I learned that lesson the hard way. At the *Boston Globe*, I wrote a four-part series in 1991 called "Bungling the Basics." As part of the project, I gathered data collected by the FBI for its Uniform Crime Report on "clearance" rates of violent crimes. My editors did not understand that clearance meant police solved cases, sometimes by arrests or through forensic evidence that attributed deaths to natural causes or suicides. Instead, my editors wanted to use the easier-to-understand term "arrest rate," which was misleading because it suggested that all of the crimes were solved when culprits were caught and charged.

The FBI data supported a minor finding in the series, which revealed far more serious problems in the department that I uncovered by reviewing years of court records and by conducting numerous interviews. I should have done a better job of explaining the difference between the two terms. By using "arrest" instead of "clearance" in a sidebar on day one of the series, we opened ourselves up to criticism by the department, which later managed to get the FBI to write a letter attacking my entire series when it was nominated for a Pulitzer Prize. I learned that a Pulitzer judge used the FBI's letter to argue with other members of the panel that my series should not make the cut to finalist.

You will make people mad, and they'll come after you. Boston cops picketed outside the *Globe*, carrying signs that said, "Locy Lies." They'll dissect every word you write. Do not stoop to their level of nastiness. I always talked to readers who called me, and I enjoyed it. Some became regular callers who often suggested questions that had not occurred to me. But calling someone on the phone takes more guts than shooting a profanity-laced email through cyberspace. You must maintain your composure. You don't want your response taken out of context and posted on a blog that portrays you as an arrogant, biased reporter. It's a trap. Don't step in it.

In the Internet age, a deadline passes every second. Despite the pressure, you must keep reporting to ensure that your stories are accurate and fair. You must call the lawyer for the defendant indicted for murdering his wife. Police and prosecutors will give you their spin on an investigation or an indictment. Go beyond their press releases. Don't ever rush into print, online or on the air with a prosecutor's summary of an indictment you could read for yourself. Try to talk to the suspect himself, his relatives, people in the neighborhood and witnesses. There's no doubt you'll often strike out. People will refuse to talk to you, but you must never stop trying. One phone call or email won't cut it. You must keep reaching out to those people. Do the legwork. Don't allow government officials to spoon-feed you like a baby.

Reporters also must avoid falling for the hype of an ongoing investigation. Thanks to former Attorney General John Ashcroft, practically every police chief and sheriff in America uses the term "person of interest" to describe a suspect or witness in a case. The term has no legal significance, but it can be used to smear an innocent person. The authorities can use "person of interest" in place of suspect or target, which has a legal definition that requires police and prosecutors to follow specific steps to ensure that constitutional rights are honored.

Why would they do something like that? Cops naturally want to put the public at ease. Prosecutors, many of whom are elected and politically motivated, want the public to see them as tough on crime and in control. This kind of motivation can cost taxpayers when an innocent person is tarred with such a label and ruined. Ashcroft used the term to describe Dr. Steven Hatfill, a former Army scientist who was the main subject for years in the FBI's investigation into the 2001 anthrax attacks that killed five people. The FBI eventually admitted it was wrong in focusing on Hatfill and revealed that agents believe the real killer was another scientist, Bruce Ivins, who worked at the same facility in Maryland as Hatfill. Ivins committed suicide, and the Justice Department agreed to pay Hatfill nearly $6 million to settle a civil lawsuit he had filed.

If you hear a police chief use the "person of interest" label, ask him what he means. Is the person being sought as a suspect or a witness? There's a big difference. Force the police to justify their actions. Do they have evidence, and if so, what specifically? Are they grandstanding? When Ashcroft used the term, I searched the *U.S. Attorneys Manual*—the federal prosecutors' bible—for any mention of person of interest. I found none, and I wrote a story saying so.

See the Building, Take the Building

Like other news reports, court stories must contain answers to most, if not all, of the Five W's—who, what, where, when and why—and how. Who was charged with murder? What happened? Where did it happen? When? My favorite W is why. When you ask why, you often produce stories with the most depth and nuance. Life isn't simple, and your stories shouldn't be either.

I also constantly second-guessed myself:

- What do I know? How do I know it?
- Who do I believe? Is someone trying to use me?
- What is the "evidence"? Do I have enough to write a story?
- Are there gaps in the information I have? Am I taking this on faith in someone or something?

- Am I being misled by jargon? Do I really understand the terms I am using, and am I using them correctly?
- Am I reaching the proper conclusion based on the facts?
- Are my sources reaching the proper conclusions based on what they know?
- Am I being logical?
- Am I being intellectually honest?

Journalists will ask themselves these questions in a matter of minutes, often without realizing it. Gathering the news is not a science. It is an art that requires a great deal of practice.

When you cover a courthouse beat, you need to take pride in what you do. That means you should look at the courthouse as if it were *your* house. Nothing should move in the building unless you know about it. If you miss a story, you should be embarrassed.

Today reporters can sit at computers in their homes or offices and access websites and databases containing federal and state court records—unless they're sealed—almost anywhere in the country. While advances in technology are supposed to make our lives easier, they aren't supposed to make us lazy. You need to go to the courthouse, walk the halls and talk to people. If you weren't in the courtroom for the former city housing official's sentencing, you would've missed it when she fainted as the judge announced a lengthy prison term that meant she'd have to trade in her designer suits for orange jumpsuits.

You also need to be early and stay late because it pays off. While working at the *Philadelphia Daily News*, I saw another side of mob boss Nicodemo "Little Nicky" Scarfo when an elderly woman entered the courtroom. "Ma!" he shouted, taking the woman's hands tenderly in his. Had I not arrived early, I would've missed the moment. Being a reporter means you will put in long hours. You cannot leave work until you write the day's stories, no matter how tired you are or whether you have plans for dinner. As I used to tell myself, *can't* is not an option at the *Washington Post*.

Challenging the Corporate Culture

Most of the reporters I worked with were deeply suspicious of authority. That's why most of us went into journalism. We loved to question people with power, including our editors. This give-and-take is crucial to gathering the news. How else can we be sure that our news organizations are doing the right thing by naming a teenage rape suspect or in identifying the mayor's mistress the day before the election?

For the first half of my career, it was a normal day at the office if someone cursed or kicked a trash can across the room because an editor had rewritten a lead. Newsrooms were places to laugh about stories that had better punch lines than the best jokes, such as the time the Philly mob tried to hire a Frank Sinatra impersonator to perform at a benefit to raise money to pay their locked-up boss's legal bills.

There also were more serious moments. In Philadelphia, suspects often showed up at the *Daily News* to turn themselves in to senior editor Chuck Stone. A staff photographer took pictures of the suspects to document that they were in good health, with not a mark on their bodies, before the police were called to take them into custody. At that time, the Philly cops had a documented track record for beating people up—or worse, turning their police dogs loose on them.

Throughout my career, I questioned my editors about issues big and small. Could I have been more diplomatic? Absolutely. But I do not regret the disagreements I had with any of them. Editors sit in offices all day, shuffling from one meeting to another. They don't know what's happening in the courthouse. Only you do. One of the reasons I became a beat reporter was to avoid assignments dreamed up by editors who didn't leave the building for lunch. Good reporters, particularly those working beats, come up with their own story ideas. They don't wait for an editor to tell them what to do. It's called original reporting.

But be warned. Corporate-owned news organizations tend to establish rigid chains of command in newsrooms. At *USA Today,* reporters were so disenchanted by the corporate culture that they stopped sounding the alarm about the work of Jack Kelley, the foreign correspondent who resigned in shame in 2004 after fabricating stories for years. When I raised questions about the validity of Kelley's work a year or so earlier, an editor told me, "You're just jealous because Jack's a star and you aren't." I didn't press the issue, and I wish I had.

Reporters need the freedom to question editors. There's no doubt in my mind that good work will happen—and horrendous mistakes will be avoided—if reporters can do what they do best, and that is to question authority anywhere and everywhere.

· *Chapter* ·

Cops, Lawyers, Judges and Reporters: Who Does What and Why?

■ ■ ■

Laws reflect the public's morality. When people break the rules, criminal laws specify how violators must atone for their offenses and whether they will face the ultimate punishment, the death penalty. The classic reasons for punishment are deterrence to send a message to other potential violators of the law, rehabilitation to help those who may or may not want it and retribution to avenge a wrong.

It all starts with police officers, of whom we ask and expect a great deal, all in the name of protecting and making us feel safe. They see us at our worst—when we are victims, witnesses or perpetrators of crimes. They risk their lives each time they pull over a driver who runs a red light or when they try to stop a drunken husband from beating his wife. And citizens want police officers to play by the rules, except when they don't, such as when a child goes missing.

Nearly all of the other key players in a courthouse have law degrees—prosecutors, plaintiffs' lawyers, defense attorneys and judges. Prosecutors and plaintiffs' attorneys level accusations, while judges serve as referees who are supposed to make sure the rule of law is followed. Defense attorneys are usually the last people to arrive at the party, assigned to or hired by a defendant after criminal charges have been brought or a lawsuit has been filed.

In the past, justice was hyper-local, defined and enforced by police, prosecutors, judges and jurors who lived in neighborhoods affected by crime. Today, suburban voters and their elected officials dictate how justice is served on inner-city streets. Beginning in the late 1970s and early 1980s, lawmakers in state capitals and Washington orchestrated a seismic transfer of power from judges and juries to police and prosecutors by passing laws with easily manipulated procedures and harsh penalties that led to increasing numbers of plea bargains, fewer trials by jury, and an explosion in the nation's prison population. In this chapter, we will examine the state and federal court systems and how they resemble each other in structure but differ in style.

The Power of the State

In the 1840s and 1850s, the nation's largest cities created police departments to keep order during the first major wave of immigrants from Europe, who crowded urban neighborhoods and stretched resources. Police officers were needed to deal with an increase in crime caused primarily by gangs that competed to control neighborhoods. Today's police officers exercise wide-ranging power, which they often decide to use in a matter of seconds when they fire their weapons at fleeing suspects, stop and search young black men walking on the streets and arrest protesters outside a political party's convention.

Cops do not need warrants to talk to people or test evidence they find on the street. They can conduct sweeps of buses and trains, asking people during highly stressful confrontations to consent to searches for drugs. They can stop you on the street and pat you down if they think you look suspicious. They can pull over your car if you commit a minor traffic violation with the intent of searching your vehicle for drugs. They need to wait only seconds before kicking down a door to search a suspect's apartment. They can peek in your windows if you've failed to pull your blinds all the way down. They can lie during interrogations, telling one suspect that his partner has copped a deal when he hasn't.

All of it is legal; the U.S. Supreme Court has said so.

As a reporter, you must remember that the standards for a good story are not the same as the prerequisites for a lawsuit or an indictment. Journalists are not bound by convoluted legal definitions in deciding what's fair or unfair. Justice is about more than semantics; it's about people. It's also important to keep in mind that the U.S. Supreme Court has made its share of mistakes throughout history, such as validating the property rights of slave owners before the Civil War and the roundup and internment of Japanese Americans during World War II.

When cops abuse their power, they can destroy the public's confidence in the judicial system. In New York, veteran police officers have been indicted and convicted of working secretly for the Mafia. In Boston, an FBI agent went to prison for helping James "Whitey" Bulger run his criminal enterprise out of South Boston for decades. In my career, I wrote about a citywide squad of elite drug investigators in Philadelphia who skimmed cash and narcotics when they searched homes of suspected drug dealers.

Crooked cops grab headlines, but police officers' mistakes, biases and incompetence are far more common. Their missteps during an investigation can gut a case or lead to dismissal of all charges against a defendant, if it gets that far. More alarming, the mistakes and abuses may never be revealed because plea bargains far outnumber trials in the American criminal justice system, and evidence—or lack of it—isn't tested in court.

Rights Aren't Technicalities

Cops and prosecutors can exacerbate their errors by trying to cover them up or by blaming someone else. They often dismiss their failures as mere "technicalities" and label judges as soft on crime if they throw flawed cases out of court.

Constitutional rights are not technicalities. Beating a confession out of a suspect is a violation of the Fifth and Eighth Amendments' promises of due process and ban on cruel and unusual punishment, respectively.

Breaking into someone's home without a warrant violates the Fourth Amendment's restrictions on unreasonable searches and seizures. Hiding evidence of a defendant's possible innocence contradicts the Sixth Amendment's guarantee of a fair trial.

Covering an investigation into a crime that captivates the public is one of the toughest assignments a reporter will receive. It is crucial that reporters understand the dynamics of a high-profile criminal investigation, in which facts change as witnesses contradict each other or make honest mistakes. New leads can be discovered that alter the direction of an investigation. Corners also can be cut if police fear they may lose a chance to catch a killer, rescue a victim or locate the body of a missing child to bring closure to her family.

You may feel as much pressure to break stories as the detectives experience in trying to solve the crime. To protect yourself from reporting bad or old information, you must cultivate a large group of police sources at every level in the department, from the patrol officer on the street up to the chief's office.

Above all else, you must remain skeptical of your sources and never forget that they want to look good with the public. They want people to feel safe. You can't blame them for that, but you can never allow yourself to forget that their agenda differs from yours.

For the People

As with police departments, elected prosecutors didn't emerge in America until the 1840s and 1850s. Until then, prosecutors were hired when needed and paid by the case. In most states today, prosecutors are called district attorneys, state's attorneys or commonwealth's attorneys, who rise with great solemnity in court to remind all present that they represent "the people."

State and county prosecutors typically run for election, which means they need to raise money to fund their campaigns. If you cover elected prosecutors, you must pay close attention to the political side of their lives. People usually don't give money away without a reason. You must review your DA's campaign contributions to figure out who is putting the big bucks behind him. Remember, if you follow the money, you'll often wind up with a good story.

At the federal level, the top prosecutor in a particular geographic area is called the U.S. attorney. The president appoints U.S. attorneys with the advice and consent of the U.S. Senate. Don't for a second think that politics aren't part of presidential or gubernatorial appointments. An appointee came to a politician's attention in some way, but the connection may be harder to find.

Not every lawyer working in a prosecutor's office carries the title of DA. There's only one top dog. The rest of the prosecutors working there are assistant district attorneys. The same goes for the feds: There is one U.S. attorney in an area, and there are assistant U.S. attorneys working for her. Get the titles right.

I'm not giving away any secrets of journalism by telling you that prosecutors can be key sources for reporters. With their help you can lead your newscast or home page with scoop after scoop. But be careful. Don't get overconfident and fool yourself into believing that prosecutors are on your side. If they're DAs, they want to be re-elected. If they're federal prosecutors, they want to look like hard-charging crime-fighters. You only fit into that equation if you help them meet their goals.

Always remember that reporters also represent the people. Prosecutors spend taxpayers' money on all kinds of investigations. How is the money spent? Are prosecutors abusing the public's trust in them to be fair and honest in administering justice?

Raw Power

Today's big-city prosecutors command small armies of assistants and investigators. They review evidence gathered by cops and decide which cases to pursue and which matters to drop. In other words, they decide whom to charge with a crime—or not. They also can ask a judge to force a witness to testify in court. Prosecutors are the government, at the county, state and federal levels.

In several cases spawned by the so-called War on Drugs, the U.S. Supreme Court has made it difficult, if not impossible, for defendants to challenge state prosecutors about their decisions to charge white defendants in state courts and refer black drug suspects to federal courts, where the possible penalties are more severe.

The Court also has erected high barriers for defendants who believe racial bias played a role in prosecutors' decisions, such as when they seek the death penalty and the potential jurors they choose to eliminate from a panel.

Unless a prosecutor makes a blatantly racist remark in public, he has wide latitude to try cases as he sees fit, as Michelle Alexander wrote in *The New Jim Crow: Mass Incarceration in the Age of Colorblindness*. It's up to journalists to inform the public when the law doesn't make sense, is applied unfairly or has unintended consequences by favoring one group over another.

Piling On

In late November 2001, Americans had little patience for John Walker Lindh, an idealistic teenager who converted to Islam, left his Marin County, California, home and headed to Afghanistan, where he wound up fighting for the Taliban. Lindh was already there on September 11, 2001, when al-Qaeda launched its stealth attack on the United States. He was still there when U.S. troops invaded Afghanistan several weeks later. He was captured with Taliban fighters and nearly died when he was wounded in an inmate uprising at the notorious Mazar-e Sharif prison.

At several news conferences, Attorney General John Ashcroft portrayed Lindh as a traitor who "chose terrorists" over his fellow Americans and deserved no mercy. A federal grand jury made sure of it in a 10-count indictment that was "tightly drafted," as a former prosecutor told me for a story I wrote for *USA Today*. The lawyer, Frank Bowman, said prosecutors structured the indictment in a way that guaranteed Lindh would spend many years in prison even if he went to trial and was convicted of only a few of the charges. "If I'm the defense attorney in this case, I read this thing and say to myself, 'This is about as bad as it gets,'" Bowman said.

The indictment squeezed Lindh into a plea bargain and a 20-year sentence by bookending a weapons charge typically used against drug dealers and another count that accused him of conspiring to murder U.S. nationals that could've sent him away for life plus 30 years. Federal prosecutors did not accuse Lindh of killing anyone in particular, but they listed the death of CIA officer Johnny "Mike" Spann as an element of one of the charges. Spann had interviewed Lindh shortly before Spann was killed during the riot at the Afghan prison. It didn't matter whether prosecutors had any evidence—which a federal judge later said they lacked—to prove Lindh had anything to do with Spann's death. Under the law at the time, they could use it against Lindh at sentencing because the standard of proof was much lower than it would've been at trial.

Lindh's case might have been handled differently, with more compassion, had he been captured later and held by military instead of civilian authorities. Yaser Hamdi, who was both an American and Saudi citizen, also was captured while fighting with the Taliban, but he was never charged with a crime. Instead he was detained as an "enemy combatant" by the U.S. military and held at a Navy brig in South Carolina before he was eventually released. Even a man who was detained as a suspected terrorist at the prison at Guantanamo Bay, Cuba, and faced a trial by military commission received a far lighter sentence than Lindh. Australian David Hicks pleaded guilty to terrorism offenses and was sentenced to serve nine months on top of the five years he had been held by the military.

How could this happen? It is legal for prosecutors to bring several different charges stemming from one criminal act as long as each offense requires proof of at least one fact that the others don't.

Over the past 30 years, state and federal legislators have narrowed the definitions of several crimes, including gun and drug charges, to the point that defendants are left with little, if any room to argue that they did not intend to harm anyone. In doing so, legislators have provided prosecutors with long lists of overlapping offenses they can charge for one criminal act. This means the balance of power has tilted in favor of prosecutors, who can threaten defendants with long prison terms if they do not agree to plead guilty and forgo a trial. Today's prosecutors have enormous discretion—or put another way, raw power—to dictate the ending of a case by manipulating the beginning in choosing the charges to include in an indictment.

In over Their Heads

Each year, police arrest more than 27 million people. There are 900,000 lawyers in the United States, of which only a small percentage specializes in criminal law. That means there aren't enough lawyers to represent people charged with crimes. The ratio gets worse when you factor in that the overwhelming majority of criminal defendants cannot afford to pay for a lawyer.

Why does the United States provide court-appointed and state-paid counsel for poor defendants? In 1932, the U.S. Supreme Court ruled in the famous "Scottsboro Boys" case that judges were required to appoint counsel, whether asked or not, in death penalty prosecutions. It wasn't until 1963 that the justices finally admitted that criminal trials present far too complicated issues for the average person, especially an indigent, to act as his own lawyer. The landmark case of *Gideon v. Wainwright* required states to provide court-appointed counsel to poor people facing felony charges. A decade later, the Court applied the same logic to misdemeanors, or cases in which a defendant faces a minimum of a day in jail. The theory is that if a defendant could lose something as precious as his freedom, even for one day, he needs a lawyer to help him fight the charges.

Defendants do not have the right to pick a court-appointed lawyer, but they are entitled to be represented by the attorney of their choice if they are paying the bills, unless a judge believes a conflict of interest exists. The U.S. Supreme Court hasn't concerned itself with whether lawyers receive adequate pay, but in a decision in 1989 the justices upheld a federal law that allowed the government to seize all proceeds of drug crimes, including fees paid to defense attorneys.

The overwhelming majority of people who graduate each year from law schools won't ever step inside a courtroom, but will confine themselves to corporate offices. There are problems among some of the lawyers who choose criminal law, with many documented cases of defense attorneys who showed up drunk in court or slept through testimony. In such instances, prosecutors easily outgun defense attorneys not only in resources but also in talent. If a defendant is poor, he may get what he pays for, which is not much.

Between a Rock and a Hard Place

The defense lawyer is both an advocate for his client and an officer of the court, which carries a duty to uphold the law and administer justice. To some people, advocacy means winning at all costs. To others, it's more of a delicate ethical dance.

The rights to a fair trial and a lawyer are fundamental American ideals that predate the Revolutionary War. The British soldiers accused of killing five colonists in the Boston Massacre in

1770 were represented by one of the premier lawyers of the time, John Adams, who became the second president of the United States. The Unabomber, Ted Kaczynski, who mailed or hand-delivered bombs that killed three people and injured several others, had defense attorneys who were nationally known experts on death penalty cases.

Reporters can expect defense attorneys to challenge evidence if the right to counsel was violated at any stage leading up to a criminal prosecution, starting with police questioning of a suspect in custody. If a person is a target of a grand jury investigation and he is subpoenaed to testify, he has a right to consult with an attorney.

A suspect has a right to a lawyer if he has been charged with a crime and is placed in a line-up for victims or witnesses to view. If he hasn't been charged, he generally doesn't have a right to a lawyer's presence during the line-up.

There also is no right to counsel during an initial appearance in court because that is usually when lawyers are appointed. Defendants have a right to a lawyer to represent them at preliminary hearings, where judges decide the sufficiency of charges, and they are entitled to counsel during trial and when they are sentenced.

A defendant is not required to have a lawyer at all and has the right to represent himself and proceed *pro se*, or on his own, if he is competent. Defendants employing an insanity defense also can represent themselves, if they understand they are facing trial and they are capable of consulting with a lawyer. Sometimes judges will allow a defendant to represent himself, but appoint standby counsel to help if he is struggling with the complexities of the law.

Promises to the Poor

If a defendant cannot afford to hire an attorney, one will be appointed for him, as the U.S. Supreme Court said in its famous *Miranda v. Arizona* decision of 1966. If a county has an office of public defender, the defendant will be assigned a lawyer who works there. If there is no public defender, or not enough of them, judges will appoint lawyers who are engaged in private practice to represent indigent defendants.

Those attorneys receive a pittance to take cases, and some of them match their effort to the low pay scale, which is typically set by state lawmakers. Federal and state appellate court files contain many stories about court-appointed defense attorneys who didn't take the time to meet their clients until a few minutes before trial, or of lawyers who didn't bother to interview witnesses who might have contradicted the prosecution's evidence and swayed a jury to impose a life sentence instead of death.

Before they retired, U.S. Supreme Court Justices Sandra Day O'Connor and John Paul Stevens raised concerns about the quality of defense representation of indigents, particularly in cases where defendants face the death penalty. Reporters should examine the quality of representation a defendant receives. The *Chicago Tribune* and *Austin American-Statesman* have published in-depth stories about lackluster defense work in capital cases. It can be done if you're willing to cull through court files, read transcripts and talk to people.

Your stories can make a difference, especially in the digital age of video, audio, slideshows and interactive graphics that bring people and issues alive in a way that a gray newspaper page cannot. Besides that, the Internet displays your story to millions of people around the world, well beyond the finite number of subscribers to hard copies of the daily newspaper or viewers who tune in for the 6 o'clock local newscast.

Here Comes the Judge

The courtroom is a judge's fiefdom, where people sit, speak and shut up when he or she tells them to. If the public suspects a judge is partisan or biased, people lose respect for the rule of law. In several high-profile cases, judges have been ridiculed for losing control of their courtrooms: Judge Thomas Trenchard in the trial of Bruno Hauptmann, the accused kidnapper and killer of aviator Charles Lindbergh's baby; Judge Edward Blythin in the first trial of Dr. Sam Sheppard, a Cleveland surgeon accused of killing his wife; and Judge Lance Ito, who presided in the *State of California v. Orenthal James Simpson,* the former football star who was acquitted of stabbing to death his wife and her friend.

Self-preservation and hopes for re-election lead many judges to dislike or fear press coverage of cases assigned to them. Some judges respond by trying to control the flow of information about court cases, shrouding the proceedings in secrecy or placing restrictions on participants to prevent leaks.

Understanding the roots of this distrust is important for a reporter who is new to a court beat. When I began covering the federal courthouse in D.C. for the *Washington Post,* I called every judge on the trial court and the appellate bench and asked to set up what I called a meet-and-greet. In those informal meetings, I chatted with the judges and explained my philosophy and approach to journalism: I didn't need handholding, and I didn't need to be spoon-fed. Just let me know when something interesting was happening, and I'd do the rest. I'd read the court records. I'd talk to the lawyers for both sides. I'd show up in court and listen to the judges explain their rulings. I'd write stories based on all of that legwork.

Most important, if I made a mistake, I wanted them to call me so I could correct the error. They knew my phone number, and they knew where to find my office in the courthouse.

Guardians of the Law

Judges keep prosecutors and defense attorneys in line, as well as watch over grand juries and trial juries to make sure they are not misused by the prosecution or misinformed by either side about the meaning of the law.

A grand jury is convened by the court at a prosecutor's request and is generally comprised of up to 23 citizens who decide whether there is probable cause, which is a reasonable belief that a crime was committed and that a particular person committed it. Petit, or trial juries in criminal cases, are comprised of 12 citizens. In civil trials, the number of jurors varies and can be as few as six. Avoid using the word "petit" in your stories. Call it a jury.

In the United States, judges do not arrest people. That's what cops do. Judges don't issue indictments; that's a grand jury function. They don't try to prove guilt, like prosecutors, or raise the possibility of a defendant's innocence, as a defense attorney might. Judges are supposed to act as neutral as umpires, calling the shots as they see them. They make sure the dueling sides follow the rules on what evidence is admissible or not. They instruct juries on what law pertains to a case and how it should be applied.

Although grand juries are widely considered tools of the prosecution, the chief judge of a court usually has the power to intervene if there is a problem, such as with a witness who refuses to testify, or if company executives believe they should not be forced to comply with a subpoena for sensitive documents.

In those instances, judges have the power to weigh in. They can grant "immunity" to a witness in exchange for testimony. The term is misleading because some witnesses don't want immunity, and if they are ungrateful and refuse to accept it, they can be jailed for the life of the grand jury, which is usually up to 18 months. Judges also can look at company or government records privately in chambers, in their offices, to decide whether a prosecutor is using overly broad language in a subpoena to conduct a "fishing expedition."

Politics of Judging

In most states, judges stand for election at some point. Sometimes the governor appoints judges for an initial term, but they can keep the jobs only if they win retention by the voters. In Virginia and South Carolina, state legislators choose judges. The president appoints federal judges with the approval of the U.S. Senate, and they serve for life as long as they behave themselves.

Yet we expect our judges to be independent and above politics, to serve, as Alexander Hamilton explained in *The Federalist Papers*, as a "barrier to the encroachments and oppressions of the representative body," by which he meant Congress. Hamilton also considered the judiciary "the weakest of the three departments" and believed incorrectly that "from the nature of its functions, will always be the least dangerous to the political rights of the constitution; because it will be least in a capacity to annoy or injure them."

At the federal level, judicial nominations have turned more caustic since President Ronald Reagan's nomination of appellate Judge Robert Bork to the U.S. Supreme Court failed amid partisan bickering in 1987. A new verb emerged—"borked"—to describe the outcome in intensely political confirmation hearings. Millions of dollars are spent in judicial elections to get voters worked up about the death penalty, abortion, gun rights and a host of other hot-button issues.

The challenge for reporters is to separate hype from substance in determining whether a candidate is suitable to sit on the bench in judgment of others. You'll want to keep track of campaign contributions to judicial candidates. Who is giving them money, and why? Who is leading the charge against them, and who is bankrolling those special-interest groups? Check with your county or state elections office. You'll also want to examine judges' financial disclosure records, usually kept by a county or state ethics commission. Federal judges also must file financial disclosure forms that you can review by submitting a request with the Administrative Office of the U.S. Courts. Are they investing in companies whose representatives are appearing before them in civil or criminal matters?

You likely will hear the term "judicial activism" leveled by liberals and conservatives to characterize a decision they don't like, regardless of whether it is legally sound. Reporters must guard against efforts by people on all points of the political spectrum to spin and use them. Read the decisions yourself. Talk to law professors and practicing attorneys with a wide array of opinions to help you understand how the judge applied or didn't apply the law. Investigate the real-world impact of the rulings by talking to the people and businesses that are affected.

Report the real facts, not the spin.

Trust Your Eyes and Ears

In your first few months on a court beat, you'll notice that trials are rare because criminal defendants plead guilty and civil litigants settle cases. But what happens if you suddenly begin seeing more jury acquittals than usual in the few trials held in your courthouse? Does it mean the legal gods are evening the playing field and knocking prosecutors down to earth? That's unlikely, and you need to find out why. Do the juries distrust police officers, as they did in Washington in the 1990s? How do you prove it? Pull the case files and talk to defense attorneys, prosecutors, judges, and especially jurors. All you have to do is ask my favorite W—why? Why was the defendant acquitted?

What happens if jurors are hopelessly deadlocked and cannot reach a unanimous verdict, and the judge declares a mistrial? Prosecutors may try to shift the blame to jurors, suggesting they were not savvy enough to understand the evidence. That may be true, but you should talk to jurors and ask why they couldn't reach a unanimous decision.

In Philadelphia in the late 1980s, I covered both federal trials of City Councilman Lee Beloff, who was accused of conspiring with a mob boss to shake down a local developer for $1 million in exchange for a promise of no labor troubles on a waterfront project. The first trial was a mess. I was as confused as the jury, and I understood most of the prosecution's evidence.

The prosecutors made a fatal mistake: They didn't tell a story. Jurors, as much as readers, need the case to come to them like chapters in a book. That's not always possible, depending on the availability of witnesses and evidence, but prosecutors should provide jurors with an easy-to-follow table of contents. I wrote a story saying as much about the Beloff case, which angered the prosecutors, who told me I didn't know what I was talking about because I'm not a lawyer.

I was there in the courtroom for the entire trial. I watched how prosecutors presented their evidence. Your observations in court are a key part of your reporting. Journalists bear witness to history, and we recount what we see, hear and feel for our readers, viewers and listeners. If a reporter who has followed a case closely is confused, it shouldn't be a surprise that jurors are lost. Trust your instincts.

In the second trial of the Philadelphia city councilman, prosecutors did a better job of telling the story of an attempted extortion. He was convicted and sentenced to prison.

Parallel Universes

State and federal courts are similar in structure, with trial courts at the bottom, appeals courts in the middle and supreme courts at the top. They also have the same hierarchy: Intermediate-level appeals judges outrank trial court judges and tell them what they've done wrong, when they need to correct their mistakes, and how. Supreme court judges can second-guess the appeals courts and the judges who presided over trials.

By handling the majority of the nation's legal business, state courts have a greater impact on communities and the people who live in them. Testimony about shocking acts of cruelty and profound moments of bravery is heard in state courtrooms across the nation on everything from murders, rapes and robberies to child abuse, drunk driving and speeding. State courthouses often are crowded, rundown, grimy places where defendants, victims and their families come together in a combustible mix.

For the sake of the story and your safety, make sure you understand the dynamics of the cases you cover. All hell can break loose when the jury announces its verdict or when a key witness identifies the defendant as the culprit. In 1996, an accused gang leader in Washington jumped from his wheelchair and used a homemade knife to stab his former girlfriend as she left the witness stand after testifying against him. She survived because he hit her in the sternum and a deputy U.S. marshal wrestled him to the floor before anyone else was hurt. In Georgia in 2005, a defendant grabbed a deputy sheriff's gun in a courtroom and opened fire, killing a judge and two others. You want to protect yourself, but also be in a position to observe what happens and accurately report it.

Federal courthouses usually are as quiet as libraries. As I walked the deserted hallways of the U.S. courthouse in Washington, I often thought my body wouldn't be discovered for days if I col-

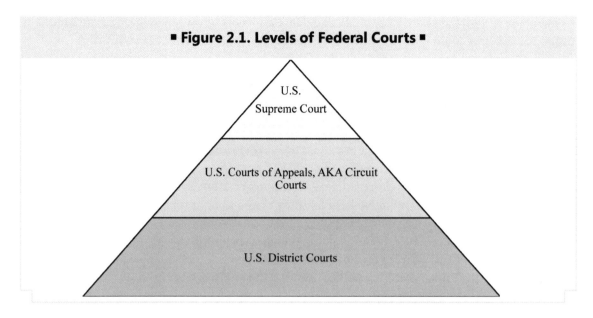

■ Figure 2.1. Levels of Federal Courts ■

U.S. Supreme Court

U.S. Courts of Appeals, AKA Circuit Courts

U.S. District Courts

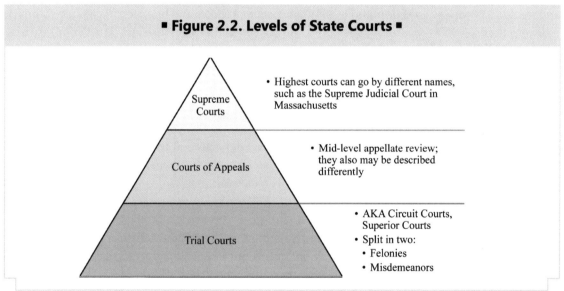

■ Figure 2.2. Levels of State Courts ■

Supreme Courts
- Highest courts can go by different names, such as the Supreme Judicial Court in Massachusetts

Courts of Appeals
- Mid-level appellate review; they also may be described differently

Trial Courts
- AKA Circuit Courts, Superior Courts
- Split in two:
  - Felonies
  - Misdemeanors

lapsed and died in my fourth-floor office. Don't let the sounds of silence fool you into thinking there's nothing going on. Federal judges are appointed to positions of lifetime tenure by the president for a reason; they act as checks on federal law enforcement agents in their use of covert surveillance to gather evidence against people suspected of dealing drugs, bankrupting pension funds or ripping off taxpayers. The most complex blue-collar and white-collar criminal conspiracies also land in federal court, including gang-bangers in baggy pants who peddled drugs on street corners and stockbrokers in Armani suits who promoted worthless securities out of their corner offices. On the civil side, federal judges preside over lawsuits filed by consumers against large corporations that deliberately dumped toxic waste into creeks, ignored warnings from engineers about substandard brakes on cars, and sold toys with attachments knowing that babies could choke on them.

Felonies and Misdemeanors

Cases enter the state court system at the bottom rung of the ladder, which is the trial court level. Many states split their trial courts into two sections. One side of the house deals with civil claims, generally of less than $500, and misdemeanors, which are less serious criminal offenses. The other section handles felonies, which are serious crimes that are punishable by more than a year in prison, or by death.

Misdemeanors, such as bouncing checks, are typically punishable by no more than a year in jail, a small fine or both. In many states, misdemeanor cases are heard in district courts, not to be confused with federal district courts, where serious felonies are handled. The state district courts are often set up along county lines. A small county might be combined with a neighboring county or city. In many states, defendants who are convicted in a district court can appeal by asking for a *trial de novo*, a new trial, at the next level where felonies are handled.

For reporters, the felony trial court is where the action is. Judges in courts of general jurisdiction preside over civil lawsuits seeking significant dollar damages or criminal cases that are considered felonies. In many states, this level is called the circuit court. The number of felony trial courts in a state also depends on geography. Some trial courts operate at the town or city level, while others cover counties or regions. Pennsylvania calls this level the Court of Common Pleas. New York keeps you on your toes by using the term "Supreme Court" to describe its trial courts.

If a defendant is convicted of a misdemeanor and receives a sentence of less than a year, he serves his time in jail. If a defendant is convicted of a felony and receives a sentence of more than a year, he serves his time in prison. If a state's prisons are crowded, he may spend time in the local jail, waiting for a bed to become available in a prison. Jail and prison are not interchangeable terms. There is a huge difference. Inmates at the county jail in Rockbridge County, Virginia, are likely to prefer to mix with small-time thieves and other less serious offenders rather than the convicted murderers and rapists housed in a state prison like the one in Gatesville, Texas.

In the federal system, felonies are heard in the district courts, of which there are 94. The courts range in size from a couple of judges to a dozen or more members of the bench. District courts also have magistrate-judges, but they do not have all of the power of an Article III judge, a reference to the section in the U.S. Constitution that created the judiciary. But magistrate-judges keep the trains running on time, handling returns of grand jury indictments, presiding over initial appearances of defendants after they are arrested, and meeting with civil litigants to keep cases from getting bogged down.

When a court hears testimony about a petty offense, there usually is no transcript of the proceeding. If the city council president sues her hairdresser over a bad haircut, you probably won't find a transcript of the hearing if you miss it. You might, if you're lucky, find an audio recording. Make sure you ask whether one exists. If nothing else, you should be able to find a copy of the original complaint. The same goes for proceedings in magistrate courts, justices of the peace and traffic courts. If there is no audio recording, you must rely on the participants to tell you what happened. Proceed with great caution. You must talk to as many people who were in the courtroom as you can to avoid being misled.

In state and federal felony courts, stenographers usually produce transcripts of the proceedings, or recordings are made. Transcripts aren't normally filed as part of the publicly available felony file. They are expensive and most news organizations cannot afford to buy them. That means you need to get good at taking copious notes. Hearings before federal magistrate-judges usually are recorded, but the audiotapes are not always easy to access. In some federal courts, the audio recordings are filed as part of the case docket and you can access them, for a fee, through the PACER, the Public Access to Court Electronic Records system. But it may take time for the recording to show up on the electronic docket sheet. If you ask nicely, the magistrate-judge, his secretary or clerks will let you listen to what you missed, but you shouldn't count on it. There may not be time in the clerk's schedule or a convenient place for you to listen to the recording. You also may not have enough time before deadline to listen to the tape. This is another reason to make sure you stay on top of what's happening in the courthouse. It's easier if you are there for the hearings.

Taking an Appeal

Not every defendant has a right to appeal. State constitutions and legislatures define the types of cases that can be appealed and when. This means that state appellate courts can decide what cases to accept or reject. There are exceptions, including death penalty cases, for which state legislatures have provided automatic rights to appeal.

State and federal appellate judges usually do not hear new testimony. They read trial transcripts, review briefs filed by lawyers on all sides of an issue and listen to oral arguments. Appeals court judges confine themselves mainly to two issues: Did the trial judge give the jury proper instructions on the law? Was the law followed? Lawyers in criminal and civil cases rely on precedents, or prior legal decisions, to support their positions. By looking to the past to fight today's legal battles, the law evolves as society changes its responses to violations of its rules. Forcing a woman to wear a scarlet letter on her clothing is no longer an acceptable punishment for adultery; nor is hanging a man for stealing a horse.

Some states have two levels of intermediate appellate courts, separating criminal and civil appeals. Most states have one court that handles both. When appeals are filed, the cases are assigned randomly to three-judge panels. If a litigant dislikes the outcome, he can file an appeal within an appeal by seeking *en banc* review of his case. That means he wants all of the judges on the appellate court to hear his appeal. A state's supreme court has final say on the meaning of its laws and constitution. In most states, supreme courts have seven members. Many states use the term "supreme court" to describe their highest court, but there are exceptions: In Massachusetts, the highest court is called the Supreme Judicial Court. In New York, the top court is known as the Court of Appeals. Regardless of the name, a state's highest court monitors lower courts' performance, telling judges if they've made mistakes and how and when to correct them. State supreme courts also set rules for lawyers' behavior.

There is one limitation on their power: The U.S. Supreme Court can reverse state high courts when they interpret the meaning of the U.S. Constitution and federal laws. The U.S. Supreme Court, however, cannot tell a state high court what its state constitution means. Some legal observers say they believe that is what happened in *Bush v. Gore* in 2000, when the U.S. Supreme Court told the Florida high court that it was wrong in finding that its constitution required recounts of votes, a decision that halted the battle over the presidency between Vice President Al Gore and Texas Governor George W. Bush.

The federal judicial system's intermediate appellate level is called the U.S. Court of Appeals. There are 13 federal appeals courts, or circuits, divided into geographic regions across the nation. They include the U.S. Court of Appeals for the District of Columbia Circuit, specializing in disputes involving government agencies, and the U.S. Court of Appeals for the Federal Circuit, which handles controversies over international trade, government contracts, trademarks and patents. A decision in one appellate court is not binding on another. For example, the decisions of the U.S. Court of Appeals for the D.C. Circuit are binding on the trial court judges in Washington but not on the district court judges in New York, which is part of the First Circuit. When the circuits disagree on an aspect of the law, lawyers call it a "circuit split," and often try to use it to persuade the U.S. Supreme Court to accept an appeal to resolve the confusion.

Federal and state appellate judges work largely unnoticed by journalists and the public. Trial courts are fast-paced, while appeals focus on complex legal arguments that can hurt your head, and decisions often aren't reached for months. That doesn't excuse a lack of coverage, especially because of the importance of appellate court decisions. Increasingly, the federal appeals courts are exerting more influence over the law, how it is applied and who it affects because the U.S. Supreme Court hears fewer cases than it has in the past.

Cold, Hard Facts

In criminal cases, prosecutors generally cannot appeal a defendant's acquittal because of the U.S. Constitution's ban on double jeopardy, trying someone twice for the same crime. But either party in a civil case can appeal a jury's verdict. The party who files the appeal is called the appellant, or the petitioner. The other side is known as the appellee, or the respondent.

While an appeal is pending, the losing party can seek a stay, or a temporary halt in enforcement of the judgment. In other words, the losing party can ask the appeals court to allow him to wait to pay the damages or report to prison until it decides the case.

The three-judge panel sets deadlines for each side to file a brief, a document that outlines the party's legal position, and schedules oral arguments, a hearing during which judges question lawyers about points of law.

The appellate court will not grant a new trial if it finds that the trial judge committed a harmless error, meaning the mistake did not prejudice the rights of the losing party by denying him a fair trial. A reversible error is a significant mistake that could've changed the case's outcome, such as admitting improperly obtained evidence.

The appeals court judges take a vote and then decide which one of them will write the majority opinion, which explains the ruling of the judges on the prevailing side. Judges who agree with the majority may write a concurring opinion if they arrive at the same result but got there by a different legal route. Judges who disagree may write dissenting opinions to explain why they think the majority was wrong.

If the appeals court reverses a trial judge, the case is likely to be sent back to him or her on remand, which will require further action to comply with the appellate ruling. If the judgment of the trial court is affirmed, the losing party can try to get the U.S. Supreme Court's attention, which is no easy task, unless the legal questions are novel.

· Chapter ·

3

A Crime Occurs: Help! Police!

■ ■ ■

Solving crime in America is mostly a reactive business. When a crime occurs, a citizen seeks help by placing a 911 call to an emergency services line, and police officers rush to the scene. At that moment, an investigation begins, often in chaos, with injured or dead victims, frightened witnesses, hysterical relatives and armed perpetrators milling around within arm's length of one another.

The investigation can end as quickly as it begins if a police officer exercises his judgment and makes an arrest on the spot or a short distance away. Or the hunt for the culprit can take days, months or years. It depends on the complexity of the crime and the police's resources and brain-power to solve the mystery. Luck also can be a factor if an offender makes a mistake; a state trooper captured Oklahoma City bomber Timothy McVeigh because he didn't have a license plate on his beat-up yellow Mercury Marquis.

How do reporters learn that a crime has been committed? For decades, editors and reporters tracked emergencies by monitoring scanners that broadcast the communications among dispatchers, cops and firefighters as they responded to calls for help. Today reporters and editors also must pay close attention to Twitter, Facebook, YouTube and email to find out about breaking news from citizens who witness accidents, shootings and robberies.

Listening to a scanner isn't easy because the dispatchers, cops and firefighters often mumble, and they speak in code, usually numbers that identify various types of emergencies. If all hell's breaking loose, you will hear the stress in their voices. They'll huff and they'll puff. And they'll yell—but not always. Sometimes the quieter they are, the bigger the story. Cops know reporters are listening, and they will use cryptic references to keep you away from their crime scenes as long as possible. This chapter will take you through the steps of an investigation, from arrests to booking to indictment by a grand jury. If you understand how it all works, you'll be able to identify the pressure points in the process, and know what questions to ask, and when.

You're Under Arrest

Police need probable cause to arrest someone. Probable cause is the lowest standard of proof in the law. It means the cop has a reasonable belief that a crime was committed and a particular person did it. Officers don't always need a warrant, which is a court order authorizing an arrest. If a crime's committed in a cop's presence, whether it's a felony or a misdemeanor, the cop can make an arrest without a warrant.

If a cop did not witness a felony, which is a more serious offense than a misdemeanor, he still can make an arrest without a warrant. A cop needs a warrant before making an arrest for a misdemeanor that was not committed in his presence, mainly because we don't want cops taking people into custody for less-serious offenses whenever they feel like it. Even so, police possess enormous power to make arrests. That is a key reason why states must provide defendants with a hearing, usually called an initial appearance, before magistrates within hours of an arrest, to double-check the work of cops.

There is a large, complicated body of law that outlines what police officers can search, and when, after they make an arrest. Essentially, after a suspect has been arrested, a cop can search the suspect personally, including all body cavities, and the area around him, primarily to protect the officer and ensure that evidence is not destroyed. If a suspect moves, the geographic area that can be searched also expands. For example, courts approved the use of evidence obtained by police as they accompanied a naked mob boss from one part of his house to another while he got dressed.

Cops cannot storm into someone's home to make an arrest without a warrant unless there is an emergency, such as if they are chasing an armed robbery suspect. When people are arrested in cars, police can search the entire passenger compartment because the area is accessible to all riders who could've hidden contraband. The U.S. Supreme Court has issued several rulings about when cops can and cannot search cars during traffic stops and after police chases. The Court has said the police's powers depend on the circumstances.

Chasing Cops

When reporters go to crime scenes, they usually wind up standing around, waiting for a ranking police officer to give a statement. Use the opportunity to introduce yourself to police officers and make small talk with people in the community who could help you on this story and in the future.

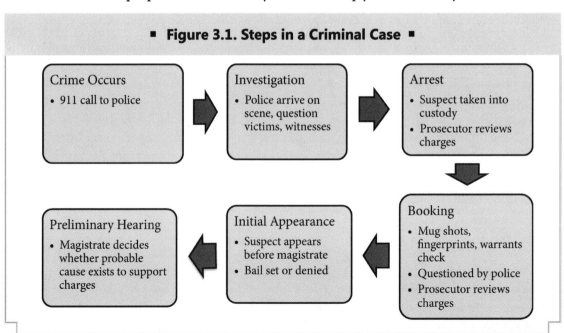

■ Figure 3.1. Steps in a Criminal Case ■

Crime Occurs
- 911 call to police

Investigation
- Police arrive on scene, question victims, witnesses

Arrest
- Suspect taken into custody
- Prosecutor reviews charges

Booking
- Mug shots, fingerprints, warrants check
- Questioned by police
- Prosecutor reviews charges

Initial Appearance
- Suspect appears before magistrate
- Bail set or denied

Preliminary Hearing
- Magistrate decides whether probable cause exists to support charges

I was only a couple years out of college and working the four-to-midnight shift in Pittsburgh, when a night editor asked me to go with a photographer to a normally quiet section of town. The editor said the police scanner had gone suspiciously quiet after homicide detectives had been dispatched to the neighborhood. When we arrived, we discovered that no one was dead, but there was a seriously injured man, along with numerous pipe bombs in a basement. I subsequently learned that the man was preparing to defend himself if his neighbors decided to attack him—that is, if the neighbors got to him before the evil spirits living in his windowsills did. The man had miscalculated as he built one of his bombs, causing an explosion that sent a hand in one direction and a foot in another.

The cops were asking people to leave their homes because they feared the explosives could blow at any moment. A woman who lived next door refused and opened her home to those of us who had work to do. The detectives set up their informal headquarters in her kitchen, and I took the living room, not that I needed a lot of space for my pen and notebook. The lady of the house shuttled between the two rooms, sharing with me snippets of what she'd overheard the cops saying, while she drank shots of sherry that increased in frequency as she realized that her neighbor had enough firepower in his basement to erase her street from the map.

Making an entrance also can help. I joined the staff of the *Boston Globe* in the winter of 1990 when young men, mostly gang members, were shooting up parts of the Roxbury, Dorchester and Mattapan neighborhoods during disputes over control of drug corners. My editors at the *Globe* were in a tizzy because the city's homicide rate was on pace to hit 100. I had moved to Boston from Philadelphia, a city plagued by so much violence that 100 homicides would've been cause for an impromptu mummer's parade to celebrate. One night, I headed to an address in South Boston that we heard about on the scanner and found detectives milling around on the sidewalk in front of a house. As I walked toward them, I hit ice and began skidding down the hill. I wasn't wearing my trademark high heels this night; I had on sensible but stylish boots. A high-ranking police officer reached out, catching me in his arms before I careened into the bowels of South Boston. Later, he became a sounding board for a four-part series I wrote about the Boston Police Department's inability to solve serious crime.

What if you can't find the crime scene? That's not as silly as it sounds. In September 1993, I was scheduled to work weekend duty when an overnight editor at the *Globe* called and woke me up at 4 a.m. after he heard a dispatcher send detectives to check out a report that a police officer had been shot. The editor had heard nothing more on the scanner because the cops had switched to a secure channel. We decided that I'd head to the Roslindale–Roxbury line, where we thought the shooting had occurred.

At that time of night, I didn't think it would be hard to find a crime scene, especially if a cop had been shot. "Officer down" is one of the most serious calls that can go out on a scanner. I thought I could roll down my car windows and track the sound of sirens, or look up in the night sky and follow the flashing police car lights. Unfortunately, Boston police officers were unusually low key that night. They had turned off their lights and sirens, but they weren't observing the speed limit. I caught a glimpse of a Ford Crown Victoria, a favorite of police detectives, as it whished past me at a deserted intersection. I floored it and followed the Crown Vic to a large parking lot in front of a strip mall. There, outside an all-night pharmacy, police found the body of Detective John Mulligan, one of the most frequently investigated cops on the force, shot to death execution-style in his car.

Allegations and Myths

When a suspect is arrested, how do you refer to him? Some reporters and editors don't like the term "allegedly" because it doesn't make clear where you obtained the information. I think you can use it after you've cited the source of the allegations, such as a police news conference, an arrest warrant affidavit, a grand jury indictment, or a lawsuit. If you want to avoid repetitive use of the word allegedly, attribute the accusations to the police, to the indictment, or to the grand jury.

I cannot stress this point strongly enough: You must attribute accusations to someone in authority or to a court document. Absent attribution, your readers won't know the source of the allegations and you will appear to be acting as judge and jury, trying and convicting a suspect before he or she steps inside a courtroom.

If a suspect is arrested without a warrant, he is taken to the police station where he is booked. The booking procedure has no legal significance. But it is an important phase to cops because it buys time for them to search for evidence while the suspect is fingerprinted and officers conduct computerized searches or make phone calls to determine whether the suspect has any outstanding warrants issued by other law enforcement agencies.

The U.S. Supreme Court has said police may not hold a suspect longer than 48 hours generally without taking him or her before a magistrate for an initial appearance. At that hearing, a suspect is informed of the charges. In some states, cops have a narrower timeframe, such as in Pennsylvania, where it is six hours. In reality, this rule is often broken to allow police more time to gather evidence against a suspect.

Significantly, cops also use this time to question a suspect in hopes of obtaining a confession. My criminal law professor at the University of Pittsburgh's School of Law, John Burkoff, says the public has a misperception about how cops solve crime because of what he calls "the myth of clues." What he meant is this: Most crimes in America are not solved by fancy high-tech scientific tests, but when police extract confessions from suspects. This makes the booking process a legal minefield for suspects.

Defense attorneys usually aren't involved at this stage unless and until a suspect invokes his right to remain silent, and he asks for a lawyer under the famous *Miranda v. Arizona* Supreme Court decision—and sticks to the request.

The Devil's in the Details

Not all arrests are spontaneous reactions to crime. Police officers can delay making arrests until they complete investigations that vary in length from a few days (to set up an undercover drug buy and bust) to several years (to take down a Mafia family on racketeering and murder charges). Police use a variety of tools to gather evidence to make a criminal case. They use subpoenas to demand documents to track a criminal enterprise's cash flow. They install wiretaps and pen registers to listen to phone conversations and keep track of incoming and outgoing calls to figure out who is involved in illegal activity. They enlist the help of informants. They ask courts to approve warrants to search for evidence. And finally, they seek a judge's approval of an arrest warrant.

Warrants are usually accompanied by affidavits in which detectives justify their requests to search a home, office, or computer, or to arrest a suspect. An affidavit is a sworn statement, pledged under oath by the author, or affiant. Lawyers, witnesses and parties in a civil lawsuit also can file affidavits to explain their actions. Police, prosecutors, defense attorneys and witnesses can file affidavits

▪ Figure 3.2. Sample Search Warrant ▪

(Source: U.S. District Court for the District of Columbia)

AO93(Rev.5/85)Search Warrant

UNITED STATES DISTRICT COURT
FOR THE DISTRICT OF COLUMBIA

[1-1] In the Matter of the Search of

Residence at ▮▮▮▮▮▮▮▮▮▮
Frederick, Maryland,
owned by Bruce Edwards Ivins,
DOB ▮▮▮▮, SSN ▮▮▮▮

SEARCH WARRANT **[1-2]**

CASE NUMBER: $07\text{-}524\,M\text{-}01$

[1-3] TO: __Postal Inspector Thomas F. Dellafera__ and any Authorized Officer of the United States

[1-4] Affidavit(s) having been made before me by __Postal Inspector Thomas F. Dellafera__ who has reason to believe that ☐ on the person or ☒ on the premises known as (name, description and or location)

Single Family Residence at ▮▮▮▮▮▮▮▮ Frederick, Maryland, and large white shed on rear of property, owned by Bruce Edwards Ivins, DOB ▮▮▮▮ SSN ▮▮▮▮

[1-5] in the District of Maryland there is now concealed a certain person or property, namely (describe the person or property)

trace quantities of Bacillus anthracis or simulants thereof, hairs, textile fibers, lab equipment or materials used in preparation of select agents, papers, tape, pens, notes, books, manuals, receipts, financial records of any type, correspondence, address books, maps, handwriting samples, photocopy samples, photographs, computer files, cellular phones, phone bills, electronic pager devices, other digital devices, or other documentary evidence.

I am satisfied that the affidavits(s) and any recorded testimony establish probable cause to believe that the person or property so described is now concealed on the person or premises above-described and establish grounds for the issuance of this warrant. **[1-6]**

[1-7] **YOU ARE HEREBY COMMANDED** to search on or before $\underline{November\ 9, 2007}$
(Date)

(not to exceed 10 days) the person or place named above for the person or property specified, serving this warrant and making the search ☐ (in the daytime - 6:00 A.M. to 10:00 P.M.) ☑ (at any time in the day or night as I find reasonable **[1-8]** cause has been established) and if the person or property be found there to seize same, leaving a copy of this warrant and receipt for the person or property taken, and prepare a written inventory of the person or property seized and promptly return this warrant to the undersigned U.S. Judge/U.S. Magistrate Judge, as required by law.

OCT 31 2007 @ 5:08 PM

Date and Time Issued in Washington, DC pursuant to the domestic terrorism search warrant provisions of Rule 41(b)(3)

DEBORAH A. ROBINSON
U.S. MAGISTRATE JUDGE
Name and Title of Judicial Officer

United States District Court
For the District of Columbia
A TRUE COPY **[1-9]**
NANCY MAYER WHITTINGTON, Clerk **[1-10]**
BY
Deputy Clerk

Signature of Judicial Officer

DEBORAH A. ROBINSON
U.S. MAGISTRATE JUDGE

1-1 Location of search	**1-6** Search deadline
1-2 Case number	**1-7** Timing of search
1-3 Law enforcement official asking for the warrant	**1-8** Warrant officially filed
	1-9 Warrant approval date and time
1-4 Description of location	**1-10** Magistrate's signature
1-5 List of what agents believe they will find	

▪ Figure 3.3. Sample Search Warrant Affidavit ▪

(Source: U.S. District Court for the District of Columbia)

<u>AFFIDAVIT IN SUPPORT OF SEARCH WARRANT</u>

1-1

I, Charles B. Wickersham, being duly sworn, depose and say:

1-2

I have been a Postal Inspector of the United States Postal Inspection Service (USPIS) for approximately twenty months. I am authorized to investigate crimes involving violations of Title 18 U.S.C. Sections 2332(a), 1114, and 1512(a)(2).

This affidavit is respectfully submitted in support of an application for warrants to search the following premises and vehicles, pursuant to the domestic terrorism search warrant provision found at Rule 41(b)(3) of the Federal Rules of Criminal Procedure, in that it involves threats to witnesses in, and obstruction of, a domestic terrorism investigation, pending in the District of Columbia.

1-3

(1) A warrant to search wall locker number 55, located in Room 127, Building 1412, United States Army Medical Research Institute of Infectious Diseases (USAMRIID), Fort Detrick, Maryland. Wall locker number 55 is labeled "Bruce Ivins", and is secured by a combination lock.

(2) A warrant to search wall locker number 10, located in Room B301, Building 1425, USAMRIID, Fort Detrick, Maryland. Wall locker number 10 is labeled "Bruce Ivins X34927", and is secured by a combination lock.

(3) A warrant to search the office area of Dr. Bruce Edwards Ivins, office number 19, located in Building 1425, USAMRIID, Fort Detrick, Maryland.

(4) A warrant to search Dr. Bruce Edwards Ivins's laboratory space in Room B303, B313 and B505, Building 1425, USAMRIID, Fort Detrick, Maryland.

1-4

As discussed below, there is probable cause to believe that a search of the aforementioned premises may result in the collection of evidence relevant to an ongoing criminal investigation into the dissemination of a Weapon of Mass Destruction (anthrax) through the U.S. mail system in September 2001 and October 2001 in violation of Title 18, United States Code, Sections 2332(a) and 1114, which killed five people and infected at least 17 others, and into tampering with a witness or informant in connection with that ongoing domestic terrorism investigation, in violation of Title 18, United States Code Section 1512(a)(2).

<u>Overview</u>

The Federal Bureau of Investigation and the U.S. Postal Inspection Service (hereinafter "Task Force") investigation of the anthrax attacks has led to the identification of Dr. Bruce Edward Ivins, an anthrax researcher at the U.S. Army Medical Research Institute for Infectious Diseases, Fort Detrick, MD (hereinafter "USAMRIID"), as a person necessitating further investigation for several reasons: (1) At the time of the attacks, he was the custodian of a large flask of highly purified anthrax spores that possess certain genetic mutations identical to the

1

1-1	Name of agent requesting permission of court to conduct search	
1-2	Investigating agency	
1-3	Locations to be searched	
1-4	Reason for search	

▪ **Figure 3.3. Sample Search Warrant Affidavit (continued)** ▪

(Source: U.S. District Court for the District of Columbia)

anthrax used in the attacks; (2) Ivins has been unable to give investigators an adequate explanation for his late night laboratory work hours around the time of both anthrax mailings; (3) Ivins has claimed that he was suffering serious mental health issues in the months preceding the attacks, and told a coworker that he had "incredible paranoid, delusional thoughts at times" and feared that he might not be able to control his behavior; (4) Ivins is believed to have submitted false samples of anthrax from his lab to the FBI for forensic analysis in order to mislead investigators; (5) at the time of the attacks, Ivins was under pressure at work to assist a private company that had lost its FDA approval to produce an anthrax vaccine the Army needed for U.S. troops, and which Ivins believed was essential for the anthrax program at USAMRIID; and (6) Ivins sent an email to a friend in ▭▭▭▭▭▭ a few days before the anthrax attacks warning her that "Bin Laden terrorists for sure have anthrax and sarin gas" and have "just decreed death to all Jews and all Americans," language similar to the anthrax letters warning "WE HAVE THIS ANTHRAX ... DEATH TO AMERICA ... DEATH TO ISRAEL." In his affidavit dated October 31, 2007, submitted in support of an initial search of the residence and vehicles of Bruce Edwards Ivins, Supervisory Postal Inspector Thomas F. Delafera described in greater detail information regarding Bruce Edwards Ivins, and his probable connection to the anthrax mailings. I hereby incorporate this affidavit by reference herein. *See* Exhibit A.

[2-1]

<u>Factual Background</u>

Over the course of the past few years, Dr. Ivins has become aware that the Task Force considers him a person who warrants further investigation in connection with the anthrax attacks. He has been interviewed a number of times by law enforcement throughout the course of the nearly seven-year investigation, most recently in the presence of his attorney on June 9, 2008. In addition, on November 1, 2007, Task Force agents executed search warrants at his residence, his office at USAMRIID, and his vehicles, for evidence linking him to the anthrax attacks, and seized a number of items, including numerous letters to members of Congress and the media, along with handguns. Finally, in recent months in particular, he has told co-workers and friends that he is a suspect in the investigation, even revealing to one friend a few weeks ago that his attorney has told him to prepare to be indicted for the anthrax attacks.

[2-2]

His most recent statement regarding the attacks came two days ago on Wednesday, July 9, 2008. While at a group therapy session in Frederick, Maryland, he revealed to the Licensed Clinical Social Worker and other members of the group that he was a suspect in this investigation. He stated that he was a suspect in the anthrax investigation and that he was angry at the investigators, the government, and the system in general. He said he was not going to face the death penalty, but instead had a plan to kill co-workers and other individuals who had wronged him. He said he had a bullet-proof vest, and a list of co-workers, and added that he was going to obtain a Glock firearm from his son within the next day, because federal agents are watching him and he could not obtain a weapon on his own. Based on these statements, the Social Worker called the Frederick, Maryland, police department, and they took custody of Bruce Edwards Ivins on Thursday, July 10, 2008, for a forensic evaluation at Frederick Memorial Hospital, where he remains as of this writing.

2-1 Facts used by agent to justify search	**2-2** Agent presses case for search approval

in criminal cases to vouch for the authenticity of evidence. Sometimes prosecutors and police want to hold their cards close and an affidavit will contain bare-bones details to justify the arrest. Other times an affidavit will overflow with titillating tidbits of information. Be warned: In an affidavit, a police officer or an FBI agent describes what he thinks happened and who did it. It is one side of the story with facts yet to be proven. A well-written affidavit can result in a front-page or lead story on a website. I scooped other reporters in Pittsburgh when I obtained a police affidavit used to justify

▪ Figure 3.3. Sample Search Warrant Affidavit (continued) ▪
(Source: U.S. District Court for the District of Columbia)

Further, with respect to backyard at the residence, at approximately 10:30 p.m., in early June 2008, Bruce Edwards Ivins was observed walking in the rain out into an area of his backyard near his back fence. He was then observed making a raking or digging motion in that area. Subsequent visual scrutiny of that area revealed that it was an untended area of grass and other vegetation.

Finally, with respect to the three vehicles, over the course of the past several months, visual surveillance has been conducted regularly at the residence of Bruce Edwards Ivins at ▮▮▮ ▮▮▮▮▮▮, Frederick, Maryland. Such surveillance has revealed that all three vehicles are regularly parked in front of the Ivins residence or in the driveway on the property.

The Task Force submits that a search Subject Residence and Subject Vehicles may reveal physical or documentary evidence that will assist the investigation into these threats to witnesses related to the anthrax investigation, and obstruction of that investigation. The search is for firearms and other weapons, ballistics vests or other protective gear, and any writings identifying a plan to kill witnesses or names of intended victims, or any other relevant documents, notes, photographs, and records in various formats, including computer files and other electronic media, as more fully described in the Attachment to this affidavit.

<u>Conclusion</u>

Based on the foregoing, I submit that there is probable cause to believe that a search of the Subject Offices and Wall Lockers may result in collection of evidence relevant to the investigation of threats to witnesses in, and obstruction of, the investigation into the dissemination of a weapon of mass destruction (anthrax) through the U.S. mail system in September and October 2001 in violation of 18 U.S.C., Sections 1512(a)(2), 2332a and 1114. Specifically, there is probable cause to believe that a search of the Subject Residence and Subject Vehicles as described in the Attachment to this affidavit, may reveal firearms and other weapons, ballistics vests, and writings identifying a plan to kill witnesses, names of intended victims, photographs, and other relevant documents.

Because this affidavit is part of an ongoing investigation that would be jeopardized by premature disclosure of information, I further request that this Affidavit, the accompanying Order, and other related documents be filed under seal until further order of the Court. 〔3-1〕

The statements contained in this Affidavit are based in part on information provided by FBI Special Agents and U.S. Postal Inspectors, on observations made by law enforcement agents, and on my experience and background as a Postal Inspector. I have not included each and every fact known to me concerning this investigation. I have set forth only the facts that I believe are necessary to establish the necessary foundation for the search warrant.

CHARLES B. WICKERSHAM
Postal Inspector
U.S. Postal Inspection Service

Sworn to before me this
_11_ day of _July_, 2008   〔3-2〕

U.S. MAGISTRATE JUDGE
United States District Court
for the District of Columbia

3-1 Request to keep affidavit secret	**3-2** Date and signature of magistrate who approved search

the arrest of a man who allegedly tried to kill his wife and himself when he drove the wrong way on a highway, causing a four-car pileup that killed a 22-year-old prospective bridegroom the night before his wedding. The affidavit said the suspect's blood-alcohol level was more than three times the legal limit and that he wanted to kill his wife because she had asked for a divorce.

Sometimes affidavits are written by cops and other times, if police are smart, they'll ask a prosecutor to draft the document. A prosecutor or police officer then presents the affidavit to a magistrate or a judge who decides whether investigators have met the probable cause standard, meaning there is slightly better than a 50-50 chance that a crime occurred and the subject of the search or arrest warrant committed the offense. It is not much of a hurdle to overcome. Search warrants should explain exactly what the police want to search, why and what they think they might find. Once a search is concluded, police are supposed to file a return, which is an inventory of every item that officers took out of a home, office, car or off a computer.

Prosecutors often ask judges to seal affidavits and warrants out of fear that suspects could be tipped off, prompting them to destroy evidence or flee the area, before a search or arrest occurs. Once the search is conducted or the arrest is made, reporters should try to obtain the affidavit. By writing stories based on affidavits, reporters publicize the reasoning behind searches and arrests and serve as an additional check on the judgment of police, prosecutors and magistrates. Sometimes search warrants aren't sealed but are hiding in plain sight on the public record. In many courts, search warrants aren't filed in the criminal case index under the name of the subject of the investigation. Instead, you'll find the paperwork by going to the court's miscellaneous docket and looking up the address of the building that was searched. Many courts keep this additional docket to log searches of cars, computers, homes and businesses, and to keep track of emergency matters. Figure out how your court uses its miscellaneous index. Does the court spell out house numbers, does it use numerals, or does it rely on a combination of both? Chances are that clerks have used both methods over the years. You'll need to run the address several ways to make sure you haven't missed it.

If affidavits and search warrant returns remain under seal after an arrest or a search, journalists should ask judges to make the records public or explain in writing why they should remain secret. Unfortunately the news media's financial difficulties have led to reductions in the money set aside to wage legal fights over access to records and proceedings. You may find that your news organization lacks the funds, guts, or both to seek access to a sealed record. If that happens, your best option could wind up costing a lot more: If you obtain the records from a confidential source, you could be subpoenaed to testify before a grand jury, and that will cost more money because you and your news organization will need a lawyer. Good reporters put aside the fear, gather the news and deal with the fallout later, if it occurs. Worrying about what could go wrong will paralyze you. Do your job and gather the facts to inform your readers, viewers or listeners.

If you can't get your hands on the affidavit, ask a trusted source to read it to you or summarize what it says. When I worked at the *Boston Globe*, I covered the story of a retired minister who dropped dead of a heart attack when cops, heavily armed and dressed in black ninja outfits, burst into his home by mistake because of bad information from a drug snitch. It was a weekend and I couldn't get into the courthouse to obtain a copy of the search warrant affidavit, although I tried by tracking a clerk I knew to his girlfriend's house on Cape Cod. When he couldn't get back to Boston in time to help me gather details for the next edition, I dispatched a couple of my cop sources to sneak peeks at a copy of the affidavit that the police brass were keeping at headquarters. I remember sending one of my sources back to re-read the affidavit several times to clarify the details.

■ Figure 3.4. Sample Search Warrant Return ■

(Source: U.S. District Court for the District of Columbia)

1-1

AO 109 (2/90) Seizure Warrant

RETURN

1-2

DATE WARRANT RECEIVED	DATE AND TIME WARRANT EXECUTED	COPY OF WARRANT AND RECEIPT FOR ITEMS LEFT WITH
10/31/2007	11/1/2007 6:45 PM	IN Residence

1-3

INVENTORY MADE IN THE PRESENCE OF
Kellie OBrien

INVENTORY OF PROPERTY SEIZED PURSUANT TO THE WARRANT

See attached

CERTIFICATION

1-4

I swear that this inventory is a true and detailed account of the property seized by me on the warrant.

FILED

NOV 0 9 2007

1-5

1-6

Subscribed, sworn to, and returned before me this date.

NANCY MAYER WHITTINGTON, CLERK
U.S. DISTRICT COURT

11-09-07
Date

U.S. Judge or U.S. Magistrate Judge

1-1 Time and date search conducted
1-2 Reveals whether agents left list of items confiscated
1-3 Name of person present during the search
1-4 Name of agent filing inventory

1-5 Proof that return was filed with court and when
1-6 Magistrate who accepted formal filing of inventory of seized items

▪ Figure 3.4. Sample Search Warrant Return (continued) ▪
(Source: U.S. District Court for the District of Columbia)

U.S. DEPARTMENT OF JUSTICE
FEDERAL BUREAU OF INVESTIGATION
Receipt for Property Received/Returned/Released/Seized

On (date) _____

At (time) _____

(Name) _____

(Location) ██████████████████

Item(s) listed below were:
- ☐ Received From
- ☐ Returned To
- ☐ Released To
- ☐ Seized

ITEM#	DESCRIPTION
1	One (1) small cardboard box labeled "Paul Kemp...Attorney client privilege"
2	One (1) small cardboard box labeled "Paul Kemp...Attorney Client Privilege"
3	One (1) small cardboard box labeled "Paul Kemp...Attorney Client Privilage" Contains scientific research documents. RMR-1029
4	Photo copy of hand drawn map; application for guns-found in lock box
5	Spector Pro internet monitoring software
6	two (2) 5x7 cards with writing
7	Check transaction Register
8	Glock 27 stock barrell-G6026
9	5x7 card with writing
10	Handwritten and mapquest directions to 37 Anderson Ave Warwick, RI
11	US Department of State-Bruce Edwards Ivins; Social Security Card Lebanon, OH; Two (2) newspaper articles
12	Counter surveillance package/equipment
13	Five (5) cards from Respect Life Committee
14	Four (4) VHS tapes found in third shelf from the bottom; right side
15	VHS tape found in VCR
16	Eight (8) VHS tapes, bottom shelf, right side
17	Eight (8) VHS tapes found in second shelf from bottom, right side
18	Laboratory supplies
19	Photo negative
20	Business cards, contacts, email addresses
21	Make-up & false hair, costume type

Page 1 of 3

2-1   List of confiscated items

Gathering information isn't easy. You will run into dead ends, but don't give up. Keep asking yourself, who else would know what I want to know, and who else has access—or can get access—to what I want to know?

Prosecutors Punt

In a country of 300 million people and fewer than one million cops, it should be no surprise that most crimes go undetected, uncharged and unpunished. Of the small percentage investigated and charged by police, prosecutors choose to pursue only a fraction. When prosecutors decide to *nolle prosequi*, or abandon a case, they punt and dismiss charges. Before making such a decision, a prosecutor usually asks two questions: Did the police have probable cause to make the arrest? Will the evidence convince a jury beyond a reasonable doubt that the suspect committed the crime? Proof of a crime beyond a reasonable doubt is the highest standard in the law, meaning as close to 100-percent certainty as possible. Prosecutors care most about meeting the top standard. If they lose a high-profile case, they may not get re-elected.

Sometimes prosecutors decline to pursue a case because the crime is *de minimis*, or not serious enough. They also may reject a case because the witnesses are unreliable or the cops committed misconduct. If all of the witnesses are drug addicts, a prosecutor might worry that a jury won't believe them. A prosecutor might abandon a case if the police beat a confession out of a suspect or violated the parameters of a search warrant.

When that happens, the exclusionary rule comes into play. This rule is a part of American criminal law that makes the United States unique in the world. By relying on a series of U.S. Supreme Court decisions, judges can exclude, or throw out evidence because it is what's known as the "fruit of the poisonous tree," information that was improperly obtained by police. When cops complain that cases were thrown out of court on technicalities, this is what they're usually talking about.

If the DA decides to pursue a case, the suspect must appear before a magistrate or other judicial officer who will explain the charges. At this point, the charges are not cast in stone and can change if the investigation turns up additional evidence. The magistrate tells the suspect that he has a right to a trial by jury and an attorney.

Depending on the charges and how serious the prosecutor makes them sound, the magistrate also decides whether to release or detain the defendant pending trial. In high-profile cases, prosecutors will ask magistrates to set high bail or bond, terms that are often used interchangeably. Bail includes all of the conditions a magistrate sets to ensure a defendant's appearance at future hearings. The magistrate also can release a defendant on his own recognizance. If released on OR, as it's known, a defendant pays nothing and gives his word that he will behave himself and show up for subsequent hearings.

Defendants typically need only to raise a percentage of the amount of the bond, the price tag a magistrate sets on a defendant's release, with cash or property. Many defendants cannot afford to pay even a small percentage of a bond, and they're locked up in jail before trial.

Peek-a-Boo

In most states and at the federal level, people facing criminal charges have a right to be indicted by grand juries. A suspect can be arrested and charged before that happens, and prosecutors usually have about a month to present the case to a grand jury for indictment. If the prosecutor can't make the deadline, doesn't want to or is in a state that doesn't require grand jury indictments, he makes his case before a magistrate or judge during a preliminary hearing.

The purpose of the preliminary hearing is the same as a grand jury: To provide an additional check on prosecutors and police to ensure that the probable cause standard was met, meaning there is a reasonable belief that a crime occurred and the defendant is more than likely the person who committed it. If so, the judicial officer declares that the defendant is bound over for trial, meaning he must face the criminal charges filed against him.

During a preliminary hearing, the prosecutor presents just enough evidence to meet the probable cause standard. Defendants can waive the preliminary hearing, but they usually don't, unless they are talking to the prosecutor about a plea agreement, a deal that can include a lower sentence in exchange for an admission of guilt.

In an elaborate game of peek-a-boo, defense counsel may try to use a preliminary hearing to get a look at the prosecution's case. Don't be surprised if the defense attorney calls no witnesses during a preliminary hearing because he doesn't want to reveal his evidence to the prosecutor.

Contrary to another myth about the criminal justice system, prosecutors are not required to share every tidbit of evidence with defense attorneys and can hold back information until cases are well underway.

Some judges pressure prosecutors to share early in the process to avoid delays. Many local prosecutors have "open-file" policies designed to share evidence with defense attorneys earlier than they are required by law to keep cases moving.

Down on the Farm

"I like it. It's like hogs in a pen," said Judge David B. Sentelle of the U.S. Court of Appeals for the D.C. Circuit. He was referring to 10 reporters standing behind a roped area outside the room where a grand jury heard testimony about whether President Bill Clinton had lied about his sexual relationship with White House intern Monica Lewinsky.

A grand jury stakeout can be as boring as watching paint dry. What's worse is that sometimes court officials do their best to make you as uncomfortable as possible by forbidding you from sitting on the floor. What can you possibly learn from such a frustrating duty? You can figure out the direction of an investigation by talking to witnesses about what prosecutors asked and what they said in response. Don't let a lawyer in a fancy suit and expensive shoes tell you that grand jury witnesses are sworn to secrecy. They are not. You can try to talk to them. The witnesses, of course, can refuse, but there is nothing in the law that precludes them from discussing their testimony. That is, unless they are cops, FBI agents and prosecutors, who are banned by law from revealing matters that are before grand juries. The proceedings are supposed to be secret, mainly to protect the innocent from having their reputations ruined if an investigation turns up no wrongdoing. But this doesn't stop the newsgathering process.

Prosecutors control grand juries because they present only one side of the story. No one else is allowed to appear before a grand jury unless a prosecutor says so. As a result, defense lawyers are fond of saying that a district attorney can manipulate a grand jury into indicting a ham sandwich. Through a grand jury, a prosecutor can subpoena witnesses, obtain bank records, and demand utility bills along with other information, in seeking details about virtually every aspect of a person's life. If a prosecutor abuses this power, who would know? That's why it's important for reporters to keep track of grand juries.

Hookers and Exotic Dancers

A witness appears alone when he testifies before a grand jury. It's the witness, the prosecutor and the grand jurors, up to 23 of them, crammed in a small room often made to feel more claustrophobic because there usually aren't any windows to keep prying eyes from looking in.

Sometimes a witness will fight a grand jury subpoena by filing a motion to quash. The motion asks a supervisory judge to determine whether the prosecutor is over-reaching and seeking information from someone who doesn't have it or shouldn't be forced to give it up because of testimonial privilege. Such a privilege protects communications between a lawyer and client, a minister and penitent and a husband and wife. Unless they're sealed, the motions to quash probably will show up on the court's miscellaneous docket, which gives you another reason to pay attention to it.

When a witness testifies before a grand jury, her attorney is not allowed in the room. If the witness is unsure how to answer a question, she can ask for a moment to confer with her lawyer outside the grand jury room. There also is no judge, which means there is no one inside the room to determine whether prosecutors are asking legally proper questions with a factual basis. In the late 1990s, I was among a group of reporters staking out a grand jury investigating top police officials in Washington when a witness emerged from the grand jury room and said he had been asked if he knew whether female prostitutes and exotic dancers had been procured for a lieutenant and the former police chief. The TV cameras rolled as we questioned the witness while he walked to the nearest Metro subway stop. The witness said he denied knowing anything about hookers or dancers. When asked to comment on what the witness told reporters, the former chief said he didn't know what the prosecutor was talking about. The chief's best friend and roommate, a police lieutenant, eventually pleaded guilty to wire fraud, theft and extortion for blackmailing men he saw attending gay night clubs.

Critics of the grand jury system argue that innocent people can be ruined when stories are written about the questions posed by prosecutors. My response: Prosecutors shouldn't be asking bizarre questions without some legitimate reason. If they are, they're abusing the grand jury system. Put the blame where it belongs. We won't know if prosecutors go off on tangents unless we keep tabs on grand juries and write stories about what they're asking witnesses.

If a witness has already appeared before the grand jury and the testimony is in transcript form, defense attorneys could get in trouble if they leak it to a reporter in violation of a judge's secrecy order. It happened when two *San Francisco Chronicle* reporters obtained transcripts of grand jury testimony in the federal investigation into steroid use by Major League Baseball players. The reporters were on their way to jail after being held in contempt of court for refusing to identify their source when a defense attorney admitted that he had provided the transcript to the newspaper.

Your sources probably aren't going to be as willing to give themselves up. Nor should they. Don't make a promise if you think there's a chance you won't keep it.

Smokin' (Mad) in the Ladies' Room

A witness who is subpoenaed by a grand jury can refuse to testify by invoking his Fifth Amendment right against self-incrimination. In doing so, he sets a process in motion that a reporter needs to understand to cover investigations. Early in my career, my understanding of this process had mixed results.

In one instance, I was covering a run-of-the-mill drug case in the federal courthouse in Pittsburgh, when several deputy marshals barged in and declared that no one could leave the courtroom until they said so. Naturally that got my attention. As soon as possible, I left the courtroom, but I swung past the chambers of Judge Carol Los Mansmann, whom I knew was serving as the emergency judge that day. Judges typically take turns with this duty, which requires them to handle an assortment of requests, including immunity for witnesses who don't want to testify before grand juries for fear of incriminating themselves. When I poked my head in Judge Mansmann's outer office, I saw several men in suits.

Not wanting to let them know I was on to them, I headed down to the floor below, to the grand jury room. I knew the process for granting immunity. First, the witness goes before the grand jury and invokes his Fifth Amendment rights when asked questions by the prosecutor. I guessed that I was covering the drug case when that happened. Next, the witness is taken to the emergency judge to receive the grant of immunity. With that in hand, the witness returns to the grand jury room to answer the prosecutor's questions. I had no idea who the witness was, but I thought I might recognize him and figure out what the grand jury was investigating.

It wasn't a bad plan. When I came down the staircase, I saw a court security officer. He didn't see me because he was speaking on his walkie-talkie, reporting that the hallway was clear. I slipped behind him into a ladies' restroom, which was conveniently located outside the grand jury room. I tried to time my exit to coincide with the witness's arrival at the grand jury room, but I opened the door too soon. Prosecutors and FBI agents surrounded the witness, who was too far down the hallway for me to identify. My hiding place blown, the court security officer ordered me to return to the ladies' room. He never laid hands on me, but he blocked my exit with his arms while crowding me back inside.

I was a kid, in my early 20s working at my first reporting job covering my first big beat, and I didn't know what to do. There were slats in the lower half of the door. I thought I could see through them. They were rusted shut. There was a crack between the floor and the bottom of the door. I was dressed in a suit and heels, but I got down on the floor and tried to look under the door. All I saw were wing-tipped shoes. Frustrated and angry, I started screaming for the U.S. attorney, J. Alan Johnson.

To this day, I'm not sure who the witness was. I think it was a professional baseball player, one of several who were granted immunity to testify against men who had supplied them with cocaine in the late 1970s and early 1980s. No FBI agent or prosecutor dared be seen talking to me in the days after the incident outside the grand jury room for fear of being accused of leaking the story to me. As if my humiliation that day wasn't bad enough, my competition at the *Pittsburgh Post-Gazette* broke the story. You'll win some, and you'll lose some. The point is to keep swinging for the fence.

Watch and Listen

How do you know when and where a grand jury is meeting? If you are covering an investigation, talk to a lawyer who represents someone you think has received a subpoena to testify. It will say when and where the grand jury is convening. It also may identify the number assigned to the grand jury.

In the federal court in Washington, there were several different grand jury panels, each with its own identifying number. There used to be a phone number that grand jurors could call to listen to a recorded message to find out when they were meeting. Reporters learned the phone number and used it to check the grand juries' schedules so that we would know when to stake out the third floor of the courthouse. Eventually court personnel caught on and changed the phone number.

You can figure out when the grand jury is in session if you make regular swings by the room on the floor where it meets. If you keep tabs on who goes in and out, you'll recognize grand jurors, and that will help narrow down meeting days. The designs of newer courthouses, especially federal buildings, make it harder for reporters because grand jury rooms are located in secure areas that are off-limits to the general public. That means you may be forced to conduct your stakeout from the sidewalk in front of the courthouse. You also can and should talk to other people in the courthouse who know when a grand jury meets, such as bailiffs, court security officers, clerks and even judges.

It's important to remember that you should not talk to sitting grand jurors, unless you want to be accused of obstruction of justice and wind up in jail. It may be worth the risk if a grand juror reaches out to you because she is concerned that a prosecutor is misusing his power.

Sometimes witnesses and their lawyers go to great lengths to avoid reporters who are staking out a grand jury. During the Clinton administration, at least eight separate grand jury investigations were conducted into the activities of the president, his wife, Hillary, and several members of the administration for everything from whether the Clintons had participated in a questionable land deal in Arkansas to whether a housing secretary had lied about paying off a mistress. In late October 1997, White House lawyer Cheryl Mills was called before a grand jury to explain why videotapes of Clinton's coffee klatches with large campaign donors weren't turned over to investigators. Another White House lawyer, Bruce Lindsey, accompanied Mills to the third floor of the federal courthouse, where I, along with several network TV producers, were waiting to ask her about her testimony.

But the White House lawyers headed in the other direction, away from us. Mills pressed a buzzer to be admitted into a private hallway that led to the chambers of several appellate court judges. She went to see Judge David Tatel, a former law colleague of hers and a Clinton appointee. Judge Tatel, who is blind and said later he didn't know Mills had just testified before the grand jury, told the White House lawyers they could use the judges' private elevator to leave the building. This was my turf, and I knew the layout of the courthouse. I narrowed down the possible exit routes: The TV producers and I split up to cover all of them. A CBS camera crew captured Mills and Lindsey on videotape as they left the building.

I also participated in one of the news media's worst moments when Clinton's secretary Betty Currie kicked off a grand jury investigation in January 1998 into whether the president had urged White House intern Monica Lewinsky to lie about their sexual relationship. I had never seen so many reporters in my life. My quiet courthouse was as packed as a mall at Christmastime. When Currie exited the front door of the courthouse, reporters and camera crews closed in around her. She couldn't move. At one point I was next to her, and I thought we were going to be crushed like fans during a riot at a soccer game. I looked up and saw a tall aluminum light pole that the TV people used. It was swaying wildly, and I thought it was going to fall and land on Currie's head.

Luckily it didn't, and we in the news media got our act together. We worked with court personnel and lawyers for witnesses to create a more civilized exit procedure in which attorneys and their clients would go to a bank of microphones on the front steps of the courthouse, make a brief statement and leave, mostly but not completely unmolested. The TV cameramen still followed them down the street, but the witnesses and their lawyers weren't mobbed as Currie had been.

No Guts, No Glory

My knowledge of the bowels of the courthouse came in handy again during the Lewinsky grand jury investigation when Independent Counsel Kenneth Starr conducted several private meetings with Chief Judge Norma Holloway Johnson, who was called on several times to resolve witness immunity and other legal issues.

Tipped off that Starr was in the building, I slipped away from the pack of reporters on stakeout duty outside Chief Judge Johnson's courtroom. I guessed that Starr would try to use the judges' elevator to make his escape, as Mills and Lindsey had. To reach that elevator, Starr had to walk down a private corridor from the chief judge's chambers to a door that opened into a dead end in the public hallway. I positioned myself outside that door, where a deputy U.S. marshal assigned to Starr's security team also had decided to wait. Unsurprisingly he didn't want to share the spot with a reporter, and he ordered me to leave the area immediately.

To cover courts aggressively, it helps if a reporter works for a news organization with guts. I was fortunate to work for the *Washington Post*, where I had been instructed to call the paper's legal counsel directly, bypassing my editors, if I got into a legal jam. I used my cell phone and reached Katharine Weymouth, now the *Post*'s publisher but then a lawyer in the paper's office of legal counsel. I told Weymouth that I was nose-to-nose with a rather large deputy marshal who was so angry with me that the veins in his neck were bulging.

I'll never forget what she said to me: Don't move. Make him arrest you. I was standing in a public hallway in a public courthouse, acting as a watchdog on a special prosecutor who was investigating the president of the United States. Eventually the deputy marshal backed down, possibly after someone above his pay grade decided he should avoid a showdown with a *Post* reporter. When Starr walked by me to board the private elevator, I asked him why he was meeting with the chief judge. He declined to answer, but I don't consider that a loss. Ken Starr knew we were watching, and another member of the court security crew learned that the federal courthouse in Washington remains accessible to the public and the press.

Principles matter, and you should not be afraid to stand up for them. I learned that lesson from a federal judge. While covering my first court beat in Pittsburgh in the mid-1980s, I was kicked out of several courtrooms because prosecutors routinely asked judges to clear the rooms and lock the doors so they could enter into secret deals with drug dealers who had become federal informants. Each time I did what I was taught: I stood up, objected and asked the judge to recess the proceeding to give me time to get a lawyer to the courtroom to argue on my behalf for an open hearing.

One day, Judge Carol Los Mansmann, the same judge who signed off on the immunity deal in the baseball cocaine investigation, closed a courtroom on me in an unrelated drug case. I went to her chambers to talk about it. She invited me into her inner sanctum and we sat in comfortable leather chairs. She must have been amused by the chutzpah of a 20-something reporter in asking her to explain why she had shut me out, but she didn't show it. She was polite, professional and listened patiently. She also congratulated me on doing my job and doing it well. She said that my role as a reporter was to challenge her as a judge, to force her to think twice about the ramifications of the secrecy prosecutors asked her to impose. Throughout my career, I followed her advice, challenging judges to question whether prosecutors were exaggerating danger to justify secrecy or to hide a mistake.

· *Part* ·

Chasing Paper
and People

· *Chapter* ·

The Paper Chase: Finding, Reading and Making Sense of Court Records

■ ■ ■

Every year, clerks in state and federal courthouses across the nation log millions of criminal and civil cases. That's not counting hundreds of thousands of motions filed in new and existing cases.

The federal trial court in Washington often had dozens of cases filed each day. There, the civil clerks kept a wooden box on a counter where they placed the paper versions of the day's lawsuits. On the criminal side, the clerks kept a clipboard with a list of all public grand jury indictments. I made a habit of stopping in the clerk's office several times a day to check the box and clipboard. Not every courthouse will have the same setup, and you will need to locate the spots, low-tech as some of them may be, in your clerk's office, and check them regularly.

Today attorneys can file lawsuits and motions electronically, making them accessible from a computer on a reporter's desk or in your home. It's important to remember that not every court filing may be available immediately, or easy to find because there is no digital equivalent of the box and clipboard. That means you will need to cultivate clerks, lawyers and judges to tip you off about the existence of a filing.

The federal Freedom of Information Act does not apply to records held by the U.S. courts, which means reporters cannot rely on that law to force a judge to reveal a piece of information. A judge can seal a record, or block it from view by the public and the press at the request of a prosecutor, plaintiff's attorney or defense lawyer, or take action on his own. In this chapter, we'll discuss how to find your way around a courthouse, dig for details in documents and separate the innocuous from the important in interpreting legal developments and evaluating information for newsworthiness.

A Brave New World

Before computers, there was no central repository of federal civil and criminal cases. Now there's PACER, the Public Access to Court Electronic Records system (http://www.pacer.gov). In the past, you had to beg your editor to send you to other cities if you wanted to do a "scrub," or background research on people or companies that had moved into your community to find out whether they had been charged with a crime, filed suit against anyone or been sued by others. Only then could you run their names through court indices, pull the files and read about their business or criminal dealings.

Even in the digital age, members of the public and press still can go to the local courthouse, read the files and take notes at no charge. If you want paper copies of records, you must pay for them. The PACER system isn't free either. You need to set up an account, and users pay fees based on the number of pages in a downloaded record. David Sellers, a spokesman for the Administrative Office of the U.S. Courts, says the money is used to maintain the computerized repository and the publicly available websites that individual courts have created for judges to post their opinions.

Reporters should urge judges to follow the leads of their counterparts in San Francisco, Washington, D.C., and Alexandria, Virginia, in making case filings available online for free to the public and the press. Many of the filings in the case against former San Francisco Giants slugger Barry Bonds, who was accused of lying about his use of performance-enhancing drugs, were available on the free website set up by the U.S. District Court for the Northern District of California. The U.S. District Court for the Eastern District of Virginia provided free public access to documents in the criminal case against Zacarias Moussaoui, a French citizen of Algerian descent who admitted he was a member of al-Qaeda and came to America to receive flight training for a second wave of terrorist attacks after 9/11. The U.S. District Court for the District of Columbia also ensured the public could access for free the affidavits the FBI filed in support of search warrants it obtained for the home, cars and office of Bruce Ivins, the Fort Detrick, Maryland, scientist whom the bureau blames for the deadly anthrax attacks of 2001.

More and more state courts also are posting filings in high-profile cases, as state court judges in Florida and Colorado did when they made available online documents that had been filed in the *Bush v. Gore* case in 2000, which granted public access to filings in the fight over the presidency, and the rape case against Los Angeles Lakers star Kobe Bryant that was dropped in 2004. State courts try to keep up, but it is difficult because they depend on often cash-strapped legislatures for funding to make documents available online. This means you won't have digital access to everything you need, and you'll have to cover your courthouse the old-fashioned way by being there, walking the halls, talking to people, pulling paper files and reading documents.

Ups and Downs

When a grand jury votes to accuse one or more people or businesses of wrongdoing, is the indictment handed up or handed down? The terms are not interchangeable. The difference makes sense, literally. Grand jurors hand up an indictment to a judicial officer because he usually sits on an elevated bench above them. When paperwork moves in the opposite direction, a judge hands down a written opinion to the rest of us from his perch. I usually avoided using those terms because I thought they were legalese. I relied on "returned," "issued" or "charged" because I thought those words were easier for the average reader to grasp.

When an indictment or a lawsuit is filed, go beyond a Google search and run the names of the defendants and plaintiffs through your local newspaper's morgue, or archived database, to see what's been written about them in the past. The morgue stores your community's memories, especially its bad ones about convicted murderers, rapists and other criminals. More than one young reporter has written a glowing tribute about a man who works with kids only to learn later that the hero was a convicted pedophile. Checking your news organization's archives will help you avoid a similar blunder.

Once an indictment is filed in the clerk's office, the case belongs to the court beat reporter, and the fun begins. She is responsible for monitoring developments big and small, gathering string and writing substantive stories to keep readers informed. You can bet you'll be following not one but several criminal and civil cases that are newsworthy—all at once. To do this well, it doesn't hurt to be more than a little obsessive and compulsive.

Where do you start? Keep track of the court's calendar, a daily, weekly or monthly schedule of hearings and trials before each judge. Many courts post calendars on websites they've created. If not, some judges tack a paper schedule outside their courtroom doors, or you can find a list of the day's events in the clerk's office.

One of the first steps a reporter should take is to make note of case numbers. You'll need these identifiers to follow developments online, or if you need to go to the clerk's office to pull paper files because your court doesn't provide digital access to documents. You don't want to be searching frantically for a case number while you're on deadline. I also was compulsive about keeping an up-to-date calendar of my own, listing dates for hearings and deadlines set by judges for lawyers to file motions in all of the cases I was following.

You cannot keep all of the case numbers, hearing dates and filing deadlines in your head. If you forget one, you could miss a big story. Create your own system to stay on top of what's happening in the cases of interest in the courthouse.

Treasure Hunting

How do you know what's going on in a particular case? As each case progresses, a docket, or detailed list of every development, grows in length. Dockets provide maps to a case's treasure. They can go on for pages, depending on a case's complexity, and they should include notations about every filing by the parties, every hearing and every ruling by a judge, no matter how trivial.

Docket sheets also list names, phone numbers and email addresses for lawyers for all of the parties in a case. The most technologically hip courts provide docket sheets that allow electronic access with a click of a mouse to every document filed in a case, starting with the indictment in a criminal matter and a lawsuit in civil litigation.

Entries on docket sheets provide brief summaries of motions, hearings and judicial orders. Clerks write the entries, which means they can be confusing and, sometimes, incorrect. For that reason, it is unwise for reporters to base stories solely on docket sheet entries. More reporting is necessary. If the site provides a live link to publicly available records, you should open the document, read it and rely on your own interpretation, not a clerk's summary.

Digital access can be a blessing and a curse. It's a blessing because reporters in Boston can look at filings in a case in Los Angeles. It can be a curse because such easy, instantaneous access means reporters are on duty 24 hours a day, seven days a week. In 2006, during the run-up to the perjury trial of I. Lewis "Scooter" Libby, Vice President Dick Cheney's former chief of staff, I checked PACER for new filings sometimes after midnight, and wrote stories for the Associated Press from my home.

I do not recommend covering courts solely via computer. If you're in the courthouse and the clerks and judges know who you are, you increase the odds that one of them will give you a heads up about a newsworthy filing, or slip a copy of it to you.

If you're not there, you'll also deprive yourself of the thrill of uncovering clues and unlocking mysteries of criminal investigations and civil disputes.

▪ Figure 4.1. Sample Docket Sheet ▪

(Source: U.S. District Court for the Northern District of California)

CAND-ECF   2/2/12 4:03 PM

APPEAL,CLOSED,E-Filing,RELATE
1-1

U.S. District Court
California Northern District (San Francisco)
CRIMINAL DOCKET FOR CASE #: 3:07-cr-00732-SI-1

1-3

1-2

1-4

1-5

Case title: USA v. Bonds   Date Filed: 11/15/2007
                                                     Date Terminated: 12/16/2011

Assigned to: Hon. Susan Illston

Appeals court case numbers: '09-10079',
11-10669

1-6

Defendant (1)

Barry Lamar Bonds   represented by **Allen Ruby**
TERMINATED: 12/16/2011   Law Offices of Allen Ruby
                                                        125 South Market Street, Suite 1001
                                                        San Jose, CA 95113
                                                        408-998-8500
                                                        Email: ruby@allenrubylaw.com
                                                        LEAD ATTORNEY
                                                        ATTORNEY TO BE NOTICED
                                                        Designation: Retained

                                                        Cristina C. Arguedas
                                                        Arguedas, Cassman & Headley, LLP
                                                        803 Hearst Avenue
                                                        Berkeley, CA 94710
                                                        510-845-3000
                                                        Fax: 510-845-3003
                                                        Email: arguedas@achlaw.com
                                                        LEAD ATTORNEY
                                                        ATTORNEY TO BE NOTICED
                                                        Designation: Retained

                                                        Dennis Patrick Riordan
                                                        Riordan & Horgan
                                                        523 Octavia Street
                                                        San Francisco, CA 94102
                                                        415/431-3472
                                                        Email: dennis@Riordan-Horgan.com
                                                        LEAD ATTORNEY
                                                        ATTORNEY TO BE NOTICED

file:///Users/locyt/Desktop/BondsDocketSheet.webarchive   Page 1 of 42

1-1 Court location	**1-4**	Start and finish dates
1-2 Case number	**1-5**	Judge assigned to case
1-3 Caption	**1-6**	Defense team

▪ Figure 4.1. Sample Docket Sheet (continued) ▪
(Source: U.S. District Court for the Northern District of California)

CAND–ECF   2/2/12 4:03 PM

Pending Counts

3-2

18:1503 Obstruction of Justice
(5sss)

Highest Offense Level (Opening)

Felony

Terminated Counts

18:1623(a) Perjury
(1-4)

18:1623(a) False declarations before
Grand Jury
(1s)

18:1623(a) False Declarations Before
Grand Jury
(1ss-10ss)

18:1623(a) False Declaration Before
Grand Jury
(1sss-3sss)

18:1623(a) False declarations before
Grand Jury
(2s)

18:1623(a) False declarations before
Grand Jury
(3s-7s)

18:1623(a) False Declaration Before
Grand Jury
(4sss)

18:1503 Obstruction of Justice
(5)

18:1623(a) False declarations before
Grand Jury
(8s)

18:1623(a) False declarations before
Grand Jury
(9s-13s)

18:1503 Obstruction of Justice
(11ss)

18:1623(a) False declarations before

Disposition

3-1

2 yrs probation, with conditions, including
30 day location monitoring, 250 hours
community service; $4,000 fine, $100
special assessment

Disposition

dismissed--defendant sentenced on
superseding charge

dismissed--defendant sentenced on
superseding charge

dismissed--defendant sentenced on
superseding charge

dismissed on Government's motion

dismissed

dismissed--defendant sentenced on
superseding charge

dismissed

dismissed--defendant sentenced on
superseding charge

dismissed

dismissed--defendant sentenced on
superseding charge

dismissed--defendant sentenced on
superseding charge

3-1 Outcome   **3-2** Charges

▪ Figure 4.1. Sample Docket Sheet (continued) ▪

(Source: U.S. District Court for the Northern District of California)

CAND-ECF   2/2/12 4:03 PM

Grand Jury (14s)	dismissed
18:1503 Obstruction of justice (15s)	dismissed--defendant sentenced on superseding charge

Highest Offense Level (Terminated)

Felony

Complaints   **Disposition**

None

```
                                                                                                      4-1
```

Plaintiff

USA   represented by   **J. Douglas Wilson**
                                                         United States Attorney
                                                         450 Golden Gate Avenue
                                                         San Francisco, CA 94102
                                                         415-436-6885
                                                         Email: Doug.Wilson@usdoj.gov
                                                         LEAD ATTORNEY
                                                         ATTORNEY TO BE NOTICED

                                                         Jeffrey David Nedrow
                                                         United States Attorney's Office
                                                         NDCA, San Jose Division
                                                         150 Almaden Blvd., Suite 900
                                                         San Jose, CA 95113
                                                         408-535-5045
                                                         Email: jeff.nedrow@usdoj.gov
                                                         LEAD ATTORNEY
                                                         ATTORNEY TO BE NOTICED

                                                         Matthew A. Parrella
                                                         US Attorney's Office
                                                         150 Almaden Blvd., Suite 900
                                                         San Jose, CA 95113
                                                         408-535-5061
                                                         Fax: 408-535-5066
                                                         Email: matthew.parrella@usdoj.gov
                                                         LEAD ATTORNEY
                                                         ATTORNEY TO BE NOTICED

                                                         Jeffrey R. Finigan
                                                         U.S. Attorney's Office

file:///Users/locyt/Desktop/BondsDocketSheet.webarchive   Page 4 of 42

4-1   Prosecution team

▪ Figure 4.1. Sample Docket Sheet (continued) ▪
(Source: U.S. District Court for the Northern District of California)

450 Golden Gate Avenue
11th floor
San Francisco, CA 94102
(415) 436-7200
Fax: (415) 436-7234
Email: jeffrey.finigan@usdoj.gov
ATTORNEY TO BE NOTICED

Merry Jean Chan
U.S. Attorney's Office
Appellate
450 Golden Gate Avenue
11th Floor
San Francisco, CA 94612
415-436-7200
Email: merry.chan@usdoj.gov
ATTORNEY TO BE NOTICED

Date Filed	#	Docket Text
11/15/2007	1	INDICTMENT as to Barry Lamar Bonds (1) count(s) 1-4, 5. (vlk, COURT STAFF) (Filed on 11/15/2007) Additional attachment(s) added on 11/15/2007 (vlk, COURT STAFF). (Entered: 11/15/2007)
11/15/2007		CASE DESIGNATED for Electronic Filing. (Entered: 11/15/2007)
11/15/2007		Terminate Deadlines and Hearings as to Barry Lamar Bonds: (Entered: 11/15/2007)
11/15/2007		Initial Appearance set for 12/7/2007 09:30 AM before Magistrate Judge Maria-Elena James. (Entered: 11/15/2007)
11/15/2007	2	Notice of Related Case by USA as to Barry Lamar Bonds (Finigan, Jeffrey) (Filed on 11/15/2007) (Entered: 11/15/2007)
11/20/2007	3	Summons Returned Executed on 11/19/07. as to Barry Lamar Bonds (lsk, COURT STAFF) (Filed on 11/20/2007) (Entered: 11/26/2007)
11/27/2007	4	ORDER RELATING CASE.. Signed by Judge Susan Illston on 11/26/07. (ts, COURT STAFF) (Filed on 11/27/2007) (Entered: 11/27/2007)
11/28/2007		Case as to Barry Lamar Bonds reassigned to Judge Susan Illston. Judge William H. Alsup no longer assigned to the case. (Entered: 11/28/2007)
12/03/2007	5	CLERK'S NOTICE Trial Setting Hearing set for 12/7/2007 09:00 AM before Hon. Susan Illston. Arraignment set for 12/7/2007 09:00 AM before Hon M. James. (ts, COURT STAFF) (Filed on 12/3/2007) (Entered: 12/03/2007)
12/07/2007	6	Minute Entry for proceedings held before Judge Hon. Susan Illston:The defendants appearance maybe waive at the next appearance. The appropriate waivers shall be filed in advance of the next hearing.The government indicated that there may be a

5-1   Docket entries: summaries and access to filings

Here We Go

It is important for a reporter to watch and listen carefully to who says what—and who doesn't—in a courtroom. Does the defendant personally say, "Not guilty," or does his lawyer say the words for him? It matters because the facts matter.

Within days of an indictment, a reporter needs to find out when the defendant's arraignment will take place. This hearing often makes big news because it kicks off coverage of a criminal case with the defendant's assertion that he is "not guilty" of the charges. During the arraignment, the judge usually offers the defendant a chance to have the charges read to him. In many instances, defense counsel waives this option to save time. By then the defendant and his lawyer should have a copy of the charges. The judge also may be asked to reconsider bail or alter the terms of the defendant's release. Sometimes arraignments are called initial appearances. In federal court, initial appearances have all of the trappings of an arraignment, except the defendant usually isn't asked or expected to enter his plea of not guilty. If the defendant is not asked to enter his plea, don't call it an arraignment. Call it an initial appearance or simply a hearing, and make sure you tell your readers or viewers that the defendant was not asked for his plea.

Instead of entering a not-guilty plea during an arraignment, an ornery defendant may try to plead guilty, or he may refuse to say a word and stand mute to disrespect the court because of an ideological, political or mental health reason. When that happens, the judge usually enters a not-guilty plea on behalf of the defendant. There is another possible outcome: A defendant enters a plea of *nolo contendere*, or no contest. In some jurisdictions, the prosecutor and judge must approve such a plea before it can be entered. In the end, it's the same as a guilty plea except it has implications for a civil lawsuit, if a defendant expects he's going to be sued. Essentially the defendant gives up

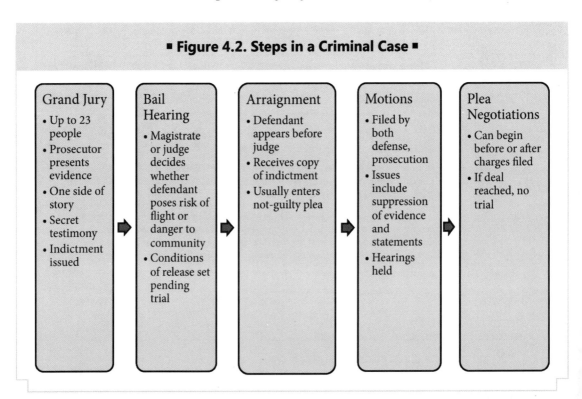

■ Figure 4.2. Steps in a Criminal Case ■

Grand Jury
- Up to 23 people
- Prosecutor presents evidence
- One side of story
- Secret testimony
- Indictment issued

Bail Hearing
- Magistrate or judge decides whether defendant poses risk of flight or danger to community
- Conditions of release set pending trial

Arraignment
- Defendant appears before judge
- Receives copy of indictment
- Usually enters not-guilty plea

Motions
- Filed by both defense, prosecution
- Issues include suppression of evidence and statements
- Hearings held

Plea Negotiations
- Can begin before or after charges filed
- If deal reached, no trial

the fight against the criminal charges, but by refusing to admit his guilt, he tries to thwart efforts to use the outcome in the criminal matter against him in a civil case. An Alford plea is similar: A defendant enters the plea, without admitting wrongdoing.

Once the arraignment is held, the criminal case takes off.

Watch, Listen and Learn

Defense attorneys file all sorts of motions, some of which make news and some of which do not. They will complain that the prosecutor hasn't given them everything they're entitled to. They'll want information about the prosecution's witnesses. They'll want more time and money to conduct their own investigations, if they're any good at what they do. They may want to move the trial to another location to avoid what they consider prejudicial pretrial publicity. They also may seek postponements for a variety of reasons, some legitimate and others not.

Reporters must understand that most of those arguments are routine. Defense attorneys often are trying to pry information from the prosecution, sooner rather than later in the process. You should read defense attorneys' filings carefully to get a sense of the strategies they may use in defending their clients.

Prosecutors also will use the pretrial phase to float theories, pressure witnesses into cooperating and coerce defendants into pleading guilty instead of going to trial. That means that both sides may try to use the news media to gain an advantage.

Lawyers perpetuate the myth that only law school graduates can read and understand legal documents. Before attendance at law schools became the accepted route to a legal career, men (and they usually were men) learned the law by reading, writing and listening to arguments in court. Like many reporters, I learned about the law the old-fashioned way by watching trials, listening to arguments and reading legal briefs. If you can read, you can understand a court document. If you know how to listen, you can cover a court hearing or a trial.

Don't think it's a piece of cake because it's not. The law is confusing and at times illogical. Don't be embarrassed to admit that you don't understand a legal term or concept. Ask a lawyer or a judge to explain it to you. Don't be ashamed to admit that you don't understand what just happened in a hearing or how a judge ruled. Most lawyers and judges want you to get it right, and they will try to help you understand what you saw, heard or read.

When reading a court record, you must first figure out its overall theme and purpose:

- What is this about?
- What does the defense attorney want?
- What does the prosecutor want?
- What's the bottom line? What did the judge rule?

Once you determine the filing's purpose, you can put the issues into context and evaluate their broader significance. That is, do they make news?

What's What

It would be nice if you had time to read an entire document before you started to write your story, but that's not the real world, especially with the Internet's insatiable demand for information as quickly as possible. You often will compose your story on the fly and under enormous deadline pressure. To help you figure out what's what, ask yourself as you read:

- What are the new nuggets of information?
- How significant are they? Are they shocking? Are they interesting? Are they amusing?
- Do they fill a significant gap in your knowledge of the case?

Keep track of the new bits of information and rank them in importance and uniqueness as you go through the document.

Be on the lookout for good quotes as you read. Select quotes that advance the story by contributing facts or context to what you want to say. Avoid rambling quotes that contain legal jargon that will require you to use parentheses to translate the terms into English. A good quote is like dialogue in a play or a punch line in a joke. It not only moves the story along, but it also spices it up and allows your readers to hear the voice of the judge who wrote the decision. As you read, rank the quotes according to their importance and potential placement in your story.

Next, ask yourself, what's my lead? As you know, the lead generally is the first paragraph of a news story, and it must tell the reader what's happened and why he or she should care. Often, figuring this out isn't as easy as it sounds. Sometimes a court document contains so much information that it's difficult to make a choice. The following questions will help you focus:

- What is the most important aspect of this document?
- Is it a particular fact or new revelation about the case?
- Or is a search or arrest in and of itself the most important element in terms of the development of the story?
- In other words, so what? Who cares?

Hoo-hah

Your next challenge is what editors call the top of the story—the first four to six paragraphs. The top has to sing, which means it has to move quickly. If not, you'll lose readers, particularly online where you have about three seconds to grab and keep a visitor's attention.

There is evidence that some online readers want more, and will read longer stories, especially on tablets. If the story is a long explanatory piece, for example, you'll want to include what one of my editors at the *Boston Globe* called the hoo-hah paragraph that puts the story into broader context by telling readers why the issues are significant. The hoo-hah, or "nut," paragraph also introduces various themes, or strands, and provides a roadmap for the reader to the rest of the story.

It may sound elementary, but you must ask yourself as you write whether you have answered the Five W's and the how questions, as needed by your subject. Who? What? Where? When? Why? How? Sometimes you won't need to answer all of them. Sometimes you won't be able to find answers to all of them, but you must tick them off in your head to be sure you've covered all of the bases.

Court and crime stories require a significant amount of vital statistics—the defendant's age, address and occupation at a minimum, exactly how many charges she faces, and how much prison time he could receive, if convicted. In other instances, you may need to find out the name of her spouse, her parents, how many children she has, their names, and the names of her dogs, cats and goldfish. Spelling every name correctly is crucial. If you misspell a name, you could implicate an innocent person in a crime. Such errors also convey to your readers that you are a sloppy reporter. If you mix up or misrepresent the facts, you display inattention or disrespect for detail. Always double-check your facts by going back through the document to make sure you haven't transposed details or misinterpreted the information during your first read.

Don't simplify and exaggerate. Legal jargon and concepts should be explained in clear language; but if you oversimplify, you run the risk of giving an inaccurate description of a legal issue. Reporters who cover courts frequently struggle with the dilemma of explaining too much or too little. If your editor asks a question about your translation of legalese, try not to dismiss him. If he doesn't get it, chances are your readers won't. Patience with editors wasn't always my strong suit, but when I talked it through with a thoughtful editor, we often came up with a better way of explaining a legal concept.

Before you hit the send button on your computer, ask yourself two important questions:

- Have I called everyone with a stake in this story?
- Have I described each party's point of view as accurately and fairly as possible?

Reading Is Fundamental

A court case is a war of words, and that means you will spend a significant portion of your time reading. Here are some of the best places to look for details you'll need to tell compelling stories:

Affidavits aren't limited in their use to support a search of a home, office or computer, or to arrest a suspect. Lawyers, witnesses and parties in civil lawsuits and criminal cases can file affidavits to make statements under oath. Remember, an affidavit is only one side of the story.

Indictments are lists of criminal charges filed against a defendant. If an indictment is well written, it reads like a novel, full of dramatic details that bring a crime to life. Other times, it can be as boring as a grocery list and makes little, if any, sense. A federal indictment may look a little different from a state indictment. An indictment in one jurisdiction also may vary slightly from that of another. The federal government and most, but not all, states require indictments to be issued by grand juries. As a result, indictments begin by announcing that "the grand jury charges," or language to that effect.

Most, if not all, indictments provide references to the laws that a defendant is accused of violating. Reporters who cover courts should consult the criminal codes that are published by state and federal governments. By looking up the law, you can find a description of the elements that a prosecutor must prove before a jury can convict, and locate an explanation of the penalties a defendant faces if he is found guilty. Increasingly, you can find the criminal codes online.

When writing stories about indictments that charge several defendants, you must be careful about making sweeping statements. In many indictments, all defendants are not charged with committing each and every offense. Indictments are divided into counts, which are separate charges. You must keep track of which defendant is charged with which count. Pro football player Michael Vick was not charged with committing every act of brutality in the dog-fighting case against him and several others. Some defendants were charged with killing specific dogs that lost matches, while Vick was not. You need to read indictments carefully to make sure you aren't accusing a defendant of committing something he isn't charged with doing.

Never forget that an indictment contains allegations—unproven charges against a defendant who has not had a chance to refute the prosecutor's claims. Make sure you say so. Don't convict a defendant before she has had her day in court. You may tire of writing "the grand jury said" or "the grand jury charged," but I don't believe you can say it too many times. If you want to break the monotony, use "the indictment said," where appropriate. Regardless of the synonym, make sure it is

▪ Figure 4.3. Sample Indictment ▪

Source: U.S. District Court for the District of Columbia

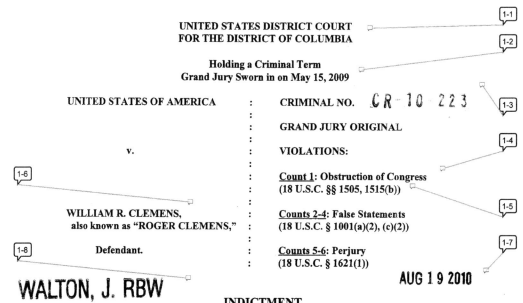

UNITED STATES DISTRICT COURT
FOR THE DISTRICT OF COLUMBIA

Holding a Criminal Term
Grand Jury Sworn in on May 15, 2009

UNITED STATES OF AMERICA   :   CRIMINAL NO. CR-10-223

:   GRAND JURY ORIGINAL

v.   VIOLATIONS:

Count 1: Obstruction of Congress
(18 U.S.C. §§ 1505, 1515(b))

WILLIAM R. CLEMENS,   :   **Counts 2-4**: False Statements
also known as "ROGER CLEMENS," :   (18 U.S.C. § 1001(a)(2), (c)(2))

Defendant.   :   **Counts 5-6**: Perjury
(18 U.S.C. § 1621(1))

WALTON, J. RBW

AUG 1 9 2010

INDICTMENT

The Grand Jury charges that:

Unless otherwise indicated, at all times material to this Indictment:

INTRODUCTORY ALLEGATIONS

Background

Major League Baseball

1. Major League Baseball ("MLB") is the highest level of professional baseball in the United

States and Canada. There are presently 30 MLB teams in 17 states, the District of Columbia and one

Canadian province. MLB operates in interstate and foreign commerce and is subject to the

jurisdiction of the United States Congress.

Defendant WILLIAM R. CLEMENS

2. Defendant WILLIAM R. CLEMENS, also known as "ROGER CLEMENS," was a

1-1	Court location	**1-5**	Federal criminal code
1-2	Date grand jury was created	**1-6**	Defendant
1-3	Case number	**1-7**	Date of indictment
1-4	Charges	**1-8**	Judge assigned to case

crystal clear to your readers and viewers that the charges have not yet been tested in court. Always remember that indictments represent prosecutors' promises to produce proof and nothing more.

Criminal complaints with accompanying affidavits are filed before an indictment, if authorities want to make an arrest quickly because they fear a defendant may flee. Police also may believe they need to wrap up an investigation immediately because they don't want drugs to wind up on the street, or they don't want to take a chance that an informant or undercover cop could be harmed. There are many other reasons, and reporters should try to find out why authorities decided to move forward before an indictment could be obtained from a grand jury. Don't assume you know. Find out why.

In the federal system and in many states, defendants must be indicted by grand juries within a month or so of arrest. The deadline is part of the panoply of rights a defendant receives in connection with a speedy trial, usually within about six months of being charged with a crime. The reason is simple: To prevent the government from arresting a person and locking him up for months or years without a trial.

In most states and in the federal system, indictments must be obtained after criminal complaints are filed. If prosecutors miss the deadline, a preliminary hearing must be held to test whether the probable cause standard has been met, or the charges must be dismissed. After an indictment is filed, compare it to the criminal complaint to identify what was added, subtracted or modified. The differences could provide angles for you to pursue in gathering more information about the investigation.

A federal *criminal information* is a document similar to an indictment in that it lists charges against a defendant, with two important distinctions: First, it contains charges filed by the prosecutor, not the grand jury. Second, it can be filed only with the defendant's consent. The filing of this document often signals that a deal calling for cooperation has been reached—but not always. It also could mean that the prosecutor and defendant have agreed to resolve the case by payment of restitution, community service or an alternative resolution. Don't jump to the conclusion that the defendant has become a snitch, although that may be what's happened. Sometimes prosecutors simply want to get a case over with and move on. More significantly, there has to be a benefit for the defendant. What person in his right mind would agree to being charged with a crime if there wasn't something in it for him? You need to ask why the prosecutor and the defendant chose this path.

A civil *lawsuit* provides one side's version of a dispute between two parties. It is important to remember that a lawsuit, like an indictment, contains allegations that have not been proven. Unlike an indictment, where a grand jury theoretically acts as a check on a prosecutor, no one reviews a lawsuit's allegations; and a complaint, another word for lawsuit, can be initiated by anyone who can pay the court's nominal filing fee. This is why reporters must do their best to get a comment from the other side when writing about a newly filed lawsuit. Often that is easier said than done. Some lawyers, particularly attorneys who specialize in civil litigation, cling to the notion that if they ignore the press, reporters will go away. Keep trying to get a comment. At least you'll know you did everything you could to be fair.

If the lawsuit is well written, it will tell a story. It's worth repeating that it is only one side of the story. Like an indictment, a lawsuit lists counts, or separate allegations of wrongdoing, that refer to state or federal laws that the plaintiff, the person or company who filed the suit, says were violated by the defendant. Reporters must be careful when summarizing the allegations in their stories, avoiding the temptation to use a broad brush to describe the dispute. You need to be especially cautious when a lawsuit names several defendants who may or may not be named in every count. You don't want to say John Doe was accused of violating three contracts when he is named in only one count of the lawsuit that deals with an entirely separate issue.

▪ Figure 4.4. Sample Lawsuit ▪

(Source: U.S. District Court for the Western District of Virginia)

Case 7:12-cv-00013-SGW   Document 1   Filed 01/12/12   Page 1 of 9   Pageid#: 1

CLERK'S OFFICE U S. DIST. COURT
AT ROANOKE, VA
FILED

JAN 1 2 2012   1-1

JULIA C. DUDLEY, CLERK   1-2
BY:
DEPUTY CLERK

IN THE UNITED STATES DISTRICT COURT
FOR THE WESTERN DISTRICT OF VIRGINIA
ROANOKE DIVISION

SONS OF CONFEDERATE VETERANS,	)
VIRGINIA DIVISION,	)
	)
Plaintiff,	)
	) **Case No:**
v.	)
	) *7: 12-CV-00013*
CITY OF LEXINGTON, VIRGINIA,	)
MARILYN E. ALEXANDER,	)
DAVID COX,	)
MIMI ELROD,	)
T. JON ELLESTAD,	)
MARY P. HARVEY-HALSETH,	)
BOB LERA,	)
GEORGE R. PRYDE,	)
CHARLES SMITH,	)
	)
	)
Defendants.	)

1-3   1-4   1-5

COMPLAINT AND PETITION FOR INJUNCTIVE RELIEF

COMES NOW the Sons of Confederate Veterans, Virginia Division, by counsel, and

states as its Complaint and Petition for Injunctive Relief against the Defendants, the City of

Lexington, and the members of Lexington City Council, the following: 1-6

I.   THE PARTIES

1.   The Plaintiff is an unincorporated, nonpolitical, fraternal organization of persons

with residences in the Commonwealth of Virginia. The Plaintiff is a division of

the Sons of Confederate Veterans, a national organization founded in Richmond,

Virginia and currently headquartered in Columbia, Tennessee.

2.   Defendant, City of Lexington, Virginia, is a city organized under the laws of the

1-1	Date lawsuit filed	**1-4**	Case number
1-2	Court where lawsuit filed	**1-5**	Defendants
1-3	Plaintiff	**1-6**	Backgrounds of parties

▪ Figure 4.4. Sample Lawsuit (continued) ▪
(Source: U.S. District Court for the Western District of Virginia)

Case 7:12-cv-00013-SGW   Document 1   Filed 01/12/12   Page 8 of 9   Pageid#: 8

8-1

V. COUNT II: 42 U.S.C. § 1983

35.   The City, by its prior practice of allowing the flag standards to be used by other organizations for the display of the flags of those organizations on occasions of significance to those organizations, created a forum for expression.

36.   The City's adoption of amended ordinance § 420-205 was in response to the request of the Plaintiff to engage in expression within the flag standard forum for expression created and maintained by the City.

37.   The City's adoption of amended ordinance § 420-205 was based upon its disapproval of the content and/or viewpoint expressed by the Plaintiff and the flags the Plaintiff flew from City flag standards in January of 2011.

38.   The City's adoption of amended ordinance § 420-205 constituted discrimination against the Plaintiff and the expression of the Plaintiff on the basis of content and/or viewpoint.

39.   The City's adoption of amended ordinance § 420-205 deprives the Plaintiff of its rights under the First Amendment to the United States Constitution, and Plaintiff is entitled to relief for this deprivation under 42 U.S.C. § 1983.   8-2

WHEREFORE, Plaintiff Sons of Confederate Veterans, Virginia Division prays for the following:

   A.   Judgment against the Defendants and for equitable relief;

   B.   A finding of civil contempt on the part of the Defendants;

8

8-1   Plaintiff's allegations against defendants | **8-2**   What plaintiff wants from court

Case 7:12-cv-00013-SGW   Document 1   Filed 01/12/12   Page 9 of 9   Pageid#: 9

C. Attorneys' fees under 42 U.S.C. § 1988, costs and sanctions;

D. Compensatory, liquidated and punitive damages;

E. For such other and further relief as may be just and equitable.

Respectfully submitted,

[9-1]

Thomas E. Strelka, VA Bar No. 75488
Correy Diviney, VA Bar No. 74833
Strickland, Diviney & Strelka
23 Franklin Road
P.O. Box 2866
Roanoke, Virginia 24001
Phone: (540) 982-7787
Fax: (540) 342-2909
Thomas@Strelkalaw.com

Counsel for Plaintiff
Sons of Confederate Veterans

Douglas R. McKusick, VA Bar No. 72201
The Rutherford Institute
1440 Sachem Place
P.O. Box 7482
Charlottesville, Virginia 22901
Phone: (434) 978-3888
Fax: (434) 978-1789
douglasm@rutherford.org

Of Counsel

9-1   Plaintiff's attorneys and contact information

Depositions are a staple of civil litigation. A witness is subpoenaed to provide sworn testimony, which means it is under oath. Depositions typically take place in a lawyer's office in the presence of counsel for all parties and the attorney for the witness. Usually a judge is not present. A court stenographer, who is also a notary public, administers the oath, and lawyers for interested parties question the witness. If lawyers object to the questions asked—and they usually do—the objections are noted on the record for the judge to resolve later, if necessary. In the interim, the witness is supposed to answer, or give a reason for declining.

A deposition can be a valuable source of information for a reporter. Nothing in newsgathering, however, is easy. Years ago courts ran out of space and decided to allow lawyers to keep transcripts of depositions in their offices. As a result, depositions aren't technically part of the official court record. That means reporters must ask lawyers to share the depositions with them. Sometimes a lawyer can comply. Sometimes he can't, if the judge imposed a protective order, which is a restriction on release of information in the case. How will you know if a deposition is worth your effort to obtain? You usually won't, unless you see a reference or an excerpt from a deposition in a motion filed by one of the lawyers.

Prosecutors occasionally will rely on depositions in place of live testimony, but that occurs if there is a concern about the health or safety of a witness in a criminal case. If that happens, you can expect a defense attorney to raise a ruckus if he hasn't had a chance to cross-examine, or subject the witness to adversarial questioning. The Sixth Amendment to the U.S. Constitution provides defendants with the right to confront witnesses against them, and that means allowing their lawyers to pose questions.

Following Bread Crumbs

Whether in the form of affidavits, motions to sever or judges' opinions, court filings contain clues to solving a case's mysteries, and that's why it's important to be thorough and careful as you read all parts of a document, including attachments and especially footnotes, where prosecutors and judges love to drop hints about an investigation's direction and make sweeping assertions about a legal issue.

In November 2003, I noticed a footnote in a document filed by prosecutors in the Zacarias Moussaoui terrorism case. Much of the filing was redacted, or blacked out, because prosecutors believed they were protecting what may or may not have been sensitive national security information. But there was enough visible to prompt me to follow up with my sources, who told me that an al-Qaeda operative, who had planned to be the twentieth hijacker on 9/11, made it to the United States but left suddenly. At that time, that's all I could tease out of my sources. Later, other pieces fell into place and prosecutors revealed that the would-be hijacker was on a flight that landed in Orlando, but an alert Customs official denied the al-Qaeda operative entry into the United States.

Here are some of the motions that often contain bread crumbs for you to follow:

Bail requests typically occur after an arrest, but defense counsel can renew the motions up to and throughout a trial. A bail hearing often resembles a mini-trial, where prosecutors provide evidence to support their claims that the defendant poses a danger to the public and a risk of flight if he is allowed to remain free pending resolution of the case. Deciding whether to release a defendant is among the toughest and most dangerous decisions a judge can make. If the defendant commits another crime while free on bail, the prosecutor, the press and the public will blame the judge.

Defense attorneys file *motions to dismiss* in criminal and civil cases. Sometimes they make news and sometimes they don't. If a prosecutor files a motion to dismiss an indictment, that's usually big news because it often means the case has fallen apart, and you need to find out why. In 2011, Dominique Strauss-Kahn, the former chief of the International Monetary Fund, was charged with forcing a New York hotel housekeeper into performing oral sex. But the case fell apart when investigators began doubting the woman's credibility after they learned of a phone call she made to her boyfriend in jail, telling him that she knew what she was doing and that Strauss-Kahn had money.

A defense motion to dismiss may be routine and rejected quickly by a judge, but it sometimes contains descriptions of previously unknown evidence that casts doubt on the strength of the prosecution's case. The motion to dismiss contains the defense's spin on the case, but you cannot and should not ignore it. Every piece of information improves a reporter's understanding of the legal issues and helps you write with authority about a case.

A *change of venue* motion is filed to seek the relocation of a trial usually because of concerns about prejudicial pretrial publicity. The trial of Timothy McVeigh, who was ultimately convicted of using a truck bomb to kill 168 people at a federal building in Oklahoma City in 1995, was moved to Denver because a federal judge believed it would've been impossible to conduct a fair trial in the city devastated by the attack. Moving a trial can be expensive. Instead of paying to put all court officials up in hotels in other cities or towns, judges sometimes agree to a *change of venire* and bring in a group of potential jurors from another county.

Postponements and *continuances* are sought by all sides, including the judge, for a variety of reasons, some newsworthy but most not. Trying cases is a logistical nightmare, as difficult at times as herding cats. Prosecutors, defense attorneys and judges have commitments in other cases. People get sick or die. Always ask why a postponement is being sought and granted. You won't know if it's worth a story unless you ask.

Severance motions are common in cases involving multiple defendants who don't want to be lumped in with others and found guilty by association. If a severance request is granted, at least two trials will be conducted on the same subject, which is not an appealing result to judges who may have other pending cases lined up like planes waiting to land at Chicago's O'Hare Airport.

Motions to suppress evidence are most often filed in drug cases, in which police have confiscated narcotics during raids and in which defendants have made incriminating statements to investigators. These motions can reveal the specifics of a defendant's admission, the circumstances surrounding a police interrogation or search, and provide hints of other evidence gathered in an investigation. Defense attorneys may allege violations of the warnings to remain silent that police must give to suspects because of the *Miranda v. Arizona* ruling by the U.S. Supreme Court. They also may accuse police of mistreating a suspect, planting evidence or other wrongdoing. If that happens, you must check out the allegations. Try to talk to witnesses, if there were any. Reach out to the cops personally. Don't rely solely on the police department's PR guy. Always call the police union when allegations of brutality are raised.

Requests to determine a defendant's mental *competency* to stand trial are usually newsworthy because they signal the possible use of an insanity defense. If defense counsel request an evaluation, prosecutors will want to bring in their own psychiatrists to conduct separate tests. The result is often dueling experts: The defense's doctor says the defendant cannot assist in his case, and the prosecutor's physician says he's fine.

Pro se motions are made when defendants want to represent themselves. Judges often will order psychological evaluations to ensure that defendants are not delusional. When a defendant represents himself, it slows the trial and increases the judge's workload by forcing him to become more involved in the questioning of witnesses than he otherwise would be. Judges will try to talk defendants out of taking this route because they know laymen will stumble and possibly hurt their causes. U.S. District Judge Leonie Brinkema displayed the patience of Job in the Zacarias Moussaoui terrorism case when she allowed the defendant to represent himself for several months. She endured a barrage of vicious personal attacks, scrawled in Moussaoui's barely legible handwriting, before she ordered him to accept real lawyers to handle the case for him.

Civil lawsuits are filed each year by *pro se* plaintiffs, people who cannot afford or don't want to hire a lawyer to represent them. The fee for filing a lawsuit can be waived by the court if the plaintiff is indigent, or too poor to pay.

Motions to quash are filed by people who want a judge to kill a subpoena for testimony or documents. These motions crop up in civil and criminal cases. Businesses file motions to quash if they object to turning over records of a top customer. Libraries file the motions if they are asked to provide a list of books a patron has checked out. Reporters will ask judges to quash subpoenas from grand juries for testimony about the identities of their sources, or their notes.

A motion to quash a grand jury subpoena can provide a reporter with clues about the scope of an investigation. In a game of keep-away, prosecutors and judges usually make sure all of the paperwork is sealed and hearings are held behind locked courtroom doors. Every once in awhile one slips through, and if you aren't paying attention and checking your traps, you'll miss it.

Motions for temporary restraining orders, or TROs, are usually filed in civil cases when one side wants the other to stop what it's doing immediately, such as draining a business's bank account or selling off assets. Government agencies, such as the Securities and Exchange Commission and Federal Trade Commission, also file lawsuits with accompanying motions for TROs against companies that allegedly are engaged in fraudulent practices. A TRO preserves the status quo until a judge can decide whether to grant a request for a *preliminary injunction*, which extends the restrictions until the lawsuit can be resolved.

Watch the docket. Check the clerk's office. Stay in contact with lawyers for all sides. Read everything that's filed in cases of interest to your news organization. If you take all of those steps, little if anything will get by you.

· *Chapter* ·

State Justice: From Birth to Death

■ ■ ■

By far, state court judges handle legal matters that affect the daily lives of more Americans than their counterparts in the federal judiciary. Local courthouses are not only filled with documents that chronicle the missteps of people who break the law. Court records also memorialize significant moments in the lives of law-abiders—when they marry, buy a house, get divorced or fight over custody of their children. In other words, courthouses are goldmines, storing nuggets of information for reporters to unearth as they research people and companies.

But it is the cases themselves—some civil, but mostly criminal—that consume the bulk of a reporter's time and energy. To cover the court beat, reporters need to be able to grasp and explain several key constitutional concepts raised by prosecutors and defense attorneys time and again in motions and arguments in felony cases, including drug offenses and homicides, where the stakes are highest.

In this chapter, we will examine a series of rulings since the early 1940s that the U.S. Supreme Court used to force states to adopt most of the provisions affecting criminal law contained in the Bill of Rights, the first 10 amendments to the U.S. Constitution. The exceptions to this doctrine, known as incorporation, are the right to be indicted by a grand jury and the right to a trial by jury in civil cases. The Court also has suggested but not ruled directly that states must abide by the Eighth Amendment's prohibition against excessive bail in pretrial detentions. If state authorities violate the incorporated procedures, evidence can be thrown out, cases can be dismissed and defendants can be set free.

We also will discuss the basic elements prosecutors must prove to earn convictions and how homicides, murder in particular, pose the biggest challenge to state courts, ethically and financially, especially when the death penalty is a possible outcome. By reading a state or federal law at issue in a trial, you'll improve your understanding of what a prosecutor must prove, and why. If you possess such a baseline of knowledge, you'll be in a better position to spot, report and write substantive, sophisticated stories about what happens when the legal process fails to work.

Know Your Rights

State constitutions can provide more legal protections for citizens than the U.S. Constitution, and some do. But states cannot provide their citizens with fewer rights than the federal Constitution. If state legislators pass a law that reduces those rights, it is likely that a federal court will find the statute unconstitutional.

The most commonly contested legal issues in criminal cases revolve around application of the Fourth, Fifth and Sixth Amendments to the U.S. Constitution, and the U.S. Supreme Court's interpretations of those areas of law.

The Fourth Amendment governs police searches of people and places, and seizures—arrests of people and collection of evidence. The Fifth Amendment provides protection for suspects during questioning by police, and the Sixth Amendment extends the grand promise of the right to a fair trial.

In a courtroom, you also will hear arguments about rights contained in two other amendments: The Eighth Amendment will be raised if a defendant says he was subjected to "cruel and unusual punishment," often after he's been locked up in prison, and the Fourteenth Amendment's guarantees of due process and fundamental fairness will come up if a suspect claims he was tortured or held incommunicado.

A Man's Home Is His Castle

The Fourth Amendment to the U.S. Constitution says: "The right of the people to be secure in their persons, houses, papers, and effects, against unreasonable searches and seizures, shall not be violated, and no Warrants shall issue, but upon probable cause, supported by Oath or affirmation, and particularly describing the place to be searched, and the person or things to be seized." Those words are as important to people today in the 21st century who travel the world with the click of a computer mouse, as they were in the 18th century when the founding fathers relied on horses and buggies to get where they wanted to go.

When police officers complain that a case was thrown out of court on a "technicality," they are often referring to a violation of the Fourth Amendment. If a cop makes a dumb mistake, lies or hides a piece of information from a magistrate, prosecutor or defense attorney, he shouldn't be allowed to get away with blaming his blunder on a judge who dares to insist that police follow the rules.

If a cop commits misconduct by violating the Fourth Amendment, a judge has the power under the so-called exclusionary rule to throw out evidence gathered during an illegal search or seizure. That means a jury won't hear about the gun the cop found in the suspect's garage, for example, because he said in a warrant that he planned to search only the man's office. The rule applies to physical evidence, not people. A person cannot seek to suppress his existence.

The United States is unique in the world in punishing police misconduct by banning use of the "fruit of the poisonous tree," a description first used in 1939 by Justice Felix Frankfurter in *Nardone v. United States* to describe evidence obtained during improper searches and seizures. In every other country, trial judges weigh the harm caused by police misconduct against the danger to society if a defendant were to be set free.

Many respected legal experts oppose the exclusionary rule's approach to policing the police. When he was a New York judge, Benjamin Cardozo famously said: "The criminal is to go free because the constable has blundered." Proponents of the rule argue that society would be in greater danger if police were not punished for wrongdoing.

State law enforcement officials weren't forced to comply with the exclusionary rule until the U.S. Supreme Court's decision in *Mapp v. Ohio* in 1961. The outcome remains one of the most famous and reviled decisions of the Warren Court, named for Chief Justice Earl Warren, who presided over the high court during its expansion of defendants' rights from 1961 to 1966. The *Mapp* decision concluded there was only one way to teach police officers a lesson when they broke the rules: Suppress, or exclude from trial, the evidence collected during illegal searches and seizures.

Knock, Knock

In 1983, a young lawyer who worked in the White House during Ronald Reagan's presidency wrote a memorandum that discussed "the campaign to amend or abolish the exclusionary rule." In 2005, the lawyer, John G. Roberts Jr., became chief justice of the United States. The following year, the Roberts Court struck its first blow to the exclusionary rule in *Hudson v. Michigan*, a case that questioned whether Detroit police violated a Fourth Amendment requirement that they knock and announce themselves before storming into a house and seizing drugs.

The practice is hundreds of years old, dating to English law, and requires that police knock, announce themselves and wait a reasonable period of time, anywhere from 15 to 30 seconds, before entering a home. Why? To spare citizens the terror of having their residences forcibly entered, especially when innocent people are caught between cops and suspects, or when police raid the wrong house. Cops worry that giving suspects too much notice could result in the destruction of evidence, or pose a threat to the officers' safety by giving people inside a house time to retrieve weapons.

When I worked at the *Boston Globe*, I wrote about a retired minister who dropped dead of a heart attack after police, heavily armed and dressed in ninja-like SWAT outfits, broke down his door and burst into his living room. The police had relied on flawed information from a snitch to obtain the search warrant. The confusing layout of the building led police to raid the wrong apartment. In other cases, police have been caught making up informants to obtain search warrants. When I worked for the *Philadelphia Daily News*, I covered a case against several members of the Five Squad, an elite citywide narcotics unit, who lied to obtain search warrants that they used to steal money and narcotics from drug dealers.

Writing for a 5-to-4 majority in *Hudson*, Justice Antonin Scalia said the crime-and-justice world had changed since the *Mapp* decision, and that violations of the knock-and-announce rule do not require judges to suppress evidence gathered during those types of searches. Justice Scalia said police departments are more professional, with sophisticated disciplinary systems in place, than they were in the early 1960s. And, he said, people who felt wronged by cops can sue today far more easily than they could 40 years ago.

In 2009, Chief Justice Roberts wrote for the majority in *Herring v. United States*, another 5-to-4 decision that chipped away at the exclusionary rule's prohibition on the use of flawed information to conduct a search or an arrest. In *Herring*, a police officer relied on faulty information kept in a neighboring county's database that led him to believe an arrest warrant was pending for a man he wanted to detain. The chief justice said the error was caused by sloppy record-keeping and not police misconduct. "To trigger the exclusionary rule," he wrote, "police misconduct must be sufficiently deliberate that exclusion can meaningfully deter it, and sufficiently culpable that such deterrence is worth the price paid by the justice system."

Police also can enter a house without a warrant when answering a noise complaint. In 2006's *Brigham City v. Stuart*, the Court considered a case involving a party that was so loud no one could hear police officers as they knocked on the door and identified themselves. Worse, some of the revelers were so drunk they didn't realize the people they saw at the door were cops. The Court said the police didn't need a search warrant to enter the house and make arrests for assault and underage drinking because they saw a juvenile being beaten by several other people. The assault was sufficient reason, the justices said.

In most instances, judges prefer for cops to obtain warrants to enter and search houses. But officers can bypass the warrant requirement if there is an emergency, or exigent circumstances, such as when cops are in pursuit of a suspect, police believe they or members of the public are in danger or they are concerned that evidence may be destroyed and a suspect might escape.

Out in the Street

Can a cop stop a person on the street—in effect, seizing him—and conduct a search? Yes, cops can stop and frisk people without probable cause, if they have reasonable suspicion that criminal activity is occurring. In 1968, the U.S. Supreme Court said in *Terry v. Ohio* that such stops are temporary and are not arrests. If a cop has a reasonable suspicion that a suspect is armed and dangerous, the officer can frisk him for a weapon.

This is one of the most controversial powers police possess and its use has been criticized in many major cities, including Boston and New York, where police officers have been accused of engaging in racial profiling, the practice of stopping and searching people of a certain race or ethnicity for drugs or guns. The encounters can be civil or demeaning, depending on how police conduct themselves when asking questions and searching people on the streets.

Don't people have a reasonable expectation of privacy to live free from the prying eyes of police? Not as much as we may think. In 1967, the U.S. Supreme Court decided *Katz v. United States*, another famous case in criminal procedure. In this case, the government secretly recorded a man talking in a phone booth. The Court said the defendant had a reasonable expectation of privacy because the booth had a door, which allowed him to carry on a private conversation.

Generally, you have a reasonable expectation of privacy if you take an action and you actually expect privacy, and other people think your expectation is a legitimate conclusion. All bets are off if you willingly reveal what you're doing. As a result, defendants must meet a heavy burden of proof to win a motion to suppress based on a Fourth Amendment violation of any reasonable expectation of privacy because the courts have created several exemptions:

- Garbage: Police officers do not need a warrant to search a suspect's trash when he places it at the curb for collection and exposes it to everyone passing by.
- Phone numbers: A suspect surrenders his right to a reasonable expectation of privacy when he dials a third party through a phone company. Cell phones raise a host of new legal issues. People tend to talk loudly on their cell phones, and, if overheard by cops and everyone else in earshot, the courts probably will consider their side of the conversation fair game.
- Mail: Police don't need a warrant to obtain the "to" and "from" information on a piece of mail because people willingly provide their names and addresses to businesses and friends, as well as the post office, FedEx or United Parcel Service. Postal inspectors need warrants to search contents of mail that is sent first class or above.
- Apartment or house windows: If a person leaves the blinds open, even a sliver, the police can look inside without violating the expectation of privacy.

- Public restrooms and store dressing rooms: These are open areas, accessible to customers—and cops—and there is no reasonable expectation of privacy for people who willingly use these areas to relieve or undress themselves.
- Email and URL addresses: People generally have a reasonable expectation of privacy regarding contents of electronic messages, but police can track websites they visit.
- Dog sniffs: This is not a search because people naturally give up their scents for all to smell, but it may make a difference if the dog sniffs outside a house or car. In October 2012, the U.S. Supreme Court was asked to decide the legality of a dog sniff at the front door of a house where marijuana allegedly was being grown. In another case, the Court was asked to determine whether officers need proof of a dog's sniffing credentials before they can establish probable cause for a search based on the animal's reaction.
- Aerial surveillance: This also is not a search as long as the police are flying in approved airspace.
- "Plain view": Police can search a car, including the trunk, without a warrant if they see evidence, such as a gun, that is obviously incriminating.
- Thermal imaging and scans: The courts consider it a search if police use this technique to locate drug-manufacturing sites and people because they give off a heat source. In 2011, a federal appeals court in Washington refused to block the use of full body scanners at airports. The judges said the government's interest in preventing terrorism outweighed an individual's privacy rights.
- GPS: In January 2012, the U.S. Supreme Court ruled that police must obtain search warrants before placing Global Positioning Systems, or GPS tracking devices, on suspects' cars. The ruling strongly favored privacy, with justices who ordinarily sided with prosecutors in criminal matters rejecting the government's contention that people driving in public waive their expectation of privacy. It remains unclear how the justices will reconcile the Constitution with technological advances that allow the pinpointing of people's locations with their cell phones, facial recognition software and other data-mining techniques that yield vast amounts of information about individuals' daily lives. In the GPS case, the justices said: Just because police have access to the technology, it doesn't mean they should use it.

Silence Is Golden

Contrary to popular culture, police do not solve most crimes with science but by eliciting confessions out of the "usual" suspects. Police tend to pick up the troublemakers in a neighborhood and lean on them to point the finger at the perpetrator. As a result, defense attorneys will file motions that attack the legality of a police interrogation if their clients confessed or made other incriminating statements. In a matter of a few hours, police can violate the Fifth, Sixth and Fourteenth Amendments to the Constitution if they coerce or beat a confession out of a suspect, fail to properly advise him of his right to remain silent or refuse to grant his request for an attorney to be present during questioning.

In the iconic *Miranda v. Arizona* ruling, the U.S. Supreme Court said in 1966 that police must advise suspects of their rights to overcome the naturally coercive effect that being questioned by officers in a police station has on a suspect. Many Americans could recite most, if not all of the *Miranda* warning: "You have the right to remain silent. Anything you say can and will be used against you in a court of law. You have the right to an attorney. If you cannot afford an attorney, one will be provided for you." Cops are then supposed to ask the suspect if she understands the rights and whether she wants to talk to police.

In 2000, the high court led by then-Chief Justice William Rehnquist refused to turn back the clock and overrule the relic of the 1960s, saying the warnings to suspects had "become part of the national culture" and "embedded in routine police practice." But in 2010, the Court ruled that suspects must speak up to invoke their right to remain silent. In a 5-to-4 decision that split along the Court's ideological fault line, the majority said judges don't need to suppress statements made by suspects who received *Miranda* warnings but sat silently through hours of interrogation before speaking up and responding to questions.

A suspect can be in custody even if he's not held at the police station. To add to the confusion, he can be in a police station but technically not be in custody. If a suspect willingly goes to the police station for questioning, it is consensual. Traffic stops also are not considered custodial because in most instances the driver is permitted to go home. Judges will try to figure out whether a reasonable person, if he found himself in the suspect's shoes, would have thought he was under arrest and not free to go.

The U.S. Supreme Court has given cops wide latitude to use trickery—and even lie—to elicit confessions from suspects, but it drew the line against torture in 1936 in a case that exemplified "southern justice" and the use of the "third degree" to beat confessions out of people. In *Brown v. Mississippi*, the high court said prosecutors could not use statements by suspects who were tortured by police officers. When former Justice Thurgood Marshall headed the NAACP's Legal Defense Fund, he won several cases from the 1940s to the 1960s in which he challenged the use of the "hole," literally a hole in the ground where police kept suspects until they confessed.

If a suspect invokes his right to remain silent but doesn't request an attorney, police officers usually can continue to question him. A key exception is if police officers take advantage of a suspect's mental illness, low IQ or other disability to obtain a confession. Once a suspect invokes his right to counsel, police officers are supposed to cease questioning, and they cannot resume the interrogation unless the suspect initiates the conversation.

In a 1977 U.S. Supreme Court decision, the justices suppressed a confession that a detective elicited by taking advantage of a suspect's low IQ and religious beliefs when he urged the man, whom he called "reverend," to reveal the location of a 10-year-old girl's body to allow her parents to give her "a Christian burial." The detective persisted with the interrogation while transporting the defendant from Davenport to Des Moines, Iowa, after promising two defense attorneys he would not question the suspect during the trip.

The (Bleeping) Death Penalty

Mob capo Francis "Faffy" Iannarella looked nervous as he wandered around the courtroom in Philadelphia's Common Pleas Court waiting for word from a jury on whether he and several other members of the Scarfo gang would be sentenced to death for killing a former pal, Salvatore Testa. While the jury deliberated, Iannarella walked over to the railing that separated spectators from trial participants and said to me, "It's the (expletive) death penalty, Tone." U.S. Supreme Court Justice Thurgood Marshall used a more socially acceptable description when he said, "death is different" to characterize capital punishment. In the United States, "evolving standards of decency" have led the Supreme Court to bar the use of the death penalty to punish the mentally retarded, juveniles who committed crimes when they were younger than 18, the mentally ill who don't understand the reason for their imminent executions and defendants who raped but did not kill adults or children.

In *Furman v. Georgia*, the U.S. Supreme Court declared in 1972 that the death penalty was unconstitutional in Georgia because state law failed to provide adequate guidance to judges and juries about the circumstances under which they could impose a death sentence. The decision led to the removal of some 600 inmates from death rows across the country, including Charles Manson, the leader of a cult-like group of young people who killed actress Sharon Tate and several others in California in 1969. In 1976's *Gregg v. Georgia*, the Court said states could impose death sentences if they met certain standards. Over the next several years, the Court said the death penalty could be imposed if a defendant deliberately killed another person; the judge or jury is permitted to consider mitigating circumstances, reasons that don't excuse a wrongful act but reduce culpability; and if a bifurcated, or two phases of a trial, are held. In the first phase, the jury decides whether a defendant is guilty, and then, if there is a conviction, a second proceeding is held to consider testimony on whether the defendant should die for what he's done.

From 1976 to 2012, more than 1,300 people were executed in the United States, according to the Death Penalty Information Center in Washington. Texas, Virginia, Oklahoma, Florida and Missouri lead the nation in executions. The federal government, U.S. military and 33 states allow juries or judges to impose death sentences. The District of Columbia and 17 states do not allow the death penalty. Lethal injection is used in 35 states and by the federal government. (Connecticut and New Mexico abolished the death penalty, but the laws were not retroactive, meaning there are people who remain on death row and could be executed by lethal injection.) In 2008, the U.S. Supreme Court upheld Kentucky's use of lethal injections and cleared the way for several other states to continue using a combination of three lethal drugs in executions. The Court rejected a constitutional challenge to the procedures that sedate, paralyze and then kill inmates. A nationwide shortage of one of the drugs has led several states, including Texas, to adopt a single-drug procedure for executions.

When a prosecutor decides to seek the death penalty against a defendant, he is maximizing his power, and he must be held accountable for how he uses it: Does he seek capital punishment against more blacks than whites? Does he decline to seek the death penalty when women are victims of domestic violence? Does he seek death sentences against blacks accused of killing whites? Does he decline to seek capital punishment against blacks accused of killing blacks? Perhaps more significant, does he use the death penalty as leverage to coerce defendants into plea agreements with lengthy sentences?

It's Latin to Me

All states have criminal codes that define crimes and, in doing so, outline the elements that prosecutors must prove to a jury to earn a conviction. You can find most, if not all, of them online.

Generally, prosecutors must prove that a defendant committed a voluntary act, or in Latin, the language of the law and ancient Rome, *actus reus*. It's not enough for a defendant to write in a diary that he wants to kill his wife. It's not enough if a defendant has a reflex motion or convulsion that sets off a chain reaction resulting in a death or injury. It is not enough for a defendant to fail to act—save a woman screaming for help as she's raped—unless he has a duty to care for the victim through a parent-child relationship or a contract, such as a lifeguard has to try to save people who are drowning. To commit a voluntary act, a defendant must take a physical action.

The second requirement is *mens rea*, which means the defendant had a culpable, or guilty, state of mind. There are four types:

- *Intentional.* This is the hardest for prosecutors to prove because it can be difficult, if not impossible, to provide evidence of what was in a defendant's mind. Here's the way John Burkoff, my criminal law professor at the University of Pittsburgh, explained it: While driving his car, Bob sees a dog and decides he wants to run over it. But the dog isn't a dog; it's a kid wearing a dog suit. The state cannot prosecute Bob for intentionally killing a kid because he thought he was killing a dog. Unless it's Halloween, and then Bob could be in big trouble.
- *Knowing.* The defendant must be practically certain that his conduct will cause a specific result. Here's an example: A defendant planted a bomb on a commuter train to kill his father. When the bomb exploded, the father and 200 other people were killed. The state can charge the defendant with one count of intentionally killing his father and 200 counts of knowingly killing the other people because their deaths were an expected result.
- *Reckless.* This means that a defendant consciously disregarded a substantial and unjustified risk and committed a gross deviation from reasonable conduct. Drag racing on the wrong side of a highway probably would be considered reckless.
- *Negligence.* This is the easiest mental state for a prosecutor to prove because a defendant should have been aware of the risk of his act. Bob should've known better than to aim his car at a figure that clearly was in a costume and not a dog.

Murder and Mayhem

The unlawful taking of the life of another is a crime that falls under the generic class of homicide. Murder, the killing of a human being with malice aforethought, is one type of homicide. Malice aforethought is a mental state encompassing the intent to kill, to inflict grievous bodily harm, to possess extremely reckless indifference to the value of human life or to commit a dangerous felony.

First-degree murder is committed with premeditation and deliberation, or it is a death that results during the commission of certain felonies.

The elements of murder are:

- *Actus reus*, a voluntary act. The defendant must have committed a voluntary action or failed to act when he had a duty to do so.
- *Corpus delicti*, or body of the crime. While there must be proof that a death occurred, a prosecutor does not necessarily need to produce proof of the existence of a corpse. He can use circumstantial evidence to prove a victim was killed.
- *Mens rea*, a guilty mental state. The prosecutor must prove that the defendant had malice aforethought, which can be satisfied by showing evidence that the defendant acted intentionally, knowingly, recklessly or negligently. It usually is sufficient for a prosecutor to show that the defendant intended to kill the victim.

A prosecutor needs only to show that a short period of time elapsed to support the element of premeditation required of first-degree murder. For most courts, five minutes is sufficient between formation of the intent to kill and the killing.

Second-degree murder is a malicious, intentional killing but not premeditated; a defendant may have acted on impulse, intended to do serious injury to a victim but not kill her, or he may have been recklessly indifferent to the value of human life.

Manslaughter is the unlawful killing of a human being without premeditation. There are two types of manslaughter: *voluntary*, in most cases a killing that occurs in the heat of passion; and *involuntary*, an unintentional killing committed recklessly, through gross negligence or during the commission of an unlawful act. Many states also have created the crime of *vehicular homicide*, which is an unintentional death caused by the driver of a motor vehicle.

Felony murder is a killing that occurs during the commission of a serious crime. Several states continue to prosecute cases of felony murder because it is the easiest type of homicide to prove. The prosecutor does not have to prove premeditation, deliberation or malice. In a robbery gone bad, for example, all a prosecutor has to prove is that a felony was committed and a person died because of it. The penalties also are usually more severe than the maximum sentences defendants face for the underlying felony, particularly in states with the death penalty. For that reason, some states have removed felony murder from their books or restricted its use if a defendant wasn't the trigger-man and didn't know his accomplice had a weapon and planned to kill anyone. In some states, an accomplice is responsible under law for a felony murder if he could have reasonably foreseen what his co-conspirators would do.

If a defendant facing the death penalty is found guilty, he is subjected to a second phase of the process in which the same jury that convicted him usually determines his sentence: life in prison or death. During the penalty phase, the prosecution will present witnesses to testify about the seriousness of the crime and about any aggravating factors, information that increases the degree of culpability, such as whether the victim was tortured. The prosecutor also may present evidence about the impact of the murder on the victim's family, and he may offer testimony about the defendant's future dangerousness even if he receives a sentence of life in prison.

The defense has the opportunity to counter by presenting testimony that offers mitigating factors to explain but not excuse the defendant's actions, including his character, childhood experiences or lack of a prior criminal history. Typically, a jury is instructed that it must impose a death sentence if it finds the existence of one aggravating factor beyond a reasonable doubt and rejects all mitigating evidence offered by the defense, or if it decides the testimony about aggravating factors outweighs the mitigating information.

Dumb and Drunker

In recent years, legal scholars and current and former members of the U.S. Supreme Court have raised concerns about the quality of representation of defendants facing death sentences. The *Chicago Tribune* and *Austin American-Statesman* exposed cases in which defense attorneys were so drunk, hung over or tired that they slept through testimony of key prosecution witnesses. Others were so incompetent that they didn't bother to meet with their clients or investigate their backgrounds to gather information to ask a jury to impose a life sentence instead of death.

Capital cases are far more complex, expensive and lengthy than other types of criminal trials. To do their jobs right, defense attorneys must spend hundreds of hours preparing, hire investigators and interview experts. Death-row inmates also need lawyers trained in the specialty of capital appeals.

DNA evidence also has created doubts about the quality of representation indigents receive and has led to releases of inmates who have spent decades in prison for crimes they did not commit. The

▪ Figure 5.1. Phase I: Direct Appeal in Death Penalty Cases ▪

Trial Court
- All states provide one automatic appeal of conviction by jury or judge that resulted in death sentence—if requested by the defendant
- The appeal limited to issues that occurred during trial

➡

State's Highest Court
- Both sides file briefs
- Court hears arguments
- Judges affirm conviction, reverse guilty verdict, nullify death sentence or remand case

➡

U.S. Supreme Court
- Losing side can file a writ of certiorari for review of federal constitutional issues raised in case
- Justices can reject request for review
- Defendant may move to next phase of appeals

▪ Figure 5.2. Phase II: Post-Conviction Appeal in Death Penalty Cases ▪

Trial Court
- Challenges to conviction and sentence outside original trial record
- Including: ineffective assistance of counsel; juror or prosecutorial misconduct; and new evidence
- Strict deadlines, if missed, may end appeal

➡

State Appeals Court
- Both sides file briefs
- Court hears arguments
- Affirms conviction, reverses guilty verdict, nullifies death sentence or remands case
- Strict filing deadlines, if missed, may end appeal

➡

State High Court
- Both sides file briefs
- Court hears arguments
- Affirms conviction, reverses guilty verdict, nullifies death sentence or remands case

➡

U.S. Supreme Court
- Defendant files writ of certiorari
- Justices may refuse to hear
- If denied, defendant has exhausted state remedies and can move to next phase

▪ Figure 5.3. Phase III: Federal Review in Death Penalty Cases ▪

District Court
- Defendant raises issues outside trial
- Briefs filed
- Possible hearing
- Judge dismisses petition, overturns conviction or nullifies sentence
- State can re-try defendant, if conviction or sentence overturned

➡

Court of Appeals
- Limited to issues in District Court
- Arguments
- Court affirms or reverses lower court ruling
- If defendant's conviction or sentence overturned, state can re-try
- If court refuses to provide relief, defendant can continue appeal

➡

Supreme Court
- Defendant files writ of certiorari
- Justices may deny request
- If so, defendant has exhausted federal remedies

➡

Clemency
- Defendant asks governor or president (in federal cases) to halt execution
- Defendant asks governor or president (in federal cases) to commute death penalty to lesser sentence, such as life in prison

Death Penalty Information Center reports that more than 140 people on death row were set free from 1973 to 2012 because of evidence that suggested they were not guilty.

But DNA is not left behind at every crime scene, despite what you see on TV, and science cannot help many defendants who were convicted of murder, rape and robbery but claim they didn't do the crime. Sometimes science is the problem: The FBI has been criticized over the years for using "junk" science to analyze bullets, hair and fibers, and several state crime labs have been accused of conducting shoddy tests of forensic evidence.

In 1932's *Powell v. Alabama*, the U.S. Supreme Court raised the possibility that a defendant not only has a right to an attorney, but also has a right to "effective assistance of counsel," a legal term of art that describes a competent lawyer who does a good job. But what does that mean? In 1984's *Strickland v. Washington*, the Supreme Court heard the case of David Washington, who had pleaded guilty to murder in Florida. Washington's lawyer had not sought character witnesses and did not request a psychiatric evaluation to present to jurors during the penalty phase of the trial. Absent mitigating circumstances, Washington was sentenced to death. The Court held that a reversal of a conviction could occur only if a lawyer's performance was deficient and caused prejudice to the defendant's right to a fair trial.

Writing for the majority, Justice Sandra Day O'Connor said the defendant carries the burden of proving that his trial lawyer's performance fell below an "objective standard of reasonableness." That is not the same thing as saying that what the lawyer did was correct. The standard gives defense attorneys a huge benefit of the doubt, unless they fail to show up for trial. The Court has since said a drunk or sleepy lawyer is not necessarily ineffective. On appeal a defendant must show cause and effect by linking the behavior with a pivotal moment in the trial.

The Eleventh Hour

There is no constitutional right to appeal in most criminal cases, but all states provide an automatic challenge of a conviction by a jury or judge that resulted in a death sentence. Inmates must exhaust the state appellate process before they can seek relief in the federal courts. Typically, there are three phases of capital appeals—guilt, post-conviction and *habeas corpus*.

In the first two phases, the defendant must file appeals first with the trial judge, then pass through all appellate levels in a state before being considered by the U.S. Supreme Court—if four justices agree to hear the case. In Latin, *habeas corpus* means that "you have the body." A writ of *habeas corpus* seeks to bring a defendant before a court to ensure that his imprisonment or detention is not illegal. In the *habeas* phase, the defendant files a petition with a federal trial court. If she loses, she can file a challenge with the intermediate federal appeals court before asking the U.S. Supreme Court to hear her case.

Applications for a stay of execution are often filed at the eleventh hour with the U.S. Supreme Court justice who oversees the circuit that covers the state that wants to execute the inmate. The justice usually refers the matter to the other eight justices who confer by phone if they are not in session or away from the Supreme Court building. Five justices must agree to grant a stay to halt the execution, but only four votes are needed for the Court to hear the inmate's entire appeal on the merits, which may challenge the legality of evidence, the trial judge's rulings and the death sentence.

In recent years, state and federal lawmakers have curtailed appeals by death-row inmates, particularly *habeas corpus* reviews, making it harder for appellate lawyers to find, assess and overcome mistakes made during trial by a defense attorney, or to uncover and raise constitutional violations committed by the judge, prosecutor or police.

Funding for defense attorneys in capital cases is another hot-button issue. Many states do not allocate funding for lawyers to hire investigators or file challenges to death sentences in higher courts beyond the one round of automatic appeals provided to death-row inmates.

If everything else fails, only one alternative remains—clemency, the executive power that can be exercised by a governor or the president. In many states, governors can grant mercy or leniency to pardon a convicted criminal, or commute his sentence. A pardon and a commutation are different. If a governor or the president of the United States grants a pardon, he officially nullifies punishment and other legal consequences of a crime. If he commutes a sentence, he reduces it or orders the release of a defendant who has served some of his prison sentence; the conviction, however, stands.

To cover an imminent execution, a reporter needs to keep tabs on the state Supreme Court, the U.S. Supreme Court and the governor's office, which are places a defense attorney may go to seek a last-minute reprieve.

· *Chapter* ·

From Janitors to Judges:
Developing and Protecting Sources

■ ■ ■

Confidential sources have helped reporters change the course of history: Think of Abu Ghraib, the Pentagon Papers, the My Lai Massacre and Watergate. Without the help of confidential sources, the *Washington Post*'s Dana Priest could not have exposed the Bush administration's secret network of overseas prisons for suspected terrorists. Without the help of government insiders, *New York Times* reporters James Risen and Eric Lichtblau could not have revealed President George W. Bush's decision to secretly spy on Americans after 9/11.

In recent years, unethical reporters have fooled editors into publishing fabricated stories by falsely claiming they had obtained information from confidential sources. The damage has been extensive, not only to the public's trust in journalists but also in the people's understanding of when and why reporters need to withhold a source's identity: *New York Times* reporter Jayson Blair sat in his New York apartment and wrote about imagined conversations with wounded soldier Jessica Lynch's family; *New Republic* writer Stephen Glass invented computer whiz kids and ambitious young political operatives to catapult his stories on to the magazine's cover; and *USA Today*'s Jack Kelley borrowed hotel workers' identities and used them as characters in stories to exaggerate his exploits as a foreign correspondent. Their sources weren't confidential. They weren't secret. They did not exist.

The Blair and Kelley scandals coincided with the beginning of a precipitous slide in the news business, the demise of a once-profitable economic model for newspapers, the rise of the Internet and the empowerment of readers and viewers. News organizations implemented strict policies on the use of confidential sources, or anonymous sources as they called them. In 25 years as a reporter, I always knew the names of my sources. They were not anonymous; they were confidential. They weren't in disguise, wearing a big nose or a funny hat, when they spoke to me. They didn't drop documents in the mail with no return address. It's true that they were "anonymous" to my readers, but I agreed to keep their identities secret to ensure that I could gather information about how government officials were doing, or not doing their jobs.

The courts, more than any other branch of government, have protected the press from threats to its ability to gather and report the news. In the past, news executives and reporters took solace in the belief that judges would rein in overzealous prosecutors and greedy plaintiffs' attorneys who tried to turn reporters into investigative arms of the government or private investigators for law firms. In recent years, judges not only have empowered prosecutors and plaintiffs' attorneys by expressing disdain for reporters and their watchdog role in America. Judges also have encouraged the use of aggressive litigation tactics against reporters to leverage large cash settlements for plaintiffs they find sympathetic. In this chapter, we will examine the importance—and dangers—of cultivating knowledgeable, trustworthy sources, how to protect yourself and your sources and what steps you can take to spot a fake.

Details, Details, Details

Information is the lifeblood of journalism. Without data and details, reporters cannot tell clear, compelling stories. Without human sources to interpret and fill the gaps often left in documents, reporters cannot provide the public with the information it needs to decide how it wants its government to act. As a reporter, your success depends on your ability to develop human sources willing to provide information that others in government want to keep secret.

When a "leak" occurs, prosecutors protest, judges pound the bench and defense attorneys howl at the injustice of it all—unanimous in their contempt for and blame of journalists for the breach of secrecy. The aggrieved public officials launch investigations to show the public how outraged they are. The Obama administration has taken leak investigations to another level in its effort to crack down on what it considers out-of-control release of classified information to the press. In six criminal cases, government employees were accused of leaking secret and sensitive information to reporters. That's more leak cases than in the administrations of all former presidents combined.

The leak investigation usually begins with subpoenas that demand reporters' notes and their testimony about the identities of their sources. The investigation can be launched by prosecutor-controlled grand juries, or by judges, legislative committees and now, increasingly, lawyers for people who have filed civil lawsuits against the government.

Not every piece of information gathered by a reporter makes it into print, online or on the air. Nor should it. But that is usually what is most prized by prosecutors and plaintiffs' attorneys who want reporters to give them information they believe will bolster and help them win their cases. Police, for example, want video footage of protests that turned violent so they can identify perpetrators. A plaintiff's attorney wants the names of FBI agents who acted as a reporter's sources to prove that his client's privacy rights were violated. Legislative committees want to know who leaked allegations of sexual harassment against a judge being considered for a higher court. Such efforts to obtain information gathered by reporters threaten to undermine the relationship between journalists and whistleblowers, the people who risk everything to reveal questionable decisions, abuses or wrongdoing by government officials and business leaders. Given the danger, it is crucial for reporters to cultivate sources inside government who know what's going on. Journalists must separate the people who are truly in the know from the pretenders, players who desperately want to be thought of as "in the loop."

Promises to Keep

There is no doubt that journalists, including myself, have relied too frequently on confidential sources, attributing information to secret operatives that sometimes could have been found on the public record. But the far more dangerous development is the institutionalized manipulation of reporters, particularly in Washington. In the so-called background briefing, a public official summons reporters and demands a promise that they will not use his name before he will share basic information the journalists need to complete their stories. It is the classic dog-and-a-bone tactic: The dog will do just about anything for the bone. Worse, it makes it appear as if journalists are relying on unnamed sources far too frequently in their stories, giving the public reason to distrust what they read and hear.

Background briefings were used extensively during President George W. Bush's administration; the Obama administration also relies heavily on the briefings in an attempt to manage the message to the public. I remember one incident in particular when I covered John Ashcroft, President Bush's first attorney general: A high-ranking official insisted on confidentiality before he would discuss the department's portion of the federal budget with reporters. There is no more of a public document than the federal budget, which describes how tax dollars are going to be spent. Several reporters, myself included, revolted and wrote a letter to Ashcroft to complain about the misuse of the background briefing. I also disrupted an FBI briefing on a computer system that the bureau had blown millions of dollars trying and failing to develop. I insisted that the FBI's press secretary go back to Director Robert Mueller and ask again if we could identify the official at the briefing by name. She came back with an answer, and it was no. More than two dozen journalists were in the room. Only one other reporter joined my objection. I often wonder what would've happened if we all had walked out and refused to cover the orchestrated news event. I tried again after the briefing to get the FBI to reconsider but failed. Back in the newsroom, I told my editors at *USA Today* what I had done—in compliance with a new policy they had implemented. Out of fear of missing a story other news organizations would have, they accepted the FBI's terms, and the official was not identified in my story that appeared the next day.

I preferred to use sources I developed on my own, not those forced on me by government agencies. For reporters, developing trustworthy sources is an art, not a science. Much of it depends on your instincts. Reporters can guard against being used by asking a series of simple questions before reporting information provided by someone who wants his or her identity kept secret:

- How did the source obtain the information? Was he or she present during an interrogation? Did he read a report? Was she in a meeting where other officials were briefed on the investigation's progress? How does the source know what he says he knows?
- Why is the source sharing the information with a reporter? What's in it for him? Is she angling for a promotion? Is he trying to embarrass a political opponent?

Once you get answers to some or all of those questions, you then must weigh the value of the information against the flaws in a source's motivation: Is the information so crucial to exposing official incompetence that the reporter can overlook a source's anger at being passed over for a promotion? A reporter often decides in a matter of minutes whether to use information. Testing the scope of a source's knowledge usually improves a story. A journalist may learn more about an interrogation or the direction of an investigation by asking those questions.

For more than 30 years, Bob Woodward and Carl Bernstein kept their promise of confidentiality to "Deep Throat," arguably the most famous confidential source in history. In 2005, the public learned from former FBI official W. Mark Felt's children that their father had helped the two *Washington Post* reporters expose the extent of President Richard Nixon's abuse of power. Felt, who provided often maddeningly obtuse hints about ways for Woodward to "follow the money," was a veteran FBI spy-hunter who was passed over for the job as director of the bureau. Why would a high-ranking official, with so much to lose if he were found out, believe a young reporter's promise of confidentiality? A government official who doesn't trust the people in his agency needs to find someone to tell his story. Why not a reporter?

The Simpler, the Better

If an interview is on the record, the information and the name of the person who supplied it can be used in a story or blog post. Usually a reporter has no obligation to grant confidentiality after the information has been provided, especially if the source is a public official, elected or appointed, who should know better than to play games.

Different rules apply if the source of information is an average citizen, such as the mother of the victim of a drive-by shooting or the father of a girl who's been kidnapped and raped. Ethically and morally, these people need to be treated differently. A reporter cannot assume that a distraught parent understands the rules of the newsgathering business. Public officials, especially those who are elected, know the risks of talking to a reporter. A greeter at Wal-Mart and a receptionist at a car dealership probably do not. When I dealt with the uninitiated, I always tried to explain exactly what I was doing, when the story would appear, how it would be displayed and where, if I knew. I also would explain that not everything a person says makes it into print because stories are not verbatim transcripts of interviews, as many people mistakenly believe.

If a source asks for confidentiality, the reporter must set clear ground rules that both sides understand. For that to happen, the reporter and the source must share the same definitions of crucial but confusing terms commonly used in the exchange of newsworthy information. Many veteran reporters get tripped up by the shifting meanings of the terms "off the record," "not for attribution" and "deep background."

Some reporters were taught, as I was, that off the record means a reporter cannot use any part of the information, not even to run by another source to try to obtain independent confirmation. In recent years, the off-the-record term has morphed into a not-for-attribution promise, allowing use of the information without a name attached to it. Deep background, information provided to guide a reporter or supplied to put details in perspective, doesn't seem to have meaning anymore.

The best way to eliminate the confusion is to ask the following simple questions:

- Can I use the information?
- Can I use your name with it?
- If not, why not?

The answers will help the reporter and source iron out the terms of the promise of confidentiality and save both parties grief later if a prosecutor or plaintiff's attorney shows up with a subpoena.

In many cities, such as Washington where politics is the main local industry, it is sometimes difficult to tell who is seducing whom. It is easy for reporters to fall in love with the idea of having high-ranking government officials as sources. Power is seductive. A reporter who gets too friendly with a source may find it difficult to keep him at arm's length when she's seated at his right elbow at a dinner table.

Romancing the Source

Good reporters put in long hours because news doesn't break on a 9-to-5 schedule. Planes crash on weekends. Disturbed employees, armed with weapons, shoot and kill their bosses at quitting time. Presidential aides orchestrate "document dumps" late on Fridays in attempts to hide incriminating details about a scandal or soften the blow by landing on Saturday mornings when the public isn't paying as close attention.

That means that reporters miss dinner dates, their kids' soccer games and other important personal events. It also means they find romance where they can—sometimes with the people they cover. Reporters and editors have had affairs with elected officials, including mayors, senators and even newsroom interns and clerks. Some have married government officials.

In 2012, a *Wall Street Journal* reporter lost her job because she did not tell her editors that she'd had an affair with a U.S. government official when she was in Baghdad covering the war in Iraq. At a minimum, she should've asked her editors to reassign her to another beat where she wouldn't have been tempted, as she was, to share copies of her stories with her boyfriend before they were printed, a serious violation of a journalist's independence. The couple eventually married, but it didn't matter. They each suffered when racy emails composed early in their relationship became public. She was forced to resign, and he was pressured into pulling his nomination to be ambassador to Iraq.

Other reporters, myself included, were luckier because we committed our youthful indiscretions at a time when journalists weren't watched as closely as they are today. I wish I had known about the reaction of A.M. Rosenthal, a legendary former executive editor of the *New York Times* who fired a newly hired political reporter after learning that she'd had an affair with a Pennsylvania state senator while she was working for the *Philadelphia Inquirer.*

Rosenthal's colorful response is one you should remember: "I don't care if my reporters are sleeping with elephants, as long as they aren't covering the circus." In other words, if you start dating someone on your beat, tell your editor and ask to be reassigned.

Friend or Foe?

In 2008, my former assignment editor at *USA Today* made a comment that prompted me to wonder about the strength of the editor-reporter relationship in today's news business. It was after I was held in contempt of court for refusing to identify sources that provided information for stories I wrote about the FBI's investigation into the deadly 2001 anthrax attacks. My former editor told me he would have rolled over and given up my sources' names, had he known them, if he had received a subpoena.

He laughed when he said it, but I don't think he was joking. He has a wife, two kids and an expensive house in the Washington suburbs. He probably wouldn't have wanted to jeopardize their financial futures by defying an angry federal judge who had ordered me to pay up to $5,000 a day in fines. Fortunately the editor never asked for the names of my sources. Back then, *USA Today*'s editors did not routinely ask for the names of confidential sources used by reporters.

At that point in my career, I'd worked for six news organizations. I recall only one time that an editor requested the names of my sources. Leonard Downie, executive editor of the *Washington Post*, asked for the identities of sources I had relied on for the first story published about the independent counsel's investigation into the relationship between President Bill Clinton and White House intern Monica Lewinsky.

I do not believe my other editors neglected their duties by failing to press me for the identities of my sources. I believe they showed how much they trusted me by not asking. Every newsroom I worked in operated under an honor code, where editors trusted that the facts in my stories were true. Editors tend to trust reporters until given a reason not to.

In most newsrooms today, reporters are required to tell their editors the names of their confidential sources, if asked. I strongly recommend that you have a heart-to-heart talk with your assignment editor to determine whether the editor will have the courage to stand with you and fight if a judge threatens both of you with fines and jail. Don't assume your editor will have your back or your source's.

Set clear ground rules with your editor in much the same way you'd set the terms of your relationship with a source. Ask your editor to think carefully about what he might do if the two of you were to find yourselves in a tough spot. Make sure you also remind your editor that he shouldn't put your sources' names in emails to his bosses because prosecutors or plaintiffs' attorneys could get their hands on the information later with a search warrant or a subpoena. That means you also shouldn't put your sources' names in emails, your notebooks or computers.

Oh, the Places You Will Go

Sources take reporters places you cannot go without an insider's help. President Richard Nixon might have gotten away with his dirty political tricks. Accounts of Lieutenant William Calley's murderous rampage in a Vietnamese village might have gathered dust in a Pentagon file room. If not for the leak of photographs taken by U.S. troops of naked, humiliated and frightened detainees at the Abu Ghraib prison in Iraq, the American public might never have known about interrogation tactics utilized by the Bush administration.

Before venturing beyond the comfort of a newsroom desk, you must ask yourself if you have the guts to do this kind of work. Will you crumble under the pressure of a subpoena and threats of bankruptcy leveled by a judge? You should not volunteer to cover courts, cops or national security if you doubt your nerve or commitment to the public's right to learn what its government is doing. The rest of the good reporters out there suffer if one among us caves under the pressure. Bad legal and ethical precedents can be set and come back to haunt others. If one reporter agrees, for example, to reveal where his source worked, the next journalist subjected to a subpoena in another case will be under enormous pressure to do the same. I know because it happened to me. This work isn't for everyone, and there is no shame in admitting it.

Throughout history, reporters have refused to give up the names of their confidential sources. In 1848, a *New York Herald* reporter obtained a copy of the secret treaty that had been negotiated to end the Mexican–American War. The U.S. Senate ratifies all treaties and took offense that a reporter had obtained a copy of the document before its members had had a chance to vote on it. When the Senate demanded to know the identity of the reporter's source, he refused and was jailed.

For the next 120 years, reporters occasionally faced efforts to unmask their sources. In the late 1960s and early 1970s, everything changed. The nation exploded in protests over civil rights, the women's movement and opposition to the Vietnam War. Government officials struggled to retain order in the face of demands by blacks for equality, and by young people for more permissive attitudes toward sex, drugs and rock-n-roll.

■ Man Up ■

In August 2007, Reggie B. Walton, a federal judge in Washington, ordered five reporters to reveal the identities of their sources for stories about the FBI's investigation into the deadly 2001 anthrax attacks. Three of those reporters—who worked for the **Washington Post**, **Newsweek** and ABC News—complied with the judge's order by persuading sources to release them from promises of confidentiality, by turning over their notes, or some combination of the two.

I refused, as did Jim Stewart, formerly of CBS News. We soon became the focus of lawyers for Dr. Steven Hatfill, a former U.S. Army scientist who sued the government after he was identified by then–Attorney General John Ashcroft as a "person of interest" in the anthrax investigation. Hatfill insisted he needed us to provide the names of our sources to prove that FBI agents had violated his rights under the federal Privacy Act by providing us with information that we used in our stories. I covered the investigation while working at **USA Today**. Even though I had left the paper in 2006, Gannett, the owner of **USA Today**, provided me with attorneys from the law firm of Nixon Peabody in Washington.

The Hatfill showdown occurred at a difficult time for the news business. Editors and publishers were coping with competition from the Internet and the collapse of a once-profitable economic model. They were afraid of high-priced plaintiffs' lawyers as well as anti-press federal judges. This fear first manifested itself in the Wen Ho Lee civil lawsuit, which was settled in 2006 when several news organizations made the mistake, in my opinion, of joining the Justice Department in paying $1.6 million to make Lee and his lawsuit go away.

Throughout the Hatfill proceedings, Judge Walton made it clear he wanted to force a settlement similar to the resolution of Lee's lawsuit. A nuclear scientist at the federal laboratory at Los Alamos in New Mexico, Lee sued after a criminal case against him fell apart, and he pleaded guilty to a minor offense. In his federal Privacy Act lawsuit, Lee sought the names of sources who provided information to journalists who reported that he was under investigation for spying on behalf of China.

None of the five media organizations—the **Washington Post**, **New York Times**, **Los Angeles Times**, ABC News and the Associated Press—that kicked into the settlement had been named as a defendant in Lee's lawsuit. Rather, reporters for the media outlets had been subpoenaed as third-party witnesses to force them to reveal their sources' identities. They also had been ordered by a federal judge to reveal their sources under threat of stiff fines that they would've had to pay out of their pockets. Their news organizations decided to settle after they lost in the federal appeals court.

Rat Race

As in the Lee case, fear spread like an infection through lawyers for reporters who had been subpoenaed in the Hatfill lawsuit. We were told that we had to try to get a waiver of our promise of confidentiality from each of our sources as quickly as possible. Judges use waivers to do an end-around freedom of the press and the thorny issue of whether a reporter has a testimonial privilege that allows her to protect her sources' identities in the same way a doctor can decline to reveal conversations about a patient's medical history.

A waiver is predicated on the misguided belief that the decision about confidentiality belongs to the source, not the reporter. There's a problem with that logic: Reporters, more than sources, understand how reneging on confidentiality agreements could impact the newsgathering process. We were told that if we didn't obtain waivers, we would face fines that could bankrupt us personally and that we could be sent to jail.

I felt pressure to race—and beat—my colleagues to obtain "original" waivers instead of the "me too" variety, in which a source revealed that he had talked to more than one of the reporters facing contempt findings. September 2007 was a blur of emails and phone calls from my lawyers, telling me to hurry, hurry, hurry and get a waiver from a source before Allan Lengel of the **Washington Post** or Michael Isikoff of **Newsweek** beat me to it.

Judge Walton exacerbated our fear with threats to hold us in contempt of court. It was a classic divide-and-conquer move, and we fell for it. By then, I was teaching journalism students, a distance away from the high-pressure environment in Washington, and I resented that we were being played to perfection by the judge and Hatfill's lawyers.

"Enough," I told my attorneys.

I stopped thinking about "me" and worrying about "we," and the effect my actions would have on how my students would gather the news in the future—aggressively, as I had throughout my 25-year career, or timidly. How could I stand in front of a class-room and urge students to hold government officials accountable if I didn't have the guts to protect the sources that had helped me remain skeptical of the FBI's anthrax investigation?

It was a battle I could wage: I am single and I enjoy a good fight, especially over a principle as important as freedom of the press. I told my lawyers that I refused to be a rat in the waiver race. I still had to reach out to as many of my sources as I could to satisfy the judge's order, but in those conversations I tried to remain as neutral as possible: I brought my sources up to speed on the case. I told them the judge was pressuring us to obtain waivers. I stressed that I would continue to honor our confidentiality agreements. I even insisted that one source talk to his wife before giving me his answer. I didn't want to coerce, trick or guilt-trip a source into granting a waiver.

Yet those conversations were the worst of my career. No matter how I sugarcoated it, I was asking these people to throw themselves under the bus to save me. Other reporters didn't see it that way. I know of one reporter who exaggerated the situation to a source we had in common, saying he had already been held in contempt and was about to lose every-thing he had. Nothing of the sort had happened yet.

Fear of the Spin

Within weeks of al-Qaeda's strike on America on September 11, 2001, anthrax-laden letters were sent through the U.S. mail. Five people died and thou-sands were forced to take antibiotics. Fear spread across the country, as restaurants stopped serving powdered sugar on French toast, and people called police to open their mail.

In the Bush administration, officials worried about the political fallout if another attack occurred. They understandably wanted to calm a jittery public, but their use of spin tactics and Ashcroft's description of Hatfill, in particular, made me suspicious and cautious because the person-of-interest term had no signifi-cance or grounding in the law.

After 9/11, I expanded the number of sources I consulted on terrorism-related subjects, including the anthrax investigation. I thought the more people I talked to, the less chance I had of being misled. I developed a practice of reaching out to 10 or more people when I did a story on anthrax. Many of my sources overlapped, with some helping me on sto-ries I wrote about anthrax, the hunt for Osama bin Laden and the administration's detention policies at Guantanamo Bay, Cuba, where hundreds of sus-pected terrorists were held without charges. Because I talked to several people on a variety of topics, I can-not remember exactly who told me exactly what in the stories I wrote about Hatfill.

Over the course of my career, I had thousands of bylines. The two stories at issue in the Hatfill case weren't memorable. Neither had appeared on page 1. They were typical of many other stories I cranked out as a productive beat reporter. I also did not have notes to refresh my memory about the four sources I relied on in the two stories. As a young reporter at the *Pittsburgh Press* in the early 1980s, I was taught to discard my notes.

During a hearing in February 2008, Judge Walton said he did not care if his order that I disclose **all** of my terrorism sources would unmask people who had nothing to do with the anthrax stories. He said those public officials shouldn't have been talking to me anyway, and they deserved what they got.

Money, Money, Money

What is particularly galling is that I did my job—and did it well. I was fair and skeptical of the FBI investiga-tion. When we talked, Hatfill's lawyer, Tom Connolly, often marveled about the quality and accuracy of my information. Several months after the Hatfill lawsuit was filed—and Connolly came up dry in his pursuit of other reporters—I was added to the subpoena list.

The quality of my reporting did not matter. Money mattered. At that time, *USA Today* was the largest-circulation newspaper in the country, owned by Gannett, the nation's largest newspaper chain. This wasn't a criminal case, where a prosecutor wanted the names of my sources to prove a suspected murderer's guilt. This was a civil lawsuit, where a plaintiff and his lawyers wanted to get paid.

By the end of 2007, only Stewart and I had not copped deals with Hatfill's lawyers. When they asked Judge Walton to hold us in contempt, he decided to split us up and handled the case against me first. In his zeal to help a man he felt quite correctly had been wronged by the FBI, the judge directed his anger at the messenger, finding me in civil contempt of court and imposing fines that escalated to up to $5,000 a day in three weeks. If personal bankruptcy didn't work, he threatened to send me to jail.

Judge Walton, in my opinion, crossed the line from using a contempt order as a pressure tactic to employing it as a coercive measure when he banned my friends, family and *USA Today* from helping me pay the fines.

Luckily, a three-judge panel of the U.S. Court of Appeals for the D.C. Circuit granted my request to stay, or suspend the fines pending my appeal of Judge Walton's order.

A Shakedown

A federal mediator called my lawyers at least three times to invite Gannett to join the Justice Department at the settlement negotiation table. Robert Bernius, one of my lawyers, asked me what I thought. I told him I understood that I couldn't tell a corporation such as Gannett what to do, but I made it clear that I did not want *USA Today* to give Hatfill or his lawyers cab fare to the courthouse, let alone contribute to a large cash settlement.

I did not want *USA Today* to be the victim of a shakedown, and I told Bernius I was prepared to keep fighting.

Nearly two months after a federal appeals court heard arguments in my case, the Justice Department made a deal with Hatfill, paying him nearly $6 million to drop his lawsuit.

But it still wasn't over. In court filings, Hatfill's lawyers threatened to come after me for their legal expenses that had mounted during the lengthy fight over the identities of my sources. They never made good on the threat, but it hung over me for months.

In November 2008, the three-judge appeals court panel granted Hatfill's request to dismiss my appeal of Judge Walton's order, while noting that I had raised "close questions under…the First Amendment."

By February 2009, it was officially over when Judge Walton formally vacated the contempt order and fines.

A Threat to the First Amendment

Civil lawsuits pose a grave danger to the news media. In the Lee and Hatfill cases, federal judges allowed plaintiffs' attorneys to place a price tag on the First Amendment.

In resisting the subpoena, I knew exactly what I was doing. I was buying time, trying to hang in there long enough for the Justice Department to settle the lawsuit with Hatfill. As a veteran courts reporter, I knew there was no way the government could take the chance of going to trial and allowing a jury to decide how much Hatfill's suffering was worth.

I still wonder what would've happened if all five of the subpoenaed reporters in the Hatfill case had stood together. Would Judge Walton have gotten away with bankrupting or jailing reporters for some of the nation's most prestigious news organizations? I think not.

In August 2009, Judge Walton spoke on a panel at an American Bar Association meeting in Chicago. He complained about the criticism leveled at him for what he tried to do to me. Apparently he received negative mail and other feedback, and he seemed surprised that anyone would stick up for a reporter. The judge failed to appreciate that there are people who want journalists to tell them what they want—and need—to know.

That's why I have no regrets, and I'd do it all again.

Every Man's Evidence

On November 15, 1969, the *Courier-Journal* of Louisville, Kentucky, printed a story under reporter Paul Branzburg's byline that described two young residents who turned marijuana into hashish, which they sold, earning, they said, about $5,000 in three weeks. A photograph accompanied the story, showing a pair of hands working with a substance identified as hashish. The story said the reporter had promised not to reveal the identities of the drug-makers.

A county grand jury promptly subpoenaed Branzburg, who showed up but refused to identify the people he had seen in possession of marijuana or the individuals he had watched transform pot into hashish. A state court judge ordered Branzburg to answer the grand jury's questions and rejected the reporter's assertions that his refusal was grounded in the state's constitution, the First Amendment and Kentucky's shield law, which, he said, protected the relationship between a journalist and a source.

Less than three months later, another grand jury in California issued a subpoena for Earl Caldwell, a reporter for the *New York Times* who wrote about the Black Panther Party and other black militant groups. The grand jury demanded that Caldwell testify and bring his notes and tape recordings of his interviews with Black Panthers. In a second subpoena served on March 16, the grand jury backed off, demanding only Caldwell's testimony.

On July 30, 1970, Paul Pappas, a reporter-cameraman for a New Bedford, Massachusetts, television station, was assigned to cover a riot. Pappas made his way through barricaded streets to a boarded-up storefront, where he covered a Black Panther leader who read a prepared statement. The reporter left but returned six hours later. The Black Panther leaders allowed him to stay inside their headquarters on condition that he would not reveal anything he saw or heard unless police raided the building.

There was no raid. Pappas stayed for three hours and left. Two months later, a grand jury subpoenaed him to testify about what he had seen and heard inside and outside Panther headquarters. Pappas testified about what he saw outside the storefront, but he refused to reveal what had occurred while he was inside the building. He argued that the First Amendment provided him with a privilege to protect confidential informants and the information they provided.

On appeal, the three cases were consolidated. By a 5-to-4 vote, the U.S. Supreme Court ruled in 1972 that reporters have no right to refuse to identify confidential sources under investigation for committing a crime. Justice Byron White, writing for the majority, sided with law enforcement and brushed aside the news organizations' concerns about threats to their independence and ability to gather news. "Fair and effective law enforcement," he wrote, "is a fundamental function of government, and the grand jury plays an important, constitutionally mandated role in this process." To do its work, the grand jury needs "every man's evidence," the majority said, except in instances where a witness has a special, legally recognized privilege against testifying. This would include a husband and wife, pastor and penitent or doctor and patient—but not a reporter and his source. There is, Justice White said, no such thing as a reporter's privilege.

The majority also rejected the news organizations' argument that forcing reporters to reveal the identities of their sources would choke the free flow of information by making whistleblowers less likely to take the risk of talking to the press. "From the beginning of our country the press has operated without constitutional protection for press informants," Justice White wrote, "and the press has flourished."

Concurring Confusion

In a brief concurring opinion, Justice Lewis Powell undercut the majority's decision by describing the ruling as "limited." Reporters have rights when gathering information, he wrote, asserting that the Court would not tolerate harassment of journalists by overzealous prosecutors or renegade grand juries. A reporter could turn to the courts by filing a motion to quash a subpoena to protect him from overly broad requests for information "bearing only a remote and tenuous relationship to the subject of the investigation," he said.

Justice Powell's caveat provided an opening for trial court judges to ignore the majority opinion and embrace the principles promoted by the losers. But it was Justice Potter Stewart who negated the majority decision, accomplishing a rarity in the law. In a dissent, Justice Stewart blasted the majority for its "crabbed view of the First Amendment" and its "insensitivity to the critical role of an independent press in our society." He warned that the majority's opinion "invites state and federal authorities to undermine the historic independence of the press by attempting to annex the journalistic profession as an investigative arm of government," a step he worried would "in the long run, harm rather than help the administration of justice."

Justice Stewart also understood that the right to publish was meaningless if reporters lacked the freedom to gather information. "It is obvious that informants are necessary to the news-gathering process as we know it today," he wrote. "If it is to perform its constitutional mission, the press must do far more than merely print public statements or publish prepared handouts." If it cannot, the press could become "a captive mouthpiece" of newsmakers, he wrote.

Worse, the dissent said, reporters could censor themselves by avoiding sensitive stories that could turn into grand jury investigations. If that happens, "valuable information will not be published and the public dialogue will inevitably be impoverished," Justice Stewart wrote.

When confronted with such predicaments, he said, judges should ensure that government lawyers:

- Show there is probable cause to believe that a reporter has information that is clearly relevant to a specific probable violation of the law;
- Prove the information sought cannot be obtained by alternative means;
- And demonstrate a compelling and overriding interest in the information.

Pro-press pundits predicted that the *Branzburg* majority opinion would destroy journalism and, in turn, democracy. But a funny thing happened on the way to the end of the free world: Trial court judges used Justice Powell's concurrence to justify rewriting the law and relied on Justice Stewart's three-part test to resolve disputes between prosecutors and reporters.

Two years later, President Nixon resigned. Justices Powell and Stewart may have swayed judges to view subpoenas of journalists with skepticism, but Bob Woodward, Carl Bernstein and "Deep Throat" romanticized the relationship between reporters and their sources. In the aftermath of Watergate, the press gained more credibility as "the Fourth Estate," with a duty to the public to act as a watchdog on the three branches of government, making presidents, senators and judges legitimate targets of scrutiny.

After the *Branzburg* decision, most of the federal circuit courts adopted Justice Stewart's balancing test and state legislatures passed shield laws to protect the relationship between reporters and their sources. At this writing, 10 of 12 federal circuit courts had ruled that the First Amendment provides at least limited protection—a qualified privilege—for reporters facing subpoenas for information and the identities of their sources in criminal and civil matters. When this book was published, 40 states and the District of Columbia had passed shield laws that provide varying degrees of protection for journalists and their sources.

There is no federal shield law. In recent years, a bill appeared to have momentum, receiving overwhelming support in the House of Representatives before encountering resistance in the Senate and Obama administration over concerns about what happens when reporters obtain information related to national security and how to define a journalist in today's changing multimedia landscape.

Just Say No

When served with a subpoena, a reporter can refuse to comply, or cooperate and reveal photographs, videos, audio or notes. If you give up the information, you could damage your reputation with a particular source or with other people in the community who might decide against revealing corruption. If you oppose the subpoena, you and your lawyer must show up in court to explain why. If your news organization is not supporting you, find a lawyer who is willing to represent you *pro bono*, or for free. Groups of journalists, such as the Reporters Committee for Freedom of the Press, at http://www.rcfp.org/, and the Society of Professional Journalists, at http://www.spj.org/, can offer guidance and advice.

A judge has a great deal of power to run her courtroom as she sees fit. She can hold a party, a spectator, a lawyer or a reporter in contempt of court to protect the rights of a litigant in a legal dispute, or to vindicate the law or her own authority. Often, the power is used in anger, such as when a reporter refuses to identify a source that a prosecutor says is crucial in a criminal case, when a defendant ignores orders to stop talking in the courtroom or when a lawyer continues to make objections despite admonishments to cease his use of disruptive tactics.

When a reporter refuses to divulge a source's identity, a judge typically will hold the journalist in civil contempt of court and impose fines or an indeterminate sentence, which is an open-ended jail term that requires that the reporter remain in jail until he or she reveals the information. With civil contempt of court, there is a fine line between coercing the journalist to reveal the source's identity and punishing the reporter for refusing. Judges are not supposed to impose fines so draconian or other conditions so harsh that civil contempt morphs into criminal contempt of court, where the sentence is supposed to be designed strictly to punish.

I am not comfortable with giving reporters special treatment. Nor do I think reporters are above the law, but judges need to look at the whole picture. Usually subpoenas of news organizations are broad, seeking anything and everything, because a lawyer is too lazy to find the information, or hasn't gone to one of the companies that keep clips and transcripts of TV broadcasts. Videotaped footage of crime and accident scenes typically top the list of the most sought-after material from news broadcasters, according to the 2003 report *Agents of Discovery*, by the Reporters Committee for Freedom of the Press. In response to the inundation of subpoenas, many TV stations no longer keep video archives of stories that have gone on the air because responding to subpoenas takes enormous time and drains their limited resources. The theory is: If we don't keep it, they can't subpoena it.

Pick Your Friends Wisely

Newspaper reporters tend to receive subpoenas from parties in criminal and civil cases that seek testimony by deposition, which is given under oath usually during questioning by attorneys for all sides of a dispute. The subpoenas also seek journalists' notes and copies of published stories. Lawyers for a news organization often can negotiate a narrowing of the request or a withdrawal of a subpoena when they call attention to a state shield law that protects journalists from being compelled to make such disclosures. Media lawyers aren't cheap. They bill by the hour, costing the news business money it doesn't have anymore.

Subpoenas aimed at reporters seek two types of information: confidential or non-confidential. Confidential information would include notes or any other paper or electronic documentation that would reveal the identity of a source you want to protect. Non-confidential information would include the published news article and aired video of an accident scene or a protest.

There are times when you must testify—if you witness something that occurs on a public street and you have footage of an event that you have already aired or sold to a TV station—and there usually is no harm to the First Amendment if you do. Journalists invoke the First Amendment to gain access to information or protect confidential sources, but they don't use freedom of the press to cover up for their buddies who went on window-smashing sprees.

Joshua Wolf, a young blogger and videographer, spent nearly a year in jail after he was found in contempt of court for rebuffing federal prosecutors' requests for footage of a violent protest in San Francisco in 2005. Wolf sold a portion of the video to a local TV station and posted other segments on his blog, but he refused to provide the rest of the footage that investigators wanted to use to identify protesters who placed a mattress under a police car and tried to set it on fire. Wolf eventually relented and posted the rest of the video online. Had he done that at the start, the police, like anyone else, could've gone to the Internet and downloaded the footage, and the young blogger wouldn't have been jailed.

If you cover an event like a protest on a public street, it makes no sense to withhold dramatic footage. Why save it? The purpose of covering the news is to show and tell people what you've seen.

Wolf wasn't protecting confidential sources. He was protecting people in a group that organized the protest. It's unfortunate he spent so much time locked in a jail cell. I applaud his spunk, but he and others like him need to understand that misguided crusades ostensibly on behalf of the First Amendment can make it easier for a judge to ridicule the next reporter caught in a battle over protecting a legitimate news source's identity.

Uncovering or Covering Up

On July 14, 2003, syndicated columnist Robert Novak reported that two administration sources said the CIA relied on nepotism to hire a former ambassador who had been critical of the quality of intelligence used to justify the U.S. invasion of Iraq. The ex-ambassador's wife was a CIA officer, and Novak named the woman, Valerie Plame, blowing her cover and destroying her career. The feeding frenzy was on, and other political reporters in Washington rushed to "match" what Novak had reported.

It is against federal law to reveal the names of intelligence operatives for one obvious reason: If identified, they could be killed. As a courts and crime reporter for most of my career, I thought every reporter knows to be careful about identifying undercover cops—or CIA officers.

New York Times reporter Judith Miller and *Time* magazine writer Matt Cooper initially refused to reveal the identities of the high-ranking Bush administration officials who had told them that Plame got her husband, Joseph Wilson, a job checking out rumors about Saddam Hussein's efforts in Africa to obtain an ingredient to make a nuclear bomb. Cooper's boss at *Time* eventually turned his reporter's notes over to a federal prosecutor, a move widely repudiated in the news media.

Unlike Cooper, Miller never wrote a story naming Plame, but she refused to give up I. Lewis "Scooter" Libby, Vice President Dick Cheney's chief of staff, and spent 85 days in jail until Libby told her he wanted her to testify before the grand jury. Miller was a polarizing figure at the *Times*, where she had made many enemies over the years. She also drew criticism for her reporting that Saddam had hidden weapons of mass destruction in Iraq, but none were ever found.

Miller insisted on protecting Libby as long as she did because she said she was suspicious of the use of waivers. In recent years, judges have pressured reporters to obtain waivers of the confidentiality agreements they made with their sources to avoid dealing with the bigger issue of whether a reporter has a privilege to protect confidential news informants. Miller said she did not believe a waiver could be truly voluntary in the coercive, high-pressure atmosphere that exists during a grand jury investigation, particularly in Washington.

In theory I agree with her, but in reality Libby was far too sophisticated a political player to be pressured into granting a waiver. He knew the rules of the road. It's the civil servants I worry about. A source of mine told me what it was like: One day, without warning, a couple of Justice Department lawyers showed up at his cubicle, shoved a piece of paper in his face and said, "Sign this." My source said he knew he was damned if he did and damned if he didn't. If he hesitated or asked too many questions about the waiver form, he could draw unwanted attention from the leak-hunters and lose his job. If he signed it and waived an important protection, he could be named as a reporter's source and lose his job.

Be Careful Out There

If you want to be a journalist, you need to understand the dangers.

The phenomenal changes in technology make me wonder whether news organizations should consider use of encrypted email and throwaway phones to protect the newsgathering process, particularly reporters and their sources. Each scientific breakthrough provides government agencies with tools to eavesdrop on all citizens, especially government employees suspected of leaking information, without anyone knowing. Federal law protects whistleblowers from retaliation, but we have no way of knowing whether agencies are violating the law.

Unless, of course, a government insider tells us—on the condition that we keep his name secret.

What's a reporter to do? Talk to your most valuable sources in person. Don't use the phone and don't use email or texts. Don't take notes on a computer. Don't put your sources names in your notes. Don't keep notes after your story has been published. If you don't have notes, they can't subpoena them. Judy Miller never wrote a story about Valerie Plame, but she was ridiculed for misspelling Plame's name as Flame in her notes. In the hands of a clever prosecutor or plaintiff's attorney, your notes can be twisted into something sinister or idiotic.

I was taught as a young reporter in Pittsburgh to come up with a system for discarding notes on all stories, not just the controversial subjects, and to stick to it. My system was straightforward: When my desk became too cluttered, I cleaned house. I usually kept public court documents so that I wouldn't waste time on deadline retrieving them again from the clerk's office or from an online database.

Once you receive a subpoena, however, you cannot throw away any notes you might have. If you do, you will be destroying evidence, which is against the law.

Police also can search your home and office. Officers could seize your computer and a plaintiff's attorney could ask a judge to force you to turn over its contents. Cops need warrants and plaintiff's attorneys need subpoenas, but they can get them easily approved by judges.

Don't ignore a subpoena. It's not a good idea to dodge a process server trying to deliver a subpoena. If you do, a prosecutor could come after you with a search warrant—which is much worse. A subpoena can be stopped before a prosecutor gets his hands on your notes, if you file a motion to quash. When a search warrant is executed, the evidence is seized, the prosecutor sees it, and by the time you ask a judge for help, it's too late.

You also need to learn the wiretapping laws in your state to avoid making a silly, embarrassing mistake. Most states require one-party consent before taping a conversation, which means that you can record someone without his or her knowledge. But about a dozen states require all parties to give consent before being recorded.

That's not why I think you should always ask for permission before you record a conversation. You should because it's the right thing to do. It's always better to be up front and honest with people. You'll get more out of them if you are.

· Part · III

Pressing the Bench

· *Chapter* ·

7

Let's Make a Deal, or Not:
Plea Bargains and Trials

■ ■ ■

Only a small percentage of criminal defendants roll the dice and go to trial before a jury of their peers. The overwhelming majority of civil lawsuits also end before they begin, often settling for secret sums of money. There is no doubt that the nation's courts would grind to a halt if forced to provide trials for each of the thousands of civil and criminal cases filed annually. There aren't enough judges or courtrooms to provide a forum for each case. But "rocket dockets," a term used to describe courts where judges are obsessed with moving cases quickly, can be dangerous, and rushes to judgment can occur.

The proliferation of plea bargains also may have a perverse effect by encouraging prosecutors and police to complete bare-bones investigations because they know they can pressure defendants into waiving trials, and law enforcement authorities won't have to prove anything. Negotiated endings to criminal cases and civil lawsuits not only prevent a thorough examination of the quality of the evidence used to support allegations, but also deprive the public of information it needs to evaluate the performance of players in court, not to mention the fairness of the process.

Why, for example, did the prosecutor make a deal with the triggerman instead of the lookout during a robbery that ended in the shooting of a security guard? Why did the FBI agree to allow a drug-dealing snitch to keep $1 million of ill-gotten profits in exchange for his promise of cooperation against mobsters? The answers will remain buried unless reporters dig deeper into the details of the deals.

Not every criminal or civil case will make headlines, but that doesn't diminish the importance of each one to the people caught up in disputes over money, property or love. In this chapter, we will deepen our appreciation for how each lawsuit and indictment tells a story about the people who live, work and die in a community. The narrative may be sad, funny or horrifying. Finding and telling those stories is the best part of being a reporter assigned to a court beat.

No Matter Where You Are, There You Are

Judges rely on similar procedures, rules and constitutional concepts in state and federal courts across the nation, regardless of whether they preside over cases in Manhattan, the borough in New York, or Manhattan, the city in Kansas. The American legal system's cornerstones—the right to a speedy trial, the presumption of innocence, the protection against self-incrimination and proof beyond a reasonable doubt—are as important in small towns as they are in big cities.

The U.S. Constitution says that criminal defendants are entitled to go to trial quickly, usually within about six months of indictment. Litigants in civil lawsuits have no such guarantee, and it means that cases can drag on for years—and many do. Defendants are presumed innocent until proven guilty by prosecutors in criminal cases. Defendants are innocent until proven liable by plaintiffs in lawsuits. In both arenas, defendants cannot be penalized for exercising their rights and refusing to testify.

Evidence generally cannot be used against a defendant if it is irrelevant, immaterial, incompetent, hearsay, opinion, privileged or not an original of a document at issue. It may sound simple, but it's not. Like the federal courts, each of the states has rules of evidence that confuse lawyers and confound judges. You don't need to tell your readers or viewers about every evidentiary skirmish, but you need to understand the reasons for disputes to report on a case's twists accurately, fairly and with confidence.

In courtrooms in big cities and small towns, the players also take similar places on stage: the judge is usually seated on an elevated bench in front of two tables. Prosecutors and plaintiffs often sit at the table closest to the jury box, while defense attorneys take their positions at the other. The places could be switched, depending on how a judge choreographs his courtroom.

Uncle! I Give Up

When a criminal case ends in a guilty plea and a civil lawsuit is settled, the public is left with an incomplete and often unsatisfactory explanation of what happened and why.

The reality is that all sides in a legal dispute may be motivated to make a deal as quickly and as quietly as possible. A prosecutor may not want to go to trial because he'd be forced to reveal that police bent the rules to gather evidence. A defendant accused of cheating little old ladies may not want all of the despicable details to get out and embarrass his family. A company's owners may not want consumers to know that executives ignored warnings about a defect in a popular product because they want to keep selling it. In civil lawsuits, plaintiffs may agree to keep quiet about a settlement because they need money now to pay their bills.

There are other practical and legitimate reasons for plea bargaining and settling cases. Defendants can avoid the cost of paying a lawyer to handle a case that could last for months. Guilty pleas save taxpayers the expense of a lengthy trial. Judges insist that people who go to trial aren't punished more harshly if they are convicted, but federal and state sentencing guidelines permit reductions in prison time for defendants who admit guilt. The guidelines also allow prison time to be increased for defendants who take longer to accept responsibility for their crimes. By making a deal, both sides are spared the uncertainty of relying on 12 strangers to decide the outcome of a case.

A plea bargain can occur in a criminal case before charges are filed and at any point up to a verdict. Plea bargaining frequently results in a defendant's admission of guilt to less serious charges or to some or all of the original counts against him or her. The guilty plea also may include a sentencing recommendation by the prosecutor and defense attorney, asking the judge to impose an agreed-upon term of probation or incarceration.

In newsworthy cases, reporters will hear rumors that the defense and prosecution are engaged in plea negotiations. Be careful. A DA could be floating the proverbial trial balloon to determine whether a deal would anger voters. The prosecutor also may spread rumors of a guilty plea to pressure a defendant into cooperating with authorities. A defense attorney may employ a similar tactic to show a prosecutor that he won't face criticism by making a deal. It's important for reporters to understand that both sides have agendas, and it's also crucial for journalists to figure out what they are.

Even if a deal is reached, it is important to remember that plea agreements can fall apart at the last minute. The prosecutor or the defendant could back out. The judge is another wild card because she must sign off on the deal before a defendant is permitted to change a plea to guilty. That means a judge has the power to nix the deal for any number of reasons.

Judges often are the last to learn that a deal has been reached, or that a case has fallen apart. Colorado Judge W. Terry Ruckriegle was several days into jury selection in Los Angeles Lakers star Kobe Bryant's trial on rape charges in September 2004 when he learned that the district attorney was dropping the case because the woman who claimed she had been assaulted refused to testify. "It didn't have that ultimate conclusion that was so repeatedly demanded by both sides," the judge said in an interview. "Everything was in place for it to come about through the trial process, and it was abandoned."

Big Breaks, Little Breaks

A prosecutor's deal with a defendant could anger the victim or the victim's family. In the past several years, many states enacted laws that require prosecutors to consider the impact on victims before entering into plea agreements with defendants. That means a reporter should try to find out whether the victim's relatives support the deal.

A plea agreement also may call for a defendant to be placed in a diversion program as part of an accelerated rehabilitation disposition, or ARD, which amounts to a second chance for less serious offenders and a way to avoid prison time. Some states have created DUI and drug courts that provide counseling and strict supervision for first-time drunk drivers and defendants caught with small amounts of narcotics. If a defendant successfully completes the program, the criminal case against him will be expunged, or erased from the public record. Who gets such a big break, and why? If reporters aren't watching, an ambitious politician could use an ARD program to do favors for big contributors and supporters, especially those with troubled and troublemaker children.

In state and federal courts, judges must take steps to ensure that a defendant knows what he's doing when he agrees to plead guilty. It's important because defendants who admit guilt waive several constitutional rights that accompany the promise of fair trials by juries of their peers. Judges ask defendants a series of questions designed to make sure they weren't pressured or threatened into pleading guilty. Of equal importance, judges must try to determine whether defendants were promised anything of value in exchange for their admissions. Judges also must satisfy themselves that defendants aren't under the influence of drugs or alcohol, which could impair their judgment.

In March 2012, the U.S. Supreme Court said in two 5-to-4 rulings that trial judges can play a bigger role in overseeing plea negotiations to ensure that criminal defendants receive effective assistance from their lawyers in striking bargains with prosecutors. As Justice Anthony Kennedy wrote,

"Criminal justice today is for the most part a system of pleas, not a system of trials," and the right to effective assistance of counsel means little if the courts don't recognize the role of plea bargaining in resolving charges.

The Q and A between a judge and a defendant during a change-of-plea hearing provides a reporter with what may be your only chance to find out what happened and why. Some judges, like Stanley Sporkin, a former federal judge in Washington, used to stray from the script and ask the obvious questions, such as, why did you do it, and what were you thinking?

When covering a guilty plea, it's important to obtain a copy of the plea agreement and all accompanying documents. A statement of facts often supplements the plea agreement, explaining the prosecution's evidence pertaining to the charge or charges to which the defendant is pleading guilty. The documents also will outline what the defendant must do, such as testify against other members of a conspiracy, or pay restitution to reimburse victims of a fraud.

But those documents will tell only the part of the story that deals with the specific charges to which the defendant is pleading guilty. If a defendant admits guilt to only one or two charges, the public may never learn all of the details about the underlying crime—especially if a reporter isn't present to gather the information that comes out in open court. If the documents are filed under seal, you will want to pursue a challenge of the secrecy order, if the case is important enough to you and your editors.

A Star Is Born

The legal profession has had a long love-hate relationship with the camera—still, film and video. Sometimes lawyers welcome cameras in the courtroom because of the educational value of giving the public a front-row seat to a trial. At other times, they liken the camera to a serpent that tempts the players in court and corrupts the outcomes of cases.

One of the most egregious examples in history is the trial of Bruno Hauptmann, a German handyman convicted and executed for the 1932 kidnapping and murder of the young son of famed aviator Charles Lindbergh. Some 700 newsmen participated in one of the first media circuses of the modern era, casting Lindbergh as an international hero and Hauptmann as a monster. Outraged by the coverage, the American Bar Association adopted Judicial Canon 35 in 1937, urging the courts to ban still cameras from all legal proceedings. In 1962, the ABA amended Canon 35 to include television cameras in the recommended prohibition.

In 1965, the U.S. Supreme Court effectively banned cameras from courtrooms with its ruling in *Estes v. Texas*, a case that involved the broadcast of a trial of a man accused of pulling off a large-scale swindle. The justices repeated their disdain for the news media, especially cameras, in their landmark *Sheppard v. Maxwell* decision in 1966, by granting Cleveland's Dr. Sam Sheppard a new trial because of the news media's behavior and the judge's failure to ensure a fair trial.

In 1981, in *Chandler v. Florida*, a case involving the burglary trial of two Miami Beach police officers, the justices changed direction and permitted states to decide for themselves if and how they wanted to allow cameras in courtrooms. Chief Justice Warren Burger wrote that states must be free to experiment and that "an absolute constitutional ban on broadcast coverage of trials cannot be justified." Today, all 50 states permit cameras in courtrooms to cover some stage of the legal process. Only the District of Columbia bans all coverage by cameras in its local trial and appellate courts. Each state has procedures that reporters must follow to request camera coverage. Reporters should check with the court to find out how they must seek approval and what rules they must follow once a judge decides to allow cameras to be used in court coverage.

Opponents of cameras in courtrooms worry most about the impact that electronic media coverage will have on participants. Will judges running for election act differently? Will lawyers preen for the cameras? Will cameras distract witnesses or make them nervous? Will they change their stories? Will cameras divert jurors' attention and make it harder for them to concentrate on testimony? Several states have studied the effects of cameras in courtrooms and found that most jurors and witnesses aren't overly concerned or affected in a negative way. In fact, the evidence suggests jurors tend to pay closer attention and stay awake in trials where cameras are present. During Dr. Sheppard's first trial, cameras were large, noisy and needed thick cables and other equipment to support hot lights that heated up a room. Thanks to technological advances, today's miniature cameras can be mounted in a corner of a courtroom where they are easy to overlook.

Cameras are not permitted in federal district courtrooms, where civil and criminal trials are held, or in the U.S. Supreme Court. But still photographers and operators of TV cameras are permitted to work outside federal courthouses, snapping pictures or shooting video of witnesses and lawyers entering and leaving the buildings.

Judges worry that their words will be taken out of context if they allow the public or the press to operate cameras and other electronic devices in courtrooms. But they are showing signs that they appreciate the need for transparency in government and the educational value of video and audio recordings of judicial proceedings. In March 2010, the Judicial Conference, the policymaking body of the federal courts, decided to allow each of the nation's 13 circuit courts, where appeals are heard, to decide whether to allow cameras in courtrooms during arguments in civil cases. The U.S. Court of Appeals for the Ninth Circuit, which encompasses California and other western states, provides free access on its website to audio and video of arguments the next day. The Judicial Conference also permitted district, bankruptcy and magistrate-judges to use digital audio recordings as official transcripts of proceedings and to make them available on PACER, the court's electronic database. The U.S. District Courts in Nebraska and the Eastern District of Pennsylvania, headquartered in Philadelphia, are the only trial courts at this writing to participate. Most bankruptcy courts and many magistrate-judges provide digital access via PACER to audio recordings of hearings. Keep in mind that it can take a clerk a day or two to post a recording on a docket sheet.

Since the October 2010 term, the U.S. Supreme Court has provided same-day access on its website, at http://www.supremecourt.gov/, to transcripts of arguments. Audio recordings of arguments are available on Fridays of argument weeks. On occasion the Court has allowed same-day releases of audio recordings of arguments in high-profile cases, including *Bush v. Gore* and the lawsuits challenging the Patient Protection and Affordable Care Act that President Barack Obama signed into law in 2010.

Who Are These People?

For defendants, the sight of a courtroom packed with average people, the sorts seen on streets, in malls or airports, finally hammers home the seriousness of the situation. Some defendants decide to plead guilty on the spot because they don't want to give a group of strangers the power to take away their freedom. If they don't plead guilty, defendants may want to take their chances with a bench trial, which means they ask the judge to take on a dual role as interpreter of the law and as finder of the facts. Why would a defendant want a judge to decide his fate? The theory is that a judge will be more likely than jurors to set aside emotions in horrific cases, such as the killing of children, or in complex matters like a massive fraud. A judge would decide whether to grant a defendant's request if a prosecutor or a plaintiff opposed a bench trial.

If a defendant wants a jury trial, officials in state and federal courts cull through voter and driver registration rolls to create a venire, or pool of potential jurors. In some areas, people can live in a community for years without being called to serve. In other cities, such as Washington, where more than one court must be supplied with jurors, citizens are summoned nearly every two years. In some states, convicted felons are barred from serving as jurors as an additional punishment for breaking the law. In recent years, several states have taken steps to restore felons' rights to vote and serve on juries.

Under law, potential jurors cannot be excluded based on race or sex, but it is difficult to prove that a prosecutor or a defense attorney set out to select an all-black female jury or an all-white male jury. If you miss the questioning of jurors, you won't know what happened if one side files what is known as a *Batson* challenge, a reference to a U.S. Supreme Court decision that requires a judge to determine whether racial bias played a part in the selection process.

I liked covering jury selection, and it paid off for me with front-page scoops. I was the only reporter who knew the jury foreman was a union president in the trial of a female Philadelphia judge accused of taking kickbacks from another union. After the verdict, he told me that his fellow jurors had asked him to describe how and when union officials interacted with public officials and whether a *quid pro quo* always accompanied a campaign contribution. He told me he answered their questions by saying, of course not. The judge was acquitted.

Let's Speak the Truth

Lawyers say that jury selection is an art, not a science. Most attorneys rely on their gut instincts, but some big law firms employ experts to determine who would be a good juror for the prosecution

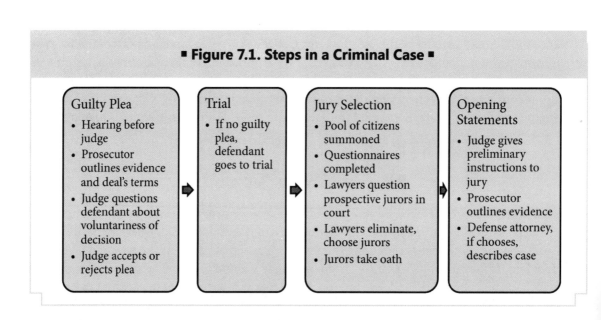

▪ **Figure 7.1. Steps in a Criminal Case** ▪

Guilty Plea
- Hearing before judge
- Prosecutor outlines evidence and deal's terms
- Judge questions defendant about voluntariness of decision
- Judge accepts or rejects plea

Trial
- If no guilty plea, defendant goes to trial

Jury Selection
- Pool of citizens summoned
- Questionnaires completed
- Lawyers question prospective jurors in court
- Lawyers eliminate, choose jurors
- Jurors take oath

Opening Statements
- Judge gives preliminary instructions to jury
- Prosecutor outlines evidence
- Defense attorney, if chooses, describes case

and who would lean toward the defense side. That means race, gender, ethnicity, occupations and class play huge roles in who gets picked and who doesn't.

It is a tedious process that some judges may rush but shouldn't. Colorado's Judge W. Terry Ruckriegle says jury selection is "a frustrating process to go through," but a judge must stay focused. "It may be burdensome. It may be time-consuming. It may be stressful. But you can always do it."

Depending on the estimated length of the trial, a judge figures out how many potential jurors will be needed to obtain a panel. The first step usually requires people in the jury pool to fill out a questionnaire. The questions are designed to uncover bias and prejudice by asking whether a potential juror has a criminal record, whether she or a family member was a crime victim, whether he trusts or distrusts cops, and if she knows any of the participants in the case. It is important to figure out, for example, if a prospective juror would disregard the testimony of a bus driver who said he saw the crime occur in favor of the version provided by a police officer who arrived on the scene 15 minutes after the assault. It's also crucial to know if a prospective juror harbors resentment toward police for failing to solve a crime committed against him.

Can reporters gain access to the completed questionnaires? The U.S. Supreme Court has not addressed the issue, but several lower courts have ruled that the questionnaires are such an integral part of the jury selection process that they should be public and available to reporters. In 2011, the judge presiding over the perjury case against baseball slugger Barry Bonds made the completed questionnaires available for inspection but not copying. In 2012, a D.C. appellate court ordered a trial judge to provide public access to the questionnaires in the trial of a man accused of killing a Capitol Hill intern. Go for it, and ask for access.

A key part of *voir dire*, the questioning of prospective jurors, occurs after lawyers for both sides have read the responses to the questionnaires, and a round of live questioning is conducted, usually in the courtroom. When a judge decides to take jurors into chambers for private questioning, reporters and their editors need to decide whether they should object on the record. Sometimes the judge will ask follow-up questions of individual jurors in open court. If the issues are considered sensitive, the judge usually calls a prospective juror up to the bench for a sidebar, a meeting with the lawyers off to a side of the bench. In some courtrooms, a clerk flips a switch and white noise drowns out the conversation, and no one in the courtroom can hear the judge, lawyers and prospective juror. The judge and lawyers also lower their voices, hoping no one can hear them. This practice presents an obstacle for reporters covering jury selection. Practically speaking, a reporter cannot go to the court stenographer during every break to ask to read the sidebar conferences if the judge hasn't sealed the transcripts. The court stenographer isn't going to have time to do that, nor is he going to be inclined to provide free access to transcripts.

It's also unrealistic as a reporter to ask your news organization to summon a lawyer to the courthouse every time a judge questions a prospective juror at sidebar. Talk to the lawyers for both sides during breaks to find out what was discussed and keep in touch with the judge to make sure you aren't missing a good story.

Strike! You're Out!

How do lawyers get rid of people they don't want on the jury? They ask the judge to strike for cause a prospective juror whose answers show obvious bias. Although jury service is considered an important civic duty, some people will say or do anything to get out of it. Sometimes they will have legitimate excuses, for example, if they are sole proprietors of a business that would suffer if they were to miss several weeks of work.

The judge can grant an unlimited number of strikes for cause, but she won't because jury selection would take days if she did. To speed up the process, the judge will force the lawyers to use their peremptory challenges, a specific number of juror strikes given to each side depending on the case's complexity and expected length. In exercising peremptories, as they are known, lawyers are not required to explain why they've eliminated a prospective juror. When each side runs out of challenges, 12 people are usually sitting in the jury box.

If the trial is expected to last several weeks, a few alternates may be chosen to step in if one of the original members falls ill or is excused from service. Judges often wait until deliberations are about to begin before they identify the alternates as a way of ensuring that everyone pays attention to testimony.

Before each break in the trial, the judge usually reminds jurors to refrain from reading or watching news reports about the case and to resist the temptation of talking about it with each other or anyone else, including family members. Increasingly, judges also must tell jurors that they should not discuss the case on Facebook and Twitter during the trial or deliberations. Some jurors can't seem to help themselves. That's why a reporter covering a trial should pay attention to the chatter online about a case—and who is doing the chatting.

If the jury is sequestered, or secluded, and not allowed to go home for any part or all of a trial, court personnel will arrange where they stay and eat and how and when they go to and from the courthouse. I caution you against trying to follow court personnel, especially deputy U.S. marshals, as they care for sequestered jurors, particularly if they are serving in a case against a suspected terrorist. An Associated Press reporter was caught following jurors in the trial of admitted al-Qaeda member Zacarias Moussaoui in 2006. The reporter was lucky the marshals didn't shoot first and ask questions later, and he was even more fortunate when the judge decided to yell at him and his editors instead of throwing all of them in jail.

Reporters need to stay out of stories. I realize that we live in a time in which everyone wants to be famous, including journalists who strive to create "buzz" or a "brand," particularly on the

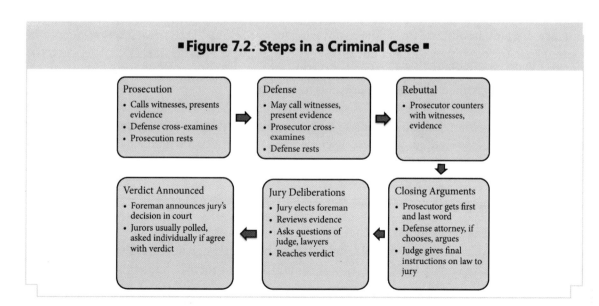

▪ Figure 7.2. Steps in a Criminal Case ▪

Prosecution
- Calls witnesses, presents evidence
- Defense cross-examines
- Prosecution rests

Defense
- May call witnesses, present evidence
- Prosecutor cross-examines
- Defense rests

Rebuttal
- Prosecutor counters with witnesses, evidence

Verdict Announced
- Foreman announces jury's decision in court
- Jurors usually polled, asked individually if agree with verdict

Jury Deliberations
- Jury elects foreman
- Reviews evidence
- Asks questions of judge, lawyers
- Reaches verdict

Closing Arguments
- Prosecutor gets first and last word
- Defense attorney, if chooses, argues
- Judge gives final instructions on law to jury

Internet. But if you do your job well, I believe you will develop something far more enduring—a reputation for integrity, accuracy, fairness and skepticism. More often than not, you will be more effective if you remain a wallflower at the orgy, as the late author and screenwriter Nora Ephron entitled one of her books.

After a clerk administers an oath to the newly chosen jurors, the judge explains basic legal terms and the scope of their duties. He tells jurors that they must consider only evidence presented in the courtroom, and he warns them against conducting their own investigations by visiting crime scenes or using Google and other Internet search engines to find information about the case. With the mini-civics lesson fresh in their minds, jurors are ready to hear testimony.

The Drama Begins

Lawyers for each side provide the jury with an introduction to the case from their respective points of view in opening statements. The attorneys are supposed to stick to the facts that they say they will prove with testimony or documentary evidence. If one lawyer crosses the line and becomes argumentative, the other attorney likely will object and the judge will admonish the offending counsel.

The lawyer with the burden of proof speaks first because he bears the responsibility for providing the evidence needed for a jury to determine guilt beyond a reasonable doubt, as close to a 100-percent certainty as possible with no nagging doubts, in criminal cases. In civil cases, the attorney for the plaintiff, the person or entity who filed the lawsuit, goes first because he must prove liability by a preponderance of the evidence, which means the weight of the evidence presented by one side is stronger than the other.

Defendants are not required to make opening statements because they have no obligation to say a word during the entire trial. Defense attorneys have the option of waiting until the prosecution finishes the presentation of its evidence before making an opening statement. Some lawyers say it can be a good tactical move, depending on the strength of the case presented by the prosecution or the plaintiff. Other attorneys say the defense should never allow the prosecution or plaintiff's story to go unchallenged for any significant period of time.

The lawyers will present two types of evidence: direct and circumstantial. Neither is better than the other. Both are given equal weight in terms of importance and reliability. Direct evidence comes from eyewitnesses, confessions, murder weapons and documents that clearly state the defendant's intent. Circumstantial evidence suggests a fact by implication or inference and is by far the most common form of proof offered by either side, especially in criminal cases. This can include testimony from police about how the crime scene looked, scientific tests that suggest a link between a suspect and victim and physical evidence that signals the presence of criminal activity.

The Brady Bunch

Unlike plaintiffs' attorneys in civil cases, prosecutors are not required by law to turn over virtually every scrap of evidence gathered in a criminal investigation, but they must share with the defense evidence that may be exculpatory, which is information that tends to exonerate a defendant. You will hear lawyers refer to this kind of evidence as *Brady* material, a nickname for a famous U.S. Supreme Court decision in *Brady v. Maryland*. The 1963 ruling and its progeny require prosecutors to disclose to the defense evidence that is favorable to the accused. Police officers are obligated to notify prosecutors when they uncover potential exculpatory evidence. Who, you might ask, decides what is exculpatory? Prosecutors. Therein lies the problem: They don't necessarily have defendants' best interests in mind, and their views of what constitutes helpful evidence can be skewed. In a post-*Brady* case, the U.S. Supreme Court urged the "careful" prosecutor to err on the side of disclosure. Prosecutors also must provide the defense with information that could impeach, or discredit a government witness. The information at issue must be material to guilt or punishment. This means that had the evidence been disclosed to a jury or a judge, it could've changed the outcome.

After a prosecution witness testifies, the government must turn over any prior statements he made regarding the case. This type of evidence is called *Jencks* material, shorthand for another Supreme Court decision that Congress later fine-tuned in a law it passed. The disclosure by a prosecutor is supposed to occur as soon as the witness finishes direct examination—before he is turned over to the defense for questioning. Often, judges will urge prosecutors to disclose this information to the defense before the witness is called to the stand to avoid delays when a defense attorney, faced with a stack of documents dumped in his lap at the last minute, asks for a break in the trial to review the material.

Not every piece of evidence is admissible, which means that a jury can consider it in reaching its verdict. State and federal courts are guided by rules that are designed to exclude evidence that is irrelevant, immaterial, incompetent or untrustworthy because it is hearsay, opinion, privileged and therefore secret, or it is not an original version of a document. Most of the fights in court between lawyers will be about the admissibility of evidence. If a suspect's confession is ruled inadmissible, the jury cannot take it into account. A jury may not be allowed to hear testimony about the discovery of a map to a body's burial site if police broke into a suspect's house without a warrant and found it there.

Reporters' use of inadmissible evidence creates one of the biggest conflicts between the press and the courts. Judges, prosecutors and defense counsel worry that jurors will see or hear stories about inadmissible evidence and allow the information to affect their verdicts. To reporters, inadmissible evidence provides insight into the workings of a police department or prosecutor's office. Journalists believe that keeping such secrets would deny the public information it needs to evaluate its public safety servants. Judges must be clear with jurors in explaining that they cannot read or watch stories about the case. Jurors, in turn, must honor the oaths they take to be fair. In other words, everyone has a job in the nation's legal system, and he or she needs to do it.

When exhibits are entered into evidence, reporters should ask for copies of the documents, transcripts of wiretaps and the recordings themselves. Be warned that you are at the mercy of the judge. In a 1978 Watergate tapes case, the U.S. Supreme Court ruled that news media do not have a First Amendment right to copy trial exhibits. Some judges have interpreted the decision to mean reporters can't even look at exhibits. To avoid problems, develop a good relationship with the judge before the trial begins. Discuss these issues ahead of time and reach a consensus on an orderly way of permitting news media access.

While covering the trials of Mafia leaders in Philadelphia, I needed transcripts to follow along when tapes of wiretaps were played in open court for the jury because the audio was of such poor quality that you couldn't understand what was said. Of course, that often led to dueling versions of the transcript, one from the prosecution and the other from the defense—and you need to read both. There's a big difference if the Mafia don said he was going out to have fun instead of going out to get a gun. TV reporters also want the recordings to play on their newscasts. Websites and bloggers will want to make the recordings and transcripts accessible to their readers.

A judge's decision on whether to grant news media access often depends on who is captured on a recording. If it's a victim or witness, a judge may rule against public access. If it's a cop, a judge probably will allow reporters to get a copy of the transcript or the recording. The news media were not allowed to get a copy of the tape-recording of passengers as they fought four terrorists for control of United Flight 93 before it crashed in a Pennsylvania field on September 11, 2001. Only a transcript was provided to reporters.

Following the Rules

State and federal rules of evidence impact who wins and who loses by regulating how facts must be proven in a case. A piece of evidence often fits into several categories, but it takes only one rule-based objection accepted by a judge to keep it away from the jury. Who can be a witness? Not just anybody. It depends on whether the person is competent to testify. Competency is a question of who can testify, not what they're going to say or how they're going to say it. Generally, witnesses can testify if they have personal knowledge of the matter: she saw, heard, touched, tasted, or felt it.

Contrary to what you might think, eyewitness testimony is among the most unreliable forms of evidence, and courts are beginning to respond to the release of defendants who were convicted based on flawed recollections of traumatized victims. In 2011 and 2012, the New Jersey Supreme Court provided trial judges with instructions to give to juries in cases in which eyewitness testimony is an issue, urging jurors to carefully consider the effect the stress of a crime could have on memory.

Before evidence can be admitted for a jury's consideration, it must be authenticated. That means the prosecutor or defense attorney must prove that the piece of evidence is what he says it is through testimony of an eyewitness, a view of a layperson or the opinion of an expert. If evidence is one of a kind, a witness needs only to look at it and identify it. If it's not, witnesses need to be called to establish a chain of custody to authenticate evidence. A witness, usually a cop, will testify that she recovered a gun at the crime scene, and that she marked, tagged and bagged it. Some items, such as newspapers and public documents, are so obvious that authentication isn't necessary.

Jurors could refuse to believe a piece of evidence even if it is authenticated because they are the finders of fact, which means they decide what is and isn't true. Jurors, not judges, also decide credibility, whether a witness or a piece of evidence is worthy of belief.

Evidence must be relevant to be admissible. In other words, the evidence must make the existence of a particular fact more or less probable in determining the outcome of a case. If evidence is relevant, it's admissible unless there's a reason to block it from consideration by a jury. Its probative value could be outweighed by prejudice—it could cause harm to a defendant—or it could confuse a jury, or it could waste the court's time. To determine whether a piece of evidence is relevant, judges ask: What does it prove? Does it establish a fact? Is the fact provable? How much does it help or hurt?

Of all of the evidentiary rules, hearsay is the most confusing because there are several exceptions that allow witnesses to testify about what they heard other people say outside of a courtroom before, during or after an incident at issue in a case. The rule exists because there may be no way to test the credibility of the person who actually made the statement. Never assume that a statement will be excluded because you think it's obviously hearsay. There's nothing obvious about the exceptions to the hearsay rule because there are so many of them, which makes it difficult to predict whether a judge will let the statement in the record or exclude it.

In many civil and criminal cases, character testimony is crucial—and dangerous, especially for a defendant because a jury could be taken off on a tangent to consider other, uncharged bad acts that he may have committed. The evidentiary rules limit this kind of testimony because jurors are supposed to decide whether the defendant committed the crime that is charged, not other offenses or whether he is a good or bad man. To decide admissibility, judges ask what the character evidence is being offered to prove. If a defendant offers evidence of his good character, he "opens the door" for the prosecutor to call witnesses to contradict him and testify about his bad side. For this reason, Jerry Sandusky, a former defensive coordinator for Penn State University's football team, changed his mind about testifying in his defense to child sexual abuse charges in 2012. Sandusky learned that if he had taken the stand, prosecutors would've called his adopted son as a rebuttal witness to testify that Sandusky also had assaulted him.

Before a trial begins, a prosecutor or defense attorney can file what is known as an interlocutory appeal with a higher court to challenge a judge's decision on legal issues that could determine a case's outcome. All other issues must wait to be appealed until after the trial ends.

Call Your Witness

In criminal cases, the prosecution kicks off testimony by calling the first witness. In civil cases, the plaintiff's attorney presents his case first. In both instances, they go first because they have the burden of proving the allegations. A witness is under direct examination while the party who called him to the stand poses questions. When a defense attorney presents her case, the witnesses she summons to the stand and questions are also on direct examination. Witnesses may testify about matters of fact, or identify documents, photographs or other items introduced into evidence. Generally, a witness cannot state opinions or give conclusions about evidence unless the judge has qualified her in advance as an expert witness, usually someone with a unique background in the topic that is being discussed.

Typically, lawyers cannot ask their witnesses leading questions, which suggest answers by providing too much information. A leading question would be: Isn't it true you saw John Doe walk across the room, pick up the gun and shoot his wife? A defense attorney certainly would object to such a question, challenging whether it was properly formed and asked under the rules of evidence. Most judges require a cursory legal reason for an objection, such as it calls for an opinion, it's hearsay or it's irrelevant. The judge is likely to rule immediately after an objection is raised, deciding to sustain or overrule the challenge. If the objection is sustained, the witness does not answer and the lawyer must rephrase the question. If the objection is overruled, the witness must answer the question as it was originally asked. The lawyer who objected can appeal the judge's ruling after the trial is over.

After the witness is questioned on direct, he is turned over to the other side for cross-examination. The main goal of cross, as it is called, is to impeach, or discredit, the witness. This can lead to fireworks in the courtroom as the cross-examiner attacks and the other side makes repeated objections to protect its witness and the story he has told. The cross-examiner must confine his questions to matters that were raised on direct examination. If the witness suffers a slip of the tongue, he "opens the door" to other issues not covered on direct, and the cross-examiner can delve into those areas. Leading questions also are permitted on cross, largely to save time and test the witness's credibility and memory. If a lawyer calls a hostile witness during the presentation of his side of a case, he can ask leading questions.

Once cross is finished, a witness could be subjected to redirect examination, which is questioning by the lawyer who called her to testify. A prosecutor often will want a witness to clear up any confusion created by questions posed by a defense attorney. Sometimes judges will allow the defense attorney to re-cross the witness and permit the prosecutor to engage in yet another round of redirect. At some point, the judge will tire of throwing the witness around like a hot potato and tell the attorneys to wrap up their questioning.

Increasingly, judges allow jurors to take notes of testimony that they can refer to during deliberations. In some instances, judges also allow jurors to write down questions after counsel for both sides have finished with a witness. The judge and lawyers will review the jurors' questions to ensure they are relevant and legally proper. If so, the judge typically poses the jurors' questions to the witness.

Frequently, the lawyers and judge will try to resolve objections to questions and other issues quickly at sidebar out of the hearing of the jury and spectators. The disputes may take time to resolve and the judge will send the jurors out of the courtroom for a break. The judge may continue the discussion off to the side of the bench, or tell the lawyers to go back to counsel tables to make arguments in front of spectators.

I broke a front-page story in the trial of former Philadelphia Judge Esther Sylvester because a lengthy sidebar caught my attention. Eventually, the judge told the jury to leave the courtroom while he and the lawyers continued their discussion at the side of the bench. This was in the late 1980s, when smoking was allowed in courthouse hallways, and most of the reporters and observers bolted for the door to grab a quick cigarette. I'm not a smoker so I stayed behind, watching the sidebar discussion become more animated. During the lunch break, I went to see the court stenographer, and he read the relevant portion of the transcript to me. The next day's headline—Judge to G-Man: I Love You—was classic *Philadelphia Daily News*. I reported that an ex-judge-turned-snitch had sent a love letter to the lead FBI agent in the investigation. The defense attorneys wanted to use the note to try to discredit the informant when she took the stand to testify against Judge Sylvester.

The End Is Near

The prosecutor or plaintiff's attorney rests after presenting all of the evidence in his case-in-chief, the material in support of his version of events. At this point, expect the defense attorney to seek a directed verdict, which asks the judge to rule that the prosecution has failed to prove its case. Judges typically refuse because they are reluctant to take a case out of the hands of a jury at this late stage.

If the defense team chooses, it can then put on its case by calling witnesses or seeking admission of various documents and other physical evidence into the trial record for the jury to consider. The jury is told repeatedly that it cannot punish a defendant who exercises his Fifth Amendment right and chooses not to testify. But in some cases, the evidence cries out for the defendant to take the stand and tell his side of the story. It is difficult to know whether jurors have punished a defendant who exercised his right to remain silent because they cannot be forced to justify their verdict.

Once the defense rests, the prosecution or plaintiff gets one more chance to call witnesses or present additional evidence in rebuttal to contradict information presented by the defendant. When the prosecutor or plaintiff finishes, the defense team is likely to renew its request for a directed verdict, reiterating its contention that the allegations have not been proven. If the motion is granted, the trial is over and the jury does not get a chance to decide on guilt or liability.

If the motion is denied, the lawyers go forward with closing arguments, which are summations of the evidence from their distinct points of view. By now the lawyers and judge have met, usually afterhours, and figured out what he will say to the jury in his final instructions, a summary of the law that must be applied in the case. The lawyer for the government or the plaintiff goes first with his closing argument because he bears the burden of proof. The defense attorney usually uses her closing argument to highlight weaknesses in the prosecution's case and to focus on facts that are favorable to her client.

The prosecution or plaintiff's attorney also gets the last word in the form of rebuttal argument, a brief attempt to counter what the other side said, before the case is finally ready to be turned over to the jury. In the rare instances where the defense declines to give a closing argument, the government does not get another chance to speak to the jury.

The courtroom is usually locked when the judge gives his charge, or final instructions, to the jury on the applicable laws. That means you can't leave to file an update to your story. If I could, I stayed to listen for one reason: If a trial judge makes a mistake, this is when it often occurs. If the errors are significant enough, an appellate court can order a new trial and the process begins again.

· *Chapter* ·

The Grand Finale:
Deliberations, the Verdict and Sentencing

■ ■ ■

A verdict is a moment that is months, if not years, in the making. It can wreck or launch careers of prosecutors, defense attorneys and judges, strip defendants of their freedom, and challenge reporters to capture the emotions that pour out of people who are shocked or relieved by the outcome. Despite a jury's best efforts, the resolution can outrage the public and lead to second-guessing of the verdict. Sometimes jurors behave less than honorably and violate the oath they took to be fair. Some jurors have accepted bribes, slept through testimony or gotten drunk or high on drugs during deliberations. At times jurors disregard judges' instructions on the law and decide cases the way they think makes more sense.

In the weeks after a verdict, reporters must turn their attention to the punishment part of crime and justice—sentencing and incarceration—as each side files motions to lobby the judge for a tough or light sentence. In this chapter, we will examine the politics of punishment and how judges' hands are often tied, particularly in drug cases because of legislatively required mandatory minimum sentences passed during the get-tough-on-crime eras of the 1970s, 1980s and 1990s. Many state legislatures and Congress also limited judges' power by passing laws that created sentencing guidelines designed to ensure that defendants charged with the same crime did the same amount of time, regardless of where the offense was committed. The guidelines were controversial, despised by some judges who complained that they lost discretion to consider a defendant as an individual.

By passing laws that define crimes narrowly, legislators empowered prosecutors to predetermine sentences by deciding which charges to level against defendants. In doing so, they can manipulate the math of the guidelines and mandatory minimums to corner defendants into agreeing to plea bargains with lengthy prison terms. Although the crime rate has decreased since the early 1990s, the United States retains the dubious distinction of leading all other nations with more than 2.3 million people locked up in its jails and prisons. China, a more populous country, has 1.5 million people behind bars. Largely because of an explosion in drug arrests over the past four decades, the United States imprisons 1 in every 100 adults, a higher rate of incarceration than any country in the world. Put another way: 1 in 30 men between the ages of 20 and 34 is behind bars in America, while 1 in 9 black males in that age group is locked up. While men are roughly 10 times more likely to be in jail or prison, the female inmate population continues to grow at a brisker pace. For black women in their mid- to late 30s, the incarceration rate has hit the 1-in-100 mark. Prisons are big business in America, but cash-strapped state governments are showing a willingness to re-examine sentencing and corrections policies, once a third rail of politics, for ways to cut spending and save money.

For 20 years, the U.S. Sentencing Guidelines required federal judges to utilize a complex mathematical formula to determine the length of punishment for defendants, often by giving weight to uncharged crimes. But in 2005, the U.S. Supreme Court ruled that the guidelines were no longer mandatory because the justices said juries, not judges, must determine guilt as to each charge that is considered in calculating punishment for an offender. For reporters, it means judges can get their groove back, if they want. Some judges may decide against straying from the guidelines, while others may relish the power and flex their muscles. Either way, it's a wild card to watch for in a court case.

The Jury Takes Charge

In federal criminal cases, there must be 12 members of a jury and they must be unanimous in their verdict. In state criminal cases, the U.S. Supreme Court has ruled that unanimous verdicts are not required as long as there are six or more people on the jury. But many states require unanimous verdicts. The Seventh Amendment to the U.S. Constitution, guaranteeing jury trials in civil cases, has not been extended to the states, which means civil juries in state courts are not required to have 12 people. In federal civil cases, the U.S. Supreme Court has left some ambiguity in the law by ruling that juries must be unanimous, but they can number as few as six people. Check with the lawyers for both sides and the judge to find out how many jurors will be used in the case you're covering and whether their decision must be unanimous.

One of the first steps a jury takes after it leaves the courtroom to begin deliberations is to elect a foreman to preside over its discussions and ensure order. Court personnel gather exhibits and other evidence for jurors to review. In some states, juries also receive copies of the judges' final instructions on the law. Reporters should note the exact time that jurors leave the courtroom to begin deliberations and the hour they return with a verdict. In lengthy trials, jurors are expected to take several days to reach a decision. That doesn't always happen: The jury in the O.J. Simpson murder case took less than four hours to reach a decision in a trial that lasted several months.

Nobody really knows what a jury is going to do until the verdict is announced, despite the rampant speculation that surrounds deliberations in every courthouse in America. More often than not, jurors take their time, methodically examining the evidence before reaching a verdict. But I always stuck around the courtroom for the first few hours of deliberations in the event there was a quick verdict. I also had developed relationships with judges and their aides who alerted me when a jury reached a verdict. It takes a little time for all of the participants in a trial to return to the courthouse from law firms or prosecutors' offices, which are usually located nearby. If you're in the courthouse, you'll know if a jury has reached a decision because the building seems to buzz with the news. If you're in a cubicle in an office across town, you may not get a call or make it back in time.

Reporters also will want to stay close to the courtroom because jurors may have questions as they re-examine evidence. Sometimes they'll ask for a transcript of a witness's testimony to be reread to them. When I first started covering courts, judges were reluctant to grant such a request and pressed jurors to be more specific about what they wanted to know. Today, judges seem more willing to comply, bringing the jury back into the courtroom where court personnel re-enact the testimony often in mind-numbing monotones for fear of influencing the jury. When a jury has a question, the foreman usually writes it on a piece of paper and gives it to the bailiff to take to the judge who summons the lawyers to court or chambers to discuss how to respond. Reporters want this part of the process to be held in open court, but judges increasingly don't. Ask your editor whether your news organization wants to fight. Whatever you decide, you'll need to find out exactly what the note said if the judge fails to read it in open court, because you'll want to tell your readers and viewers about it. Court watchers love to speculate about the meaning of jury questions. Some will predict an acquittal, while others will say the question signals a conviction. Reporters should avoid allowing such speculation to affect their coverage. Juries are highly unpredictable. They often ask questions for bizarre reasons that may lose their significance by the time a verdict is reached.

What Happens in Vegas

Most jurors are conscientious, while others, not so much. Some jurors sleep through testimony. Other jurors violate judges' admonitions against reading or watching news reports about a case. And some have been accused of discussing testimony with family, friends or strangers on Twitter. A few have been accused of drinking alcohol and snorting cocaine during breaks and deliberations. Some have been accused of making racist remarks, and others have been charged with accepting bribes in exchange for their votes.

The right to a trial by jury means that a defendant is entitled to an impartial jury. Impartiality has two parts: First, the jury must be a representative cross-section of the community. Second, jurors must be free of bias against the defendant. There are many forms of bias besides race or gender. The U.S. Supreme Court reversed a conviction in 1965 because of potential favoritism created when two deputy sheriffs who testified for the prosecution also were assigned to take care of the jury during the trial.

The nation's high court has all but barred judges from inquiring about a jury's deliberations or its verdict, no matter how outrageously jurors behave. In 1987, Justice Sandra Day O'Connor, writing for the majority, said a trial judge had not made a mistake when he refused to hold a hearing on allegations leveled by a juror who said it "felt like…the jury was on one big party." The offended juror said some members of the panel snorted cocaine and smoked marijuana, and that one juror sold pot to another, bringing his drugs and paraphernalia inside the courthouse. Justice O'Connor said what happens in the jury room stays in the jury room because "the community's trust in a system that relies on the decisions of laypeople would all be undermined by a barrage of post-verdict scrutiny of juror conduct."

In 1975, Congress approved Rule 606(b) of the Federal Rules of Criminal Procedure, which bans testimony of a juror about "any matter or statement occurring" in deliberations "or to the effect of anything upon his or any other juror's mind or emotions." The U.S. Court of Appeals for the Tenth Circuit relied on the rule in 2008 when it reinstated an assault conviction against an American Indian despite allegations that jurors lied about racial bias during jury selection. During *voir dire*, jurors said they were not prejudiced against American Indians, but during deliberations, a juror charged later, the foreman said, "When Indians get alcohol, they all get drunk." Other federal appellate courts, including the Ninth and Second Circuits, say jurors can testify about each other. A reporter will need to research how appellate courts in a particular jurisdiction have handled similar cases.

People who follow trials, like the case against Casey Anthony, the young Florida mother acquitted in 2011 of killing her two-year-old daughter, want to know what happened in the jury room during deliberations, and that is why reporters and scholars want to interview jurors. In the 1950s, the Chicago Jury Project caused a scandal when researchers tape-recorded deliberations of a jury in federal court in Wichita, Kansas, with the judge's approval but unbeknownst to the jurors. In 1956, Congress passed a law that banned the recording of deliberations of grand juries and trial juries.

Social scientists haven't given up. They use "mock" juries, panels that hear evidence in fictitious cases, or "shadow" juries, groups of citizens who follow a real trial with actual evidence and render a verdict in a parallel universe. At issue is transparency of an important part of the American legal system. Despite congressional actions and the U.S. Supreme Court's rulings, some lawyers and scholars worry that jurors possess too much unchecked power and need to be held accountable, just like everyone else.

Be Patient

It's not uncommon for jurors to get frustrated if they cannot reach a verdict quickly. When that happens, they'll send a note to the judge that says they are at an impasse. The judge usually will urge them to keep trying, but he can push only so much before he must declare the jurors are hung, or unable to reach a consensus, because they are "hopelessly deadlocked," unable or unwilling to change their minds. When this happens, the judge declares a mistrial, which means the trial cannot continue.

Prosecutors must decide whether they will retry the case. Isn't that double jeopardy, or being tried for the same crime twice? No, it is not, as long as the jury did not reach a conclusion on the charges. Sometimes a jury returns a partial verdict, reaching a decision as to some but not all of the charges. Those verdicts are accepted and recorded on the resolved charges, and a mistrial is declared on the remaining counts. If the defendant is tried a second time, he will face testimony and evidence only on the unresolved charges.

A mistrial also can occur if a witness or a lawyer blurts out a fact that was previously ruled inadmissible, or something else happens in court that the judge believes the jurors cannot forget. In the perjury case against former Major League Baseball pitcher Roger Clemens in 2011, prosecutors played a videotape of testimony before Congress that referred to an affidavit submitted by the wife of another pitcher, Andy Pettitte. The problem: The judge had ruled her statements inadmissible as hearsay because she was not subjected to adversarial questioning. A mistrial was declared; Clemens was acquitted in a second trial in 2012.

A verdict of not guilty, or an acquittal, is one of the most dramatic outcomes in court, mainly because state and federal prosecutors boast conviction rates of more than 90 percent. When they lose, it's usually big news. A not-guilty verdict is most accurately described as an acquittal, and it means that the jury decided that the prosecution failed to meet its burden of proving the defendant was guilty beyond a reasonable doubt. It does not necessarily mean the defendant is innocent, which is defined in dictionaries as free of guilt or blameless. Reporters should avoid using the word innocent and stick with acquittal and not guilty to describe the outcome. A prosecutor cannot appeal an acquittal because it would be double jeopardy to try a defendant again on charges that were resolved by a jury, like it or not.

While it's important, as a reporter, to watch for reactions to a verdict, you also must take accurate notes on the details of the decision. That is no easy task if the case has multiple charges and the verdict is a mixed bag of guilty and not-guilty results. To protect yourself from making a mistake,

■ Figure 8.1. Steps in a Criminal Case ■

Post-Trial Motions	Pre-Sentence Investigation	Sentencing
• If defendant convicted, defense files motions with trial judge • Points out possible errors • Preserves arguments for appeal • Hearing may be held • If judge denies defense motions, an appeal with higher court can be filed	• Judge asks probation officer to compile background report on defendant • Sentencing date set	• Prosecutor and defense attorney may contest Pre-Sentence Report • Hearing held • Defense calls witnesses • Prosecution may call victims to testify • Defendant may address court • Judge imposes sentence • Defendant taken into custody or allowed to report to prison to begin serving sentence

you should arrange beforehand to get a blank copy of the verdict form, the same one the jury used, so you can follow along and fill in the blanks.

Reporters also need to watch the reactions of jurors who may cry as verdicts are announced because they are overcome by the stress of the moment. Defense attorneys usually ask judges to poll jurors, which means a clerk asks each member of the panel to state publicly that he agrees with a guilty verdict. It is a way of giving a juror who feels coerced an opportunity to speak up.

Thank You for Your Support

Once the verdict is read and the jurors are polled, the judge will thank them for their service and tell them that they owe no one an explanation for their decision. Jurors are under no obligation to talk to the news media, but they retain the freedom of speech to do so if they want.

If the defendant was convicted, the judge will set a sentencing hearing date, along with a schedule for filing post-verdict motions and sentencing memoranda by both sides. By this point, defendants must draw attention on the record to concerns about the legality of the way they were treated or they may forever lose the opportunity to do so with higher courts. A *motion in arrest of judgment* questions the legal soundness of an indictment and asks that the judgment of guilt in a criminal case not be enforced. The civil counterpart is a *motion for judgment notwithstanding the verdict* and may be filed after the jury's decision but before it is formally entered on the record by the judge. The motion asks the judge to disregard the jury's verdict and rule in favor of the losing party.

A motion for a new trial explains in detail the errors that the defense says were committed by the judge or prosecutor. In some states the defense must make this motion on the record with the trial judge before it is permitted to file an appeal with a higher court. There have been numerous instances where defense attorneys failed or forgot to file the motion, particularly in death penalty cases, and defendants lost their rights to appeal.

Reporters should make note of the filing deadlines and sentencing hearing dates in their personal calendars. At this stage, a reporter also might consider writing an explanatory piece about the trial, highlighting legal issues that could come back to haunt the judge and prosecutors on appeal. By now you will have a fuller picture of the story of the crime or the civil dispute from both sides' points of view. You were in the courtroom. Trust what you saw and heard. Talk to jurors to explain why they thought the prosecution or the plaintiff proved or failed to prove the charges.

While the lawyers write their post-trial briefs in criminal cases, a probation officer will be working on a pre-sentence investigation or report, which the judge will read and use to decide the length of sentence she will impose. PSIs or PSRs, as they are called, provide the judge with information about the defendant's background and criminal history, some of which you may know as a reporter and a great deal you may not.

In the federal system and in many states, the reports are secret, but you can learn about some of the PSI findings if you pay attention to the sentencing motions filed by both sides. The lawyers will often fight over whether the probation officer got it right or wrong and whether the judge should consider the disputed facts in imposing a sentence. It also means that either or both sides will quote, sometimes extensively, from the PSI. If you read the motions before the sentencing hearing, you will understand the issues in play.

From Smack to Crack

President Richard Nixon found a receptive public when he declared a War on Crime in the late 1960s and early 1970s because the nation's major cities were rocked by riots over racial inequities and plagued by violent crime fueled by the increasing popularity of destructive drugs like heroin. State legislatures passed laws, such as the Rockefeller statutes in New York, which carried stiff mandatory sentences for drug offenses. Ronald Reagan picked up where Nixon left off, using crime as an issue in his campaign for president. In 1984, Congress approved a massive overhaul of federal criminal procedure and passed the Sentencing Reform Act, a bipartisan bill that created the U.S. Sentencing Commission to write mandatory guidelines for judges to follow in imposing sentences. At the same time, politicians and crime victims launched a movement that pressed for honesty, or truth-in-sentencing. In many states, judges imposed sentences that sounded tough to the public, but in a wink and a nod, the players in the criminal justice system moved defendants through a revolving door from prison to the street. Judges in Massachusetts, for example, engaged in the deceptive practice of imposing what was known as the Concord sentence, a reference to one of the state's prisons, knowing that defendants would serve only about a third of the punishment, if that. Lawmakers also focused on the wide disparities in sentences not only across the country but also within counties: Defendants received lighter or harsher sentences depending on where they committed their crimes and the judges who were assigned to handle their cases.

The guidelines approach seeks to play down the unpredictable human quotient by instead relying on the constancy of numbers. A complex calculation is used that adds and subtracts points for the type of offense committed, whether violence or guns were involved, the number of victims, the harm to victims, a defendant's role in the crime, his criminal history, and his acceptance of responsibility, among other factors. A grid is used to plot a sentencing range, within which the judge is supposed to stay in deciding the length of punishment.

Nearly coinciding with the sentencing movement, a potent, highly addictive form of cocaine called crack hit the streets of many major American cities, causing an outbreak of violence often in the form of "drive-by" shootings that claimed innocent bystanders from toddlers to grandmothers.

Crack swept through poor communities as quickly and mercilessly as a plague, seemingly singling out young black women with catastrophic results for their children, who wound up in foster care, tossed from one family friend to another or forced to fend for themselves. Congress responded by passing laws that carried stiff mandatory minimum sentences for offenders caught with crack. Believing crack was worse than the powder form of cocaine, lawmakers created a 100-to-1 disparity in prison time for the sister drugs. Possession of five grams of crack (about the weight of two pennies) received a mandatory minimum sentence of five years in prison, and possession of 50 grams of crack resulted in a 10-year mandatory sentence. Defendants arrested for powder cocaine charges faced similar sentences only if they were caught with 100 times those amounts. While many state legislatures mimicked Congress by approving similar mandatory minimum sentences for drug offenses, they also took aim at career criminals, passing laws that sent them to prison for life if they were convicted of three or more felonies under the popular "three strikes and you're out" approach to crime fighting.

The crackdown contrasts dramatically with how the nation dealt with concerns about alcohol abuse. When the Eighteenth Amendment to the U.S. Constitution went into effect in 1920, it banned the manufacture, sale and transportation of alcohol, but not possession. People remained free to use and serve it in the privacy of their homes. Today's drug laws criminalize possession in ways that benefit prosecutors by making cases easier to prove: To meet the threshold for distribution, a prosecutor need only show a defendant possessed more than a user's quantity of the drug. Legislators also loosened the definition of possession: A defendant does not necessarily have to have handled the drugs. Close proximity is enough. Punishment is determined by the total weight of the drugs involved, regardless of whether the defendant knew how much was being transported or sold. As a result, plea bargains with lengthy prison sentences became foregone conclusions.

Nothing to Trade

For years, defense lawyers, federal judges and civil rights groups decried the disparities in federal cocaine sentencing. In 1995, the Sentencing Commission, the agency Congress created to monitor the fairness of punishment, issued a report that found that crack sentences were the primary cause of the growing disparity between sentences for black and white federal defendants. It turned out that most crack defendants were African American and those serving time for powder cocaine charges were usually white or Hispanic. Congress ignored it, mainly because advocating leniency for criminals was, and remains, comparable to political suicide.

For African American women, it was worse. Between 1986 and 1991, the incarceration rate for black women increased nearly twice as fast as for black men—828 percent for women compared to 429 percent for men, according to U.S. Department of Justice statistics. For women of all races, the incarceration rate jumped 516 percent between 1980 and 1998. Men still far outnumbered female inmates in raw numbers, but women, many of whom were addicts, received long prison sentences for acting as drug mules, smuggling drugs for boyfriends, or playing minor roles in organizations run by men. Unlike the men, the women had little if any information to trade with prosecutors in exchange for lenient sentences. Under a provision of the federal guidelines known as 5K, prosecutors routinely asked judges to give breaks to informants, often men, by reducing prison time, sometimes significantly.

In 1999, I wrote a story for *U.S. News & World Report* that examined the consequences of the nation's drug policies on the daughters of women who were locked up for crack-cocaine offenses. I found that daughters of women inmates were following in their mothers' footsteps and getting into trouble. How did I figure out this was a story? In the mid-1990s, I noticed the skyrocketing female incarceration rates as I reviewed annual reports compiled by the Justice Department's Bureau of Justice Statistics. The federal criminal justice system collects an enormous amount of information about offenders, crimes, court caseloads and sentences. Today much information can be found online and is accessible with a keystroke or two. Every police and courts reporter should take time on a slow news day to cull through reports on the websites for the BJS, at http://bjs.ojp.usdoj.gov/. The U.S. Sentencing Commission also has useful data on its site, at http://www.ussc.gov/, and the U.S. Courts, at http://www.uscourts.gov/Home.aspx, provide access to caseload data broken down by district. State supreme courts also are increasingly providing access to similar data, and reporters should check the courts' websites to see what's there.

Tough sentences, it turned out, cost money, and lots of it. Less tangible but equally problematic is the impact that sentencing policies, particularly regarding crack, had on the public's attitude toward the courts, as Steven Chanenson and Douglas Berman explained in the *Federal Sentencing Reporter* in June 2007. "The larger problem is one of fairness and justice—both its reality and its perception," they wrote. "For nearly two decades, the crack-powder disparity has been 'Exhibit A' for those who believe that the federal criminal justice system is racially biased. It has been 'Exhibit A' for those who believe the federal criminal justice system is excessively severe."

In recent years, some politicians have decided it's safe to talk about lessening the severity of sentences if for no other reason than to cut prison costs and save taxpayers money. In 2010, Congress passed the Fair Sentencing Act, reducing the crack-to-powder sentencing disparity to 18-to-1. A year later, the Sentencing Commission took steps to allow federal judges to reduce the sentences of many crack defendants. In a June 2011 news release, Judge Patti Saris, the commission's chair, estimated that 12,000 offenders might be eligible for an average sentence reduction of 37 months. Even with the reductions, she said, the offenders' average time in prison would be about 10 years. Saris said the estimated savings to taxpayers would be $200 million in the first five years.

This seismic change in attitude may have been instigated in part by "a series of constitutional shocks," as the Justice Department described it in a June 2010 letter to the Sentencing Commission. In 2004, the U.S. Supreme Court ruled in *Blakely v. Washington* that a jury, not a judge, must find every fact that is ultimately used to enhance a defendant's sentence. The majority opinion, written by Justice Antonin Scalia, rocked the federal criminal justice system because the guidelines had permitted judges to add years to sentences by taking into consideration acts about which a jury never heard testimony. A year later, in *United States v. Booker*, the high court told trial judges that they no longer were required to follow the federal guidelines, and the rules became advisory. Since then, two categories of sentences have emerged: those imposed by judges who remain faithful to the guidelines, and those ordered by judges who are taking advantage of the restoration of their discretion. In the June 2010 letter to the Sentencing Commission, a Justice Department lawyer said disparities were appearing in sentences imposed on defendants convicted of white-collar crime, child pornography, environmental violations and offenses associated with illegal immigration and violence on the nation's border with Mexico. "These dichotomous regimes will, over time, breed disrespect for the federal courts," the Justice Department lawyer predicted.

Operation Broken Faith

In December 1993, a dozen D.C. police officers were arrested at a hotel in Washington after they accepted payments of $2,000 to escort a drug dealer's cocaine shipments. Dubbed the "Dirty Dozen," the cops had been ensnared by a fictitious drug organization concocted by the FBI in a sting known as Operation Broken Faith.

Within a year, nine of the 12 officers pleaded guilty in bargains with prosecutors that sent them to prison for no more than 20 years. Nygel Brown, the cop who recruited the others, received a 14-year sentence after agreeing within days of his arrest to cooperate with federal authorities and proving that flipping first pays off.

When the three remaining officers dared to refuse to accept plea bargains and exercised their right to a trial by jury, prosecutors brought the hammer down. They added weapons charges against the defendants for bringing their police-issued handguns to a meeting with an undercover FBI agent. As police officers, they were required to carry their guns at all times.

Before trial, U.S. District Judge Thomas F. Hogan practically begged the defendants to accept guilty pleas that would've carried 10-year sentences, but they refused.

The effect was devastating—and the outcome predictable, as the jury convicted them of the most serious charges. In June 1995, Judge Hogan used such words as "tragic," "sad" and "overly harsh" to describe the 49-year sentences he imposed on each of the three defendants, all of whom were in their mid- to late 20s at the time. The judge also criticized prosecutors for rewriting the indictment and using the sentencing guidelines to manipulate the outcome, but he said he couldn't do anything about it.

Two years later a federal appeals court stepped in and subtracted the 20 years each defendant received for the weapons charges that prosecutors had tacked on before trial. The appellate panel relied on arcane-sounding procedure, not basic fairness or prosecutorial overkill, saying it was "impossible to tell" whether the jury tied the convictions to a drug charge or, inappropriately, to a conspiracy count.

Committed to Custody

A sentencing hearing can be as emotional as a jury's verdict. Defendants learn how long they will be locked up, and victims find out how much their suffering is worth. No matter how many times a defense attorney tells a client what to expect, it's unlikely she is prepared to hear a judge say the words, "You are committed to the custody of the U.S. Bureau of Prisons." Family and friends brought Bibles to the sentencing hearing for the three former D.C. cops convicted in the FBI sting. Some defendants, victims and their families cry. Others faint. I saw a former high-ranking D.C. housing official pass out in court when a federal judge sentenced her to several years in prison. She knew what the judge was going to say, but the words still knocked the wind out of her.

The hearings can last for hours or even days, depending on how much support a defendant musters from family and friends. Reporters should check court files for letters written to judges on behalf of defendants. The names and occupations of the letter-writers can make news. Sometimes the people who don't write letters or testify on behalf of a defendant can be a story, such as when the political mentor of a prominent local politician refuses to stand up for his former protégé. Obtaining access to the letters can be problematic because the judge is likely to have them with him on the bench during the sentencing hearing. Reporters need to arrange with the judge's staff for access as quickly as possible. The letters are supposed to be part of the official court record, but you want to avoid a legal battle if possible. If you have a good relationship with the judge, you should be able to obtain copies of the letters.

A judge can sentence a defendant to a definite term, a specific number of years, or to an indefinite term, a range of years, such as three to five. In cases involving multiple charges, judges usually sentence defendants to a specific number of years on each count. They then decide whether the punishment for each charge will run concurrently, meaning it is served simultaneously with sentences imposed on all or some of the other charges. Or, judges will order that sentences must be served consecutively, or in succession. For example, if a defendant were sentenced to five years in prison for Count 1, three years on Count 2 and two years on Count 3, he would serve a five-year sentence, if the judge imposed concurrent terms. He would serve a 10-year sentence, if the judge imposed the terms consecutively.

Judges also can suspend all or part of a sentence, which means defendants get a break because they won't be locked up for the entire length of the punishment unless they get into trouble again. If that happens, they could be forced to complete the portion of the sentence that was suspended. If a defendant received a five-year sentence for robbery, with two years suspended, that means he would serve three years in prison. Most judges add a term of supervised release to apply after a defendant gets out of prison. If the defendant in our example received a two-year term of supervised release and he gets into trouble, the judge could send him back to prison for the two years that had been suspended on the robbery charge.

The biggest break a convicted defendant can receive is probation, which means he does not go to prison but is monitored by a probation officer for a specific number of months or years. In many states and at the federal level, parole, which is early release after a defendant has served part of a prison term, was abolished during the get-tough-on-crime era of politics. A panel of officials, usually appointed by a governor, decided if and when an inmate would be released early on parole. Today, a life sentence generally means life. Defendants also serve nearly all of the sentences they receive for other serious crimes, minus a few days a month of credit for good behavior. Probation and parole are different and should not be used interchangeably.

Fines and other fees can be imposed, requiring defendants to pay the costs of prosecuting them for their wrongdoing and for supervising them while they are on probation and supervised release. Some courts are hiring bill collectors to go after defendants who owe court costs, and people are being locked up because of the debts. They also can be ordered to pay restitution, which means they must compensate their victims. Who makes sure the payments to victims are made? No one. I wrote a story for the *Washington Post* in 1998 that revealed that few defendants in state courts in Maryland and Virginia ever paid a dime of restitution and suffered no consequences. In other words, a defendant who doesn't pay a court what he owes could be in trouble. If he owes a victim, he probably won't be.

Who Cares?

During the 1990s, lawmakers eliminated drug treatment and education programs for inmates. Few reporters write about prisons because information is difficult to gather, and there is a widespread belief among editors that the public could care less about what happens to inmates. I disagree. If the story is compelling, your editors and the public will care.

Prisons are nasty places. I have been inside prisons in California, Texas, Michigan and Massachusetts, and none had what I would describe as the comforts of home. In Texas, I saw inmates who slept on mattresses thinner than the Bible and ate substances the color and texture of cement. In Massachusetts, prison officials converted recreation rooms into dormitories, cramming in row after row of bunk beds to accommodate growing numbers of inmates.

In financially strapped communities, a prison means jobs for people who live there. Many states built more prisons to house the increasing number of inmates incarcerated for long periods of time because of mandatory minimum sentences and sentencing guidelines of the 1980s and 1990s. In some areas, officials overbuilt. Some states also moved to privatize, or contract out the operation of their prisons, with mixed results, including fraud, waste and allegations of physical abuse.

How does a reporter gather information to tell stories about what goes on behind prison walls? The same way she approaches other stories—by finding and cultivating sources and by researching and reading public records. The toughest part about covering prisons is getting inside, literally. Three times the U.S. Supreme Court has been asked if reporters have a right of access to prisons, and all three times the justices said no. "Newsmen have no constitutional right of access to prisons or their inmates beyond that afforded the general public," Justice Potter Stewart wrote in 1974.

Corrections officials often allow reporters to tour prisons and interview inmates—prisoners of their choosing and not the reporter's. This practice raises concerns about whether prison officials are controlling the message. I usually interviewed the inmates made available to me because I thought it was better to know something rather than nothing. As long as you understand the limits of information provided by a warden's handpicked inmates, you can figure out how much additional reporting you need to do.

When I worked at the *Boston Globe*, I interviewed inmates for stories I wrote about crowding in state prisons and an increase in gun violence involving juveniles. In those instances, corrections officials selected the inmates. But in Michigan, California and Texas, I picked the inmates I interviewed; they were mothers of young girls I had met who were getting into trouble with the law. If an inmate wants to talk to you, it's easier to get prison officials to agree to allow you inside for an interview. You should cultivate the wardens of your local jails and prisons as sources because they know a great deal about the strengths and weaknesses of the criminal justice system. Don't wait until you want something to pay attention to them.

Sources also can be cultivated in prison outreach programs, many of which are tied to religious groups and public interest law firms that represent inmates who have been sexually abused or mistreated in other ways. When I worked for the *Washington Post*, I wrote stories about lawsuits filed on behalf of women on both sides of the bars—inmates and guards—who alleged that they were sexually assaulted and harassed by male corrections officers. While covering a lawsuit filed by women guards in the District of Columbia, I developed several sources among male and female corrections officers and inmates who later tipped me off when female inmates were coerced into performing a striptease at the D.C. Jail. Despite cutbacks in treatment and programming, inmates still get to make phone calls. They can call reporters collect, and they can write letters to you.

The corrections officers' union is another potential source of information. When two inmates seized a section of Pennsylvania's Western Penitentiary, one of the toughest prisons in America in the 1980s, I had contacts in the guards' union and elsewhere who helped me figure out what was happening during the hostage situation and how and why it had occurred so that I could explain it to readers of the *Pittsburgh Press*.

· *Chapter* ·

Show Me the Money:
Civil Lawsuits, Settlements and Damages

■ ■ ■

A civil lawsuit tells a story of conflict between people, businesses or government agencies who turn to the courts to determine who was wronged and how much they should receive to compensate them for their troubles. Money is usually the goal, but not always. Sometimes a party in a lawsuit simply wants the other side to stop what it's doing. In other instances, lawsuits have protected the public by revealing dangerous defects in popular products or deadly side effects of prescription drugs.

Lawsuits also have served as instruments of change, providing the basis for challenges to segregation of the nation's public schools, anti-sodomy laws aimed at homosexuals, limitations on terrorism suspects' ability to challenge their detentions and expansion of state police power to identify illegal immigrants. The intent of a lawsuit is not always noble. It can be used to harass or intimidate because anyone who can afford to pay a filing fee can sue another person or company. Defending a lawsuit costs money, and it takes time before a judge reaches a point where he can throw it out. In the hands of a clever or vindictive business owner, politician or attorney, a lawsuit can wreck a small business's finances, silence critics or force big firms to pay the aggressor to go away.

As in the criminal side of the legal system, the majority of civil disputes are resolved without trials, resulting in settlements, which are agreements to pay money or take certain action to the satisfaction of both parties. In this chapter, we will discuss how agreements can be reached before a lawsuit is filed or at any stage after the case enters the court system up to and including a verdict. Settlements are often kept secret because the parties agree to keep them that way. This makes it difficult for reporters to inform the public about flaws in products and other dangers to consumers. Sometimes the parties ask judges to retroactively seal all of the paperwork in a case, including the original complaint, or lawsuit. On the public record it's as if the dispute never happened. In some jurisdictions there is no mention of the case at all; in others, "Sealed v. Sealed" appears on the docket with no additional information. When this happens, defendants can hide outrageous, dangerous business practices and products. Plaintiffs may go along because they want—and need—the money to pay medical bills that piled up to treat injuries caused by the defendants' behavior.

The U.S. Supreme Court has not required states to provide the right to a jury trial in civil lawsuits. Nor has it said whether civil trials are presumptively open to the public, like criminal trials.

But several state appellate courts and lower federal courts have said civil trials are supposed to be open. Does this mean documents filed in connection with a civil lawsuit are available to the public and the press? It depends.

Tort, Not Tart

A tort, a wrong that one person or a business commits against another, is the focus of a lawsuit. For years, business groups, doctors and politicians have campaigned for tort reform, changes in law designed to stop eye-popping, multimillion-dollar jury awards against big companies.

Since the late 1990s, these groups have focused on a popular form of civil litigation, the class action lawsuit, which is a case brought by a few people on behalf of a larger group that supposedly suffered similar injuries because of the defendant's actions. While working at the *Washington Post*, I covered several class action cases that had resulted in consent decrees, agreements between the parties that typically involved oversight by judges or court-appointed monitors to fix problems that had been identified by the court. I wrote a story that described how federal judges in Washington had taken over huge chunks of city government because local agencies had failed to protect foster children, the mentally ill and the mentally retarded, and provide humane conditions for prisoners. Congress passed a law in the late 1990s that placed some limits on class action lawsuits that had resulted in consent decrees. Some of those cases in D.C. remain on the docket and judges continue to monitor the city's progress.

Some parts of the country have drawn the attention of the so-called tort reform movement because they are known as plaintiff-friendly, which means juries tend to side with the underdog against big business. In other parts of the country, jurors avoid big-money awards against their area's largest employers.

Business groups and medical organizations often ask lawmakers to cap jury awards to plaintiffs, particularly for punitive damages, which are designed to punish bad behavior and deter others from engaging in similar activities. In 2010, the supreme courts of Georgia and Illinois struck down their state legislatures' attempts to limit punitive awards, mainly because the jury's role in determining damages is rooted in their state constitutions.

How Much Is Too Much?

The U.S. Chamber of Commerce and the American Medical Association have led lobbying efforts aimed at federal and state legislators to pass laws that would neutralize what they consider runaway juries by capping damages, curtailing the amount of information a business would have to share with the filer of a lawsuit, and limiting the types of cases that could be brought.

The Chamber of Commerce formed the Institute for Legal Reform, which produces annual reports that rank state and county courts from best to worst in what it considers outrageous awards against businesses. In ILR's 2012 *State Liability Systems Survey*, the group identified the courts in Chicago and Cook County, Illinois, as the worst jurisdictions for businesses. The rest of the top five included the courts in Los Angeles, the state of California generally, San Francisco and Philadelphia. A survey of in-house legal counsel for some of the nation's biggest companies identified Delaware, where many of the largest firms incorporate, as the best state for a business to defend itself. West Virginia was identified as the worst.

So far, Congress, an entity dominated by attorneys, hasn't managed to muster a consensus to cap damages, but the U.S. Supreme Court has voided what it considers exorbitant jury awards. Between 1994 and 2003, the justices issued rulings that transferred this long-standing power of the jury to judges by empowering them to reduce awards that are "too high," but the Court hasn't provided a clear definition of how much is too much.

In one case, the Court said the ratio between punitive and compensatory damages, which is the sum of money awarded to make a plaintiff whole again, must be in single digits. Some legal scholars took that to mean that punitive damages could not outnumber compensatory damages by more than 9 to 1. But in the same case, Justice Anthony Kennedy mentioned a 4-to-1 ratio, saying it might be more reasonable. Whatever the ratio, the high court has signaled that it welcomes appeals from defendants seeking to reduce or nullify multimillion-dollar verdicts in civil cases.

Justice Kennedy said people—businesses in particular—are entitled, as they are in criminal law, to fair notice about what behavior is acceptable, what is not and how severe the punishment will be for violators. He said, "punitive damages should only be awarded if the defendant's culpability…is so reprehensible as to warrant the imposition of further sanctions to achieve punishment or deterrence." The problem is that what's excessive to one person might sound about right to another.

What does this mean for reporters? No jury verdict, especially a large one, is certain, and you should be aware that a lengthy appeals process could end with a reduction in punitive damages or a new trial. When you write your story about the jury's verdict, you should ask defense counsel specifically about this issue. Your story will be far superior and smarter than your competitor's, if you explore and explain this angle.

So Sue Me

The right to sue is enshrined in the Seventh Amendment to the U.S. Constitution. Many Americans may not be able to cite the source of their right to sue, but they know they are entitled to their day in court, and a payday, if they're blinded when an eye surgeon sneezes during an operation. Filing a lawsuit is as American as apple pie. Anyone can file a lawsuit if he can pay the court's filing fee, which means journalists should report on lawsuits with a healthy dose of skepticism.

Sometimes corporations, government officials and real estate developers file lawsuits to silence citizens and community groups that oppose them on public controversies. The plaintiff usually doesn't care about winning the case, known as a SLAPP, Strategic Lawsuit Against Public Participation, but uses it to intimidate critics by forcing them to pay the legal costs of defending themselves. Several states and the District of Columbia have passed anti-SLAPP laws to provide protection against such lawsuits.

When reporting on the filing of a lawsuit, you should resist the urge to hype your reporting on how much money in damages a plaintiff seeks when he files a lawsuit. Usually the plaintiff asks for the moon, the stars and all of the planets in the solar system in the form of millions of dollars. It may sound dramatic and make for a great headline, but it's probably unrealistic. Keep it in perspective and place it in context.

Contract disputes between companies make up a significant part of a court's civil caseload. Car collisions lead to the filing of personal injury lawsuits. If someone dies, families often file what are known as wrongful death actions. For example, families successfully sued former football star O.J. Simpson for wrongful death for the murders of his ex-wife Nicole Brown Simpson and waiter

Ronald Goldman. Divorce, child support and custody battles also account for a significant portion of a civil court's docket.

When a lawsuit is filed, the plaintiff frames the dispute by providing his version of the facts and describing how he was hurt, and how much he thinks it will take to make him whole again. Like an indictment, a lawsuit includes counts, which are distinct statements or allegations of wrongdoing. Before a criminal indictment is returned, a grand jury theoretically acts as a check on the power of prosecutors by reviewing the allegations. There is no such review by anyone—other than the plaintiff and his counsel—before a lawsuit is filed. It is another reason for a reporter to be cautious, skeptical and fair. The plaintiff levels each allegation with a caveat, "upon information and belief," and specifies exactly what he wants from the judge or jury in a section of the lawsuit called a demand for judgment, or "prayer for relief." The terms are a fancy way of saying the plaintiff thinks this is what happened and this is what he deserves in return. It also means he hasn't proven anything yet.

Reporters assigned to the court beat are responsible for watching for newsworthy developments in old cases and for spotting new lawsuits that tell interesting and important stories. Here's a tip: Make printed or electronic copies of every remotely interesting document in cases you think you'll be following. The penchant for secrecy in civil litigation often means that a document that's public today can and will disappear tomorrow. If you have it, you generally can use it—unless the court comes after you and tries to retrieve it, which has happened on a few occasions, usually because a clerk has mistakenly posted or filed a document that was supposed to be sealed.

It's impossible to read every single case, but you can "eyeball" many of them if you swing by the clerk's office several times during the day, noting the names of the parties and the issues raised in the lawsuits. If you recognize a name, you should retrieve the lawsuit and read it. This is why it is important for you to know the names of the movers and shakers in your community and to keep up with news on other beats. Because we are such a litigious society, most controversial issues eventually wind up in a courthouse.

A Sense of Belonging

Before a lawsuit is filed, the plaintiff's attorney must decide where, or in what venue, she should lodge the complaint. The law dictates the venue of a lawsuit, but a judge can grant a request for a change of venue, as he can in a criminal case, and move the trial because of widespread negative pretrial publicity or for the convenience of witnesses.

To preside over a lawsuit, a judge must have jurisdiction, which means he can exercise control over the defendant or the property at issue because they are located in a geographic area covered by the court. Legal actions are often transitory, which means they can be brought wherever the defendant is located, where the incident occurred, or where the court has sufficient contact with one of the parties. A lawsuit against a company does not necessarily need to be filed in the city where it is headquartered; the case can be filed in any county where the company does business.

When a lawsuit is filed, the plaintiff includes a summons, or notice, that is sent to the defendant to alert her that she has been sued. In many courts, deputy sheriffs or private companies will serve, or deliver, the summons to the defendant. The summons will provide a deadline for which the defendant must file an answer, or a response, which is a document in which she admits or denies the allegations, paragraph by paragraph, in the lawsuit, or offers an excuse for the behavior.

Another possible reaction: "Insufficient knowledge to admit or deny," which is a legalistic way of saying, I don't know. The defendant also can file a counterclaim, which is a counterpunch aimed at the plaintiff: "If you're suing me, I'm suing you." A counterclaim can be filed separately or as part of the defendant's answer. Cross-claims may be filed if there are several parties on each side and they have separate disputes connected to the main issue raised in the lawsuit. The plaintiff can file a reply to respond to any new allegations or statements raised by the defendant in her answer.

One of the first moves by the defense will be to challenge the authority of the court to handle the lawsuit. A motion to dismiss is usually filed before the parties have gathered much, if any, information to support their positions. The defendant will argue that the lawsuit is legally deficient, but the judge must consider the facts in a way that gives the plaintiff the benefit of the doubt at this early stage. A motion to dismiss is likely to raise several issues, including:

- *Lack of subject matter jurisdiction.* This means the court lacks the power to rule on the controversy.
- *Lack of personal jurisdiction.* This means the court does not have the power to make decisions affecting a defendant who has little, if any contact with the place where the lawsuit is filed.
- *Improper venue.* This refers to places that the law says a person can and cannot be sued for a particular action.
- *Insufficient service of process.* A case can be dismissed or thrown out of court if there was a technical glitch in the summons, or if a defendant did not receive the summons or a copy of the lawsuit.
- *Failure to state a claim upon which relief may be granted.* Sometimes a defendant's negligent actions may not be against the law, meaning he had no legal obligation to look out for the plaintiff and is not liable for any wrongdoing.

The purpose of a trial is for a judge in a bench trial or a jury to decide the facts. If both sides agree on the facts, there is no need for a trial. When that happens, one side or the other will file a *motion for summary judgment*, which asks the judge to apply the law to the facts and rule in favor

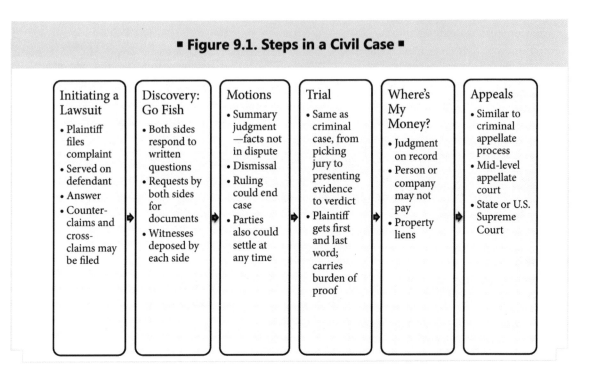

■ Figure 9.1. Steps in a Civil Case ■

Initiating a Lawsuit	Discovery: Go Fish	Motions	Trial	Where's My Money?	Appeals
• Plaintiff files complaint • Served on defendant • Answer • Counter-claims and cross-claims may be filed	• Both sides respond to written questions • Requests by both sides for documents • Witnesses deposed by each side	• Summary judgment —facts not in dispute • Dismissal • Ruling could end case • Parties also could settle at any time	• Same as criminal case, from picking jury to presenting evidence to verdict • Plaintiff gets first and last word; carries burden of proof	• Judgment on record • Person or company may not pay • Property liens	• Similar to criminal appellate process • Mid-level appellate court • State or U.S. Supreme Court

of the moving party. The case ends if the judge grants the request. To keep this from happening, the opposing side must give the judge reason to believe that key facts remain in dispute. A motion for summary judgment can be filed early in a case or later, after the parties have gathered more information about the dispute.

If a defendant ignores a lawsuit, a plaintiff could file a *motion for default judgment*. The defendant then could be found in default, which means the case would move forward without his side of the story. The only remaining issue would be how much money the plaintiff should receive in damages. Sometimes a defendant offers a valid excuse that sways a judge to vacate, or nullify, the default judgment.

Tell Me Everything

The parties in a lawsuit will spend most of their time in discovery, the process by which both sides are supposed to exchange all relevant information pertaining to the dispute. The objective is to ensure there are no surprises during trial and that one side doesn't hide key evidence, gain unfair advantage or sucker punch the other. This is the major difference between criminal and civil litigation. In criminal cases, prosecutors hold their cards close, sharing only what and when the law requires. In civil litigation, both sides reveal their hands before trial.

Discovery usually is lengthy, expensive and intrusive, and it often leads defendants to settle cases that their initial instincts may have been to fight. When money is at stake, bravado quickly gives way to practical sensibilities. Lawsuits are expensive to try. Trade secrets or other embarrassing information could be revealed. Publicity also could affect people who had nothing to do with the issues raised in the case. This is why reporters should not assume that every defendant who agrees to settle a case did something wrong. Sometimes it's easier—and more cost-effective—for a defendant to pay the plaintiff to go away. In some instances, it's a price of doing business, and when that happens civil litigation can come close to crossing the line to extortion.

Settlements usually do not lay blame but instead explicitly state that the defendant admits no wrongdoing. When you write about a settlement, make sure you find out if the deal contains this provision. You do not want to say a company admitted wrongdoing when it didn't. In some instances a defendant may settle part of a case and elect to go to trial on the remaining issues raised in the lawsuit. By agreeing to settle, plaintiffs often give up their rights to pursue additional legal action. It is also common for plaintiffs to be required to sign a pledge of confidentiality, as a condition of the settlement, promising to keep the deal's details a secret, especially its price tag.

Cases can settle at any time, providing yet another reason for reporters to stay on top of developments in important civil lawsuits. Keep in touch with lawyers for both sides and with the judge. If you don't know that negotiations are occurring, you may get caught flat-footed when an agreement is reached.

Go Fish

Civil discovery is an elaborate version of Go Fish, the game in which players must turn over cards sought by one another. Lawyers exchange information in three ways:

- *Interrogatories*, written questions that seek information about each side's version of the facts and claims;

- *Document production*, which applies to all records that are relevant to the case. It also means that one side can bury the other in paper. Since the digital revolution, judges increasingly are dealing with requests by parties for access to deleted emails and other computerized data;
- *Depositions*, out-of-court statements or testimony given under oath. The most common form of discovery, depositions usually are taken in a lawyer's office, typically the home base of the side that issued the subpoena, or demand that a person show up at a certain time to give testimony, provide documents or both. When a witness is deposed, lawyers for all sides usually are present. The lawyer for the party that issued the subpoena conducts the initial questioning before the attorney for the other side gets a shot at the witness. A judge is usually not present, which means any objections to questions are set aside for a later ruling, if necessary. Taking depositions is a key part of each side's legal strategy because the questioning locks a witness into a version of events, and it can be used to impeach, or discredit her if she changes her story later at trial. Through depositions, adversaries learn more about their opponent's strengths and weaknesses. A deposition also is good practice for a witness who will testify at trial.

How much of this is accessible to a reporter? It depends on whether the judge has entered a protective order, a restriction on information that lawyers are allowed to discuss or release. Depositions present a dilemma because they are kept at lawyers' offices, not in the court files, and a judge or the attorneys could argue that since they aren't part of the official record, they aren't accessible to the press. Talk to the lawyers for one side or the other about sharing the transcripts with you.

How will a reporter find out about the existence of an interesting deposition? During the discovery process, judges meet regularly with lawyers for both sides in what are called status conferences to manage the flow of cases and keep the parties on track. Judges also use status conferences to help them spot and avert potential problems that could derail a trial, such as an issue raised in a deposition. For those reasons, I used to attend status conferences, if they were held in open court.

Let's Make a Deal

In the majority of states, judges must refer certain kinds of civil disputes to a neutral third party to help the sides resolve their differences. This process is called alternative dispute resolution, and it is designed to save time and avoid the expense of trials.

Federal courts are required by law to use ADR to ease district court caseloads. There are two main types of ADR. In mediation, a court-appointed mediator or a magistrate guides the parties toward a settlement of their differences. In arbitration, the plaintiff and defendant agree to put their fates in the hands of a neutral third party who issues a binding decision in the case after hearing testimony and reviewing evidence. Given a choice, plaintiffs and defendants usually prefer less-binding mediation. Many litigants also favor ADR because it is usually private and confidential. Sometimes confidentiality isn't an issue, but lawyers, out of habit, insert secrecy clauses into settlement agreements, throwing up yet another obstacle for reporters in gathering information about newsworthy civil cases.

As a reporter challenging the secrecy of an ADR proceeding, you may or may not win, depending on what information you seek and at what point in the process you want access. You probably won't get access to an ADR hearing because most courts believe the process works only if the parties feel free to be honest and say whatever they want without fear of publicity. In fact, there is a rule of evidence in every state and in the federal courts that prevents statements made during ADR proceedings from being used against a party later at a trial, if one occurs.

When a settlement is reached, the parties in a lawsuit will file a joint motion to dismiss the case. The motion notifies the judge that the dispute has been resolved and that his services are no longer needed. A reporter has a good shot of obtaining access to settlement documents if the paperwork was submitted to a judge and he was asked to approve the deal. You're also more likely to obtain access to documents or information about the amount of a settlement if one of the parties is a public entity or government agency. Information often is stored in several locations. If you are shut out of one place, go to another. For example, city police departments may try to hide settlements in suits alleging brutality. The money has to come out of the city budget, where a reporter can dig around and find out how much the department paid to make the lawsuit go away.

It is more difficult for a reporter to obtain access to settlement documents if they were never submitted to the court for approval. If that happens, the settlement is not an official court record because a judge never had possession of the documents. A judge probably will not order a party to turn over a document in private possession even if it's in the office of the lawyer who filed the lawsuit.

Some states, including Texas, Virginia and Georgia, allow access to settlement agreements and other documents in cases that raise public safety issues. Other courts believe that litigants' interests in confidentiality outweigh the public's right of access, and this means the people—and the press— are kept in the dark about the resolutions of many civil disputes.

Mirror, Mirror

When they fail to make a deal, litigants go to trial before a jury or judge. As in criminal cases, trials of civil lawsuits are increasingly rare, and when a newsworthy one comes along, a reporter will want to cover it as thoroughly and aggressively as a criminal case.

At first glance, trials of civil and criminal cases are mirror images, but if you look closely you will see subtle differences. Like prosecutors in criminal cases, plaintiffs in civil lawsuits get the first and last word with juries because they have the burden of proof, which means they must prove the allegations contained in the lawsuit. The standard of proof, the level of evidence required, is different in civil cases. In criminal cases, juries must find a defendant guilty beyond a reasonable doubt, which is as close to 100-percent certainty as possible. In most civil cases, juries use the standard of a preponderance of the evidence, which means that it is more likely than not that a defendant wronged the plaintiff. In some civil cases, juries are required to use a higher standard of proof by clear and convincing evidence, meaning that it is highly probable that the defendant wronged the plaintiff.

From toughest to the least demanding, the standards of proof are beyond a reasonable doubt, followed by clear and convincing evidence, then preponderance of the evidence. The lowest standard of proof is probable cause, which is used by cops to obtain arrest and search warrants, and it means they have a reasonable belief that a crime was committed and that a particular person was the culprit.

The outcomes in civil and criminal cases differ. In civil cases, plaintiffs must convince jurors that a defendant is liable. This is not the same as guilt in a criminal case. A jury's finding of liability means that a defendant is found to be responsible for the wrong committed against the plaintiff. It may be easier to say a defendant in a civil case was convicted or found guilty, but it's incorrect.

On Your Mark

To prepare for a civil trial, a reporter should be on the lookout for filings in the days before testimony begins. Usually the judge and lawyers will get together to work out stipulations, which are agreements on undisputed facts or points of law in the case. These kinds of deals can speed up a trial, making it unnecessary for lawyers on each side to solicit testimony or introduce documentary evidence to support facts or legal points that are not in dispute.

Before trial, lawyers for each side also may file a trial memorandum, which summarizes their versions of the case. When they're done right, they can be of enormous help, providing roadmaps and insight into each side's evidence and strategy.

Juries in civil cases range from six to 12 people who are selected from a pool of potential jurors the same way as in a criminal case—from voter registration and drivers' license rolls. The size of juries in civil cases varies from state to state and sometimes depends on the type of lawsuit. Civil juries don't necessarily need to reach a unanimous verdict, and more and more states require verdicts based on the agreement of three-fourths or five-sixths of the jurors. You'll need to find out what vote breakdown it will take to win a civil case that you're covering.

As in criminal cases, alternate jurors are chosen to step in if an original member of the panel becomes ill or is dismissed for some reason. The number of alternate jurors will depend on the complexity and expected length of the trial. Some judges don't tell the alternates they are alternates until the case is ready for submission to the jury for deliberations. Judges hope jurors will pay closer attention to testimony and evidence if the panel's members think there's a chance they'll be part of the group that ultimately decides the case's outcome.

Like their counterparts in criminal cases, lawyers picking juries in civil trials also can ask the judge to dismiss a potential juror for cause if the person displays obvious bias against one side or the other. A potential juror could be the target of a strike for cause if she is related to a member of the plaintiff or defense team, or if she has a connection to the company or government agency being sued.

In a civil case, each side's lawyers receive a specific number of peremptory challenges, strikes they can exercise against a potential juror without explaining why. By the time both parties run out of strikes, the required number of people usually is seated in the jury box, ready to hear testimony and review the evidence.

Openings, Closings and Everything in Between

The plaintiff's attorney gives an opening statement to the jury, outlining the evidence he plans to present to prove the allegations against the defendant. As in criminal cases, the openings are not supposed to be argumentative. If the defense attorney chooses, he can make his opening statement immediately following the plaintiff's attorney. Or he can wait until the plaintiff has presented his case-in-chief, the heart of his evidence. The defense attorney then would present his case to the jury, if he wants.

The introduction of evidence in a civil trial resembles a criminal case in that witnesses are called to the stand, sworn and questioned by lawyers for both sides. When a lawyer for the plaintiff questions witnesses he has summoned, he is conducting direct examination. When the defense attorney questions the plaintiff's witnesses, he is engaging in cross-examination. The roles reverse when the defense presents its case and witnesses.

When I covered the federal courthouse in D.C. for the *Washington Post*, I had to juggle several cases on the calendars of multiple judges—most usually scheduled for the same hour. I couldn't be in three or four places at the same time, and I devised a routine in which I bounced from courtroom to courtroom every 15 minutes or so. I don't recall missing any dramatic moments, mainly because lawyers tend to ask the same questions repeatedly until judges get fed up and tell them to move on to another topic. I liked being in the courtroom to hear lawyers for a plaintiff or the government say the plaintiff rests, or the government rests. Once that happens, the judge usually takes a recess because he wants the jury out of the courtroom for what happens next: The defense attorney moves for a directed verdict, a finding by the judge that the plaintiff has failed to meet his burden of proof and that a judgment should be entered in favor of the defendant. If the judge grants the motion, the trial ends. This is rare because judges are reluctant to take cases away from juries at this point. If it happens, it's often news.

Once all of the testimony and evidence is presented, each side makes its closing arguments. As in criminal cases, the judge then provides jurors with final instructions, which give guidance on what law is relevant and how it should be applied. Like their counterparts in criminal cases, jurors in civil trials are fact-finders and judges are interpreters of the law. In other words, jurors decide whom or what to believe, and judges tell them what to do about it under the law.

The jury will begin deliberations and decide the case's outcome. Once jurors decide whether a defendant is liable, they then figure out how much money, if any, should be awarded to the plaintiff in compensatory and punitive damages. Compensatory damages are supposed to return a plaintiff to the financial state he was in before the defendant wronged him. Punitive damages are designed to punish the defendant and deter others from engaging in similar activities. Damages can range from nothing or $1 to hundreds of millions of dollars. That means it is possible for a plaintiff to prevail but to receive no money. In such an instance the jury is saying, "You're right. You were wronged, but what happened to you isn't worth more than bragging rights."

In complex civil cases, jurors are given detailed verdict forms to keep them on track and ensure that they approach the evidence methodically before they reach a decision. Sometimes jurors in civil cases will be asked to answer a series of questions about liability or the culpability of the parties if each side filed counterclaims and cross-claims against the other. I strongly urge reporters to get a blank copy of the verdict form and use it to follow along when a jury's decision is read in the courtroom. After the verdict is announced, jurors usually are polled at the defense's request to make sure they agree with the result. The judge will thank jurors for their service before dismissing them. Some judges will tell jurors that they shouldn't talk to reporters. They also may seal the names and addresses of the jurors. If that happens, try to catch jurors and interview them before they leave the courtroom.

When's Payday?

The jury's decision does not take effect until the judge enters a judgment, which is an order that is filed on the public record. It can take weeks for a judge to do so, and the delay gives him time to exercise his power to increase or decrease the amount of damages the jury awarded, or to modify the verdict in some other way.

A judge can use a *remittitur* to reduce damages if he finds the jury's award is grossly excessive. If that happens, a judge tells a plaintiff he has a choice: Remit or give back a portion of the award, or go to trial again. If a judge finds that a jury award is shockingly low or constitutes a miscarriage of justice, he can order an *additur*, usually with a defendant's consent, to increase the amount of a jury's award as a condition of denial of a motion for a new trial. Federal judges cannot use such tactics, but state court judges can.

During the time between verdict and judgment, a defendant can file post-verdict motions to protect his rights on appeal to raise a host of issues with judges at the next level. The losing party can file a motion for *judgment notwithstanding the verdict* after the jury's decision but before the judge enters the judgment on the record. It asks the judge to set aside the jury's verdict and find in favor of the losing party.

The losing party also can file a motion for a new trial based on errors that it believes the judge committed. If a losing party fails to raise these issues at this stage, an appeal cannot be filed in some states.

If the defendant fails to pay the damages, the plaintiff may seek an execution of the judgment, which clears the way for seizure and sale of a defendant's property to apply toward satisfying the jury's award. It is not unusual for plaintiffs to find themselves in the position of acting as a bill collector. Sometimes it is difficult to collect the damages, especially if the defendant goes out of business or files for bankruptcy protection. It is possible to garnish wages, meaning a portion of a defendant's paycheck will be seized and forwarded to the plaintiff. It is also possible to seize a defendant's property and cash to turn over to a plaintiff.

As long as a judgment remains on the public record, a defendant will be responsible for paying it. Sometimes a plaintiff must be patient; just because a defendant doesn't have the money today, doesn't mean he won't have it tomorrow.

· *Part* ·

Balancing the Checks

· Chapter ·

Secrecy in the Courts:
Gagged Lawyers, Anonymous Juries
and Locked Courtrooms

■ ■ ■

> Criminal acts, especially violent crimes, often provoke public concern, even out-
> rage and hostility; this in turn generates a community urge to retaliate and desire to
> have justice done....When the public is aware that the law is being enforced and the
> criminal justice system is functioning, an outlet is provided for these understand-
> able reactions and emotions. Proceedings held in secret would deny this outlet and
> frustrate the broad public interest.
>
> —*Chief Justice Warren Burger,*
> *Press-Enterprise Co. v. Superior Court of California (1984)*

Prosecutors, defense attorneys and judges tend to play down Chief Justice Burger's words of wisdom in favor of accentuating the pronouncement of another famous Supreme Court justice, Oliver
Wendell Holmes, who said, "The theory of our system is that the conclusions reached in a case will
be induced only by evidence and argument in open court, and not by any outside influence, whether
of private talk or public print."

To some judges who subscribe to Justice Holmes's view, nearly every piece of information
reported about a case is prejudicial. That is ridiculous. Not every tidbit about a case hurts a defendant; publicity often questions the reliability of the prosecution's evidence. The main concern is the
effect such attention could have before and during a trial on a jury's decision to convict or acquit.
Unfortunately there is no way to gather scientific proof to settle the dispute one way or another,
mainly because the law bans anyone from putting jurors in a position where they might be forced
to justify their verdicts.

At its core, the debate over pretrial publicity centers on the meaning of evidence and relevancy.
Lawyers define those words differently than reporters by relying on strict and confusing rules to
determine whether evidence is admissible in court. To journalists, any interesting information is

relevant. Reporters aren't tethered to rigid legal standards, but they are guided by journalistic ethics that require that facts are verified, sources are vetted and all sides are treated fairly. In this chapter, we will explore the seal-now, ask-questions-later attitude that pervades the courts and how it endangers freedom of the press and the public's ability to assess whether judges, prosecutors and other players in the legal system are doing their jobs with honor, integrity and courage.

Don't Trust What You Can't See

Secrecy in the courts is not new. During the so-called War on Drugs in the 1980s, judges became more receptive to sealing individual filings and entire cases from public view at the request of prosecutors and defense attorneys who worried that defendants-turned-snitches would be killed by their former partners in crime if information remained on the public record for all to see. Since the 9/11 terrorist attacks, prosecutors have sought secrecy in the name of national security, using fear to sway judges and the public into accepting restrictions on information about the government's actions.

There is another consequence: Secret orders block reporters from learning details of prosecutors' sweetheart deals with informants and about jurors who lie to hide their biases. Sealing court records also makes it easier to hide mistakes and abuses of power committed by law enforcement officials and helps businesses bury evidence that they ignored warnings about dangerous products. Such secrecy contradicts the spirit of Chief Justice Burger's majority opinions in *Richmond Newspapers Inc. v. Virginia* in 1980 and again in the *Press-Enterprise* cases of 1984 and 1986 in which the Court found that open trials and publicity about the steps in the legal process are essential checks on the power of the players in the criminal justice system. As the former chief justice wrote in all three cases, people don't trust what they cannot see.

The most powerful antidote to negative pretrial publicity is *voir dire*, meaning "to speak the truth." Judges can use *voir dire*, the questioning of prospective jurors, to keep people off juries who have preconceived notions about a case and hardened biases against a defendant or the government. In an attempt to control the flow of information to prospective jurors, judges often turn to a faster, easier remedy—the protective order, a list of restrictions on the release of information that they say is necessary to protect a defendant's right to a fair trial. A protective order also can be known as a gag order, if it restricts what lawyers can and cannot say about a case. Theoretically, judges use protective orders and gags to keep lawyers and police from trying a case in public rather than in court. Both types of orders hinder reporters in gathering and disseminating the news.

Do they work? In today's digital age, secrecy orders may backfire as some bloggers, tweeters and cable-TV hosts fill vacuums in information with inaccuracies and fabrications. Sometimes, as Chief Justice Burger observed more than three decades ago, crimes are so heinous or the outcome of a trial so shocking that it fuels the people's indignation. When that happens, no judge can stop the demand for information, especially in a world where litigants, victims and observers possess the freedom and the power to take their cases to millions of people in cyberspace.

Freedom to Listen and Report

Until 1641, Great Britain employed the secret Star Chamber to arrest and execute people who had fallen out of favor with the king. People essentially disappeared off the face of the earth. In the *Richmond Newspapers Inc. v. Virginia* decision, the U.S. Supreme Court said it was "no quirk of history" that a tradition of open trials crossed the Atlantic Ocean from England to America.

Chief Justice Burger's majority opinion declared that the public has a right to listen, as part of the First Amendment's guarantee of freedom of speech, and people have a right to attend criminal trials. The presumption of openness is not absolute, he said, but judges need good reasons to shut the public out of a courtroom. The chief justice said the rights to listen and attend criminal trials are as fundamental as the notions of innocent until proven guilty and proof beyond a reasonable doubt before conviction.

In decisions following *Richmond*, the high court said, absent a compelling reason to seal, judges should apply the presumption of openness to pretrial hearings, criminal juvenile proceedings, jury selection, and to docket sheets, plea agreements, indictments and affidavits in support of search and arrest warrants.

Chief Justice Burger also acknowledged that the public will imagine the worst, like small children who are afraid of the dark, if denied information, and people will conjure monstrous reasons for a controversial outcome, unless the press is unhindered in gathering information to explain what happened and why. A Nebraska trial judge created such a vacuum in a case involving the murders of six people that featured allegations of necrophilia and sexual assault of a young female victim. The judge allowed the press to cover a hearing, but he imposed an order of prior restraint by barring journalists from reporting on the salacious aspects of the case that they had heard in open court. The case made its way to the U.S. Supreme Court. In 1976's *Nebraska Press Association v. Stuart*, Chief Justice Burger said prior restraint is the exception, not the rule, and that there must be a clear and present danger to the defendant's ability to receive a fair trial before a judge should take such drastic steps in limiting press coverage.

The chief justice said judges have many options, short of closing courtrooms, sealing documents and telling journalists what they can and cannot report. The alternatives include: moving the trial to another jurisdiction with a *change of venue*; importing jurors from another county with a *change of venire*; postponements, or *continuances*, until the publicity dies down; in-depth questioning of prospective jurors through *voir dire*; and isolating, or *sequestering,* the jury throughout the trial or during deliberations.

After *Nebraska Press Association*, some judges aimed gag orders at lawyers to silence key sources of information for reporters. Appellate courts are split over whether news organizations have standing, or a vested interest in a case to object to a gag order imposed on attorneys, despite the adverse effect it has on the ability of reporters to gather the news. Some courts have allowed journalists to challenge gags of attorneys, but that's as far as reporters have gotten. They've lost when judges have ruled that the press has a right of access to what happens in court and nothing else. The only bright spot is that appellate courts don't like vague gag orders because they could infringe on an attorney's freedom of speech. They have ordered trial judges to be more specific about what can and cannot be discussed and why the restrictions are necessary in the first place.

Have Some Decorum

News conferences on the courthouse steps always reminded me of rugby scrums as reporters elbowed each other for position. Lawyers like to use the scrums to put their spins on the day's developments, but reporters should rely on their own recollections of testimony. Big cases draw a crowd—on the scene, the phone and in your email. Be careful of lawyers who offer themselves up as "experts." It's true that reporters rely too often on the same talking heads in their stories, leaving the public with the views of only a handful of individuals instead of a range of voices people need to hear to help them reach their own conclusions. I always looked for new voices to introduce to readers, but I checked credentials. I deliberately sought people on both sides of the political spectrum and all points in between. Diversity—in gender, race, ethnicity and politics—adds spice to stories.

Legal and media critics widely condemned California Judge Lance Ito for losing control of the O.J. Simpson trial, in which a "dream team" of defense attorneys was perceived to have run roughshod in the case because of their behavior with the news media, mostly outside the courtroom. In contrast, U.S. District Judge Richard Matsch kept a firm grip—some might say too firm—on the trial of Timothy McVeigh, who was convicted of killing 168 people when he bombed a federal building in Oklahoma City in 1995.

To control participants in the case, Judge Matsch employed a host of restrictions, including decorum orders that spelled out how the news media should behave in and out of court. Decorum orders include restrictions that range from barring the naming of a rape victim to designating where reporters can park their cars or satellite TV trucks. Decorum and protective orders may be more trouble than they're worth because they present judges with a Hobson's choice: Ignore the news media's behavior, or create a sideshow that threatens to slow the trial with hearings aimed at punishing reporters or lawyers who supply them with information.

Reporters could deny judges the reasons they need to justify decorum orders by taking the following advice:

- *Don't talk to strangers.* All trial jurors, including prospective jurors, are off limits until a judge dismisses them from further service. A reporter who tries to contact and interview a juror before a verdict could be held in contempt of court and thrown in jail. Reporters should wait to seek interviews until the judge dismisses the jurors after their verdict is reached and announced in the courtroom, or until a mistrial has been declared and the judge has dismissed the jurors. If a juror had reached out to tell me about an abuse of the legal system, I'm sure I would have listened. It never happened to me, but it could happen to you. Newsworthy information about a juror also could come your way from another source in the middle of a trial. If it casts doubt on a juror's ability to serve, you should check it out and report it if true. The important thing to remember: Absent extraordinary circumstances, you should not initiate contact with a sitting juror in the middle of a trial.

- *Watch your mouth.* Reporters need to be careful about what they say and where they say it. You shouldn't make jokes about the defendant or debate the value of a piece of evidence while standing in the courthouse's cafeteria line where jurors also may be waiting. Be aware of your surroundings and who is nearby.

- *Don't lie, cheat or steal.* Be honest about who you are and what you're doing. Don't lie to get into the lock-up or any other secure areas of the courthouse. Don't sneak electronic devices into the courtroom. You will get your story without resorting to underhanded tactics that will cost you and your news organization when you get caught, and you will get caught. If you make the judge mad enough, you could be held in contempt of court and jailed briefly or fined significantly. At a minimum, you'll likely be banned from covering the rest of the trial, and your news organization may not be permitted to send a replacement. By the time your paper, website or TV station appeals to a higher court, the trial may be over.

Now You See It, Now You Don't

Sometimes, court records disappear. One day the filings are listed on docket sheets and accessible electronically or on paper in the clerk's office. The next day, they're not. It's as if someone waved a magic wand: Poof! They're gone. It isn't magic. It's a lawyer, and it's not always a prosecutor who wants to keep secrets secret. Defense lawyers and plaintiffs' attorneys also seek to block documents from public view, and they frequently ask judges to seal records containing revelations that their clients don't want anyone else to know. There will be times when you will see a document on the public record that grabs your attention, if only for a few seconds, but you won't know exactly why. If so, don't pass on it. Trust your gut. Hit the print button or download it on your computer. If you have a copy, you have proof of its existence and you can quote from its contents.

It's difficult to know exactly how many criminal and civil cases are shrouded in secrecy in federal and state courts. In the aftermath of the 9/11 attacks, government officials removed information from public view that had long been available about power plants, infrastructure and science by arguing that terrorists could use the data to kill Americans. U.S. intelligence agents quietly removed thousands of once-public documents held in the National Archives for the same reasons. After 9/11, hundreds of men of Arabic descent also were rounded up and held secretly without charges; some were locked up in a New York jail where they were physically and verbally abused by guards, while others were moved from jail to jail to keep them from contacting their attorneys and relatives. Many other people were kept in custody on material witness warrants, a highly secretive legal maneuver designed to keep potential witnesses from disappearing before they can testify. I was among the reporters who pressed, without much success, for Justice Department officials to provide accurate counts on how many people were held as material witnesses, and why.

The Bush administration also invoked the state secrets privilege 23 times to keep information in civil lawsuits from becoming public, according to the Reporters Committee for Freedom of the Press. Were the plaintiffs trying to shake down the government by forcing large cash settlements in exchange for keeping secrets? Or were they trying to blow the whistle on government abuses of power? We may never know because the government's tactic usually winds up killing a civil lawsuit in its tracks by forcing its dismissal.

After the 9/11 attacks, frightened Americans were willing to give up many of their most precious rights to feel safe again. Unfortunately once a right is forsaken, it is difficult to get it back unless the courts step in and protect the people. If judges lack the nerve to stand up to the president in a crisis, democracy will become unbalanced, leaving one branch of government with a dangerous advantage over the others. To do their jobs and serve the public, reporters also must resist the hype—and fear—and persist in pursuit of information hidden from the public.

Hide and Seek

In 2004, dozens of detainees held at the U.S. Navy base at Guantanamo Bay, Cuba, filed legal actions, known as *habeas corpus* petitions, to demand that the Bush administration explain why they had been held without criminal charges, many of them for several years. In response to the civil actions, lawyers at the Justice Department filed what are known as returns to explain the basis of the government's suspicions that the men were terrorists who needed to be locked up indefinitely.

I was working at *USA Today* at the time, and like many reporters, I was trying to assess the quality of the evidence the U.S. government was relying on to deny trials and other legal rights to the detainees. I knew how *habeas* cases worked and that the government's returns could provide details about who these men were, how and where they were captured, and whether they posed a danger to the United States. I spent most of the summer of 2004 on PACER, the federal courts' electronic case database, checking docket sheets in the detainee lawsuits several times a day. I moved quickly. I didn't stop to read the returns on my computer screen. When I came across a return, I hit the print button and made sure I obtained copies of any and all attachments before moving on to the next case. When I had a large stack of printouts, I read through them, eventually putting together a story that revealed that many detainees hadn't been captured in Afghanistan or Pakistan, as the Bush administration wanted the public to believe, but in Bosnia, Africa and other places.

One day I noticed that a return had vanished off the docket in one of the cases; it had been there the day before and I had made a printout of it. A closer inspection revealed that the detainee's lawyer had asked the judge to seal the document. Justice Department attorneys had used the *habeas* return to unmask Bisher al-Rawi, a resident of Great Britain for 18 years, as a possible snitch by revealing that he claimed to have worked with British intelligence agents as a go-between with a radical cleric in London with ties to the al-Qaeda terrorist network.

I considered the impact of a story that revealed this detail, especially if al-Rawi had relatives in London who could face retaliation from al-Qaeda. Ultimately I decided that al-Rawi and his lawyer couldn't have it both ways: He was insisting that the U.S. government explain publicly its reasons for holding him. He couldn't insist that the reasons remain secret if they made him look bad. After my story was published, I received calls from reporters at British papers who wanted me to share the document that I, and only I, seemed to have obtained a copy before it disappeared. I refused to allow the British reporters to copy off me and told them to do their own homework—or quote *USA Today*.

The judge never called me to complain that I had written a story about a document that was under seal. Reporters aren't always that lucky. In 2004, a court stenographer mistakenly sent an email to several news outlets that contained a copy of a sealed transcript of a hearing held in chambers in the rape case against Los Angeles Lakers star Kobe Bryant. The transcript contained information about the alleged victim's name and sexual history, which are protected from disclosure under Colorado's rape shield law. Colorado Judge W. Terry Ruckriegle told me the mistake was caught quickly, and he sent a note to reporters, ordering them to destroy the transcript and banning them from disseminating its contents. The reporters wanted to publish and broadcast the details. The dispute was taken to the Colorado Supreme Court, which upheld Judge Ruckriegle's order banning publication of information about the alleged victim's sexual conduct before and after her encounter with Bryant. The state's high court struck down Judge Ruckriegle's order that the reporters destroy their copies of the transcript.

It was a loss for journalists, but not a total loss. What good is a transcript, you might ask, if you can't report what it says? Any and all information helps a reporter understand the nuances of a case, whether you can use it in a story or not.

Need to Know

Before the 9/11 attacks, the Oklahoma City bombing topped the list of the most heinous crimes committed in this country. Timothy McVeigh, a Gulf War veteran with antigovernment views, mixed a bomb out of fertilizer and chemicals, loaded it into a truck and parked it in front of a federal building. He lit the fuse and walked away.

During the run-up to McVeigh's trial, Judge Richard Matsch issued an order that explained the criteria he would use to decide whether to seal a document. He relied mainly on whether "the matter involved activity within the tradition of free public access to information concerning criminal prosecution," in other words, the tradition of openness that Chief Justice Burger referred to in several cases.

It didn't take long for the judge and news media to clash. Journalists challenged Judge Matsch's decision to seal portions of co-defendant Terry Nichols's motion to suppress statements he made to investigators, an FBI agent's notes of his interview and defense motions to sever, or try the defendants separately.

In upholding Judge Matsch's decisions, a three-judge panel of the U.S. Court of Appeals for the Tenth Circuit used a two-pronged test, which asked whether the documents in question had historically been open to inspection and if public access would have a positive impact on the trial. The panel acknowledged that a suppression hearing is "a critical pretrial proceeding," sometimes as important as the trial, because the conduct of law enforcement officers often is challenged.

Nevertheless the panel said, "Access to inadmissible evidence is not necessary to understand the suppression hearing, so long as the public is able to understand the circumstances that gave rise to the decision to suppress." Disclosing suppressed evidence, the appellate judges said, "would play a negative role in the functioning of the criminal process, by exposing the public generally, as well as potential jurors, to incriminating evidence that the law has determined may not be used to support a conviction."

McVeigh's trial featured many of today's secrecy orders *du jour* including gag orders of lawyers, protective orders banning release of pretrial documents, and an anonymous jury. The judge also listened to arguments from lawyers *in camera*, or in chambers, to resolve numerous legal issues in private and out of hearing of the jury, the press and the public.

A Public or Private Affair

Citizens have a civic duty to serve as jurors to sit in judgment of one another, and litigators will tell you that trials are often won or lost during jury selection, the process that is designed to uncover biases, prejudices or other vested interests in a case's outcome. If it's that important, and it is, it should be held in the open, not behind a locked courtroom door.

Some judges use other excuses to select juries in secret: They'll say the courtroom isn't big enough for prospective jurors and reporters, or they'll say reporters need to leave because potential jurors might be embarrassed to answer certain questions in an open proceeding. Unfortunately those excuses aren't good enough under the law, and haven't been since 1984, when the U.S. Supreme Court ruled in the *Press-Enterprise* case that concerns about juror privacy cannot justify locking the public out of a courtroom. That hasn't stopped judges from trying. In 1987, U.S. District Judge Thomas Penfield Jackson left it up to prospective jurors to decide whether they wanted to be questioned in open court in the perjury trial of former Reagan administration official Michael Deaver. It shouldn't have shocked anyone when only five of 30 prospective jurors took questions in public view. Judge Jackson justified his approach by saying, "It is not possible for me to exercise discretion in any objective fashion as to what is or what is not to be private. Things are private simply because they are private to people."

Wrong, the appellate court said. Judges must determine whether a prospective juror's concerns about privacy are legitimate. Judges can't take a juror's word for it. Instead judges must weigh the juror's concerns against the value of conducting the questioning out in the open, where spectators and the press can ensure that the courts are functioning properly and fairly. Despite the Deaver ruling, the jurors-have-privacy argument continues to gain traction among judges, who are not only closing courtrooms during jury selection, but are also sealing identifying information about jurors, including their names, addresses and occupations. When that happens, an anonymous jury decides a defendant's fate.

Why is this information so important? The credibility of the legal system depends on jurors who decide guilt in criminal cases and liability in civil lawsuits. Realizing that someone is watching you and knows your name usually encourages people to do a better job. Making the identities of jurors publicly available also increases the chances that a community member might be aware of a reason a juror is biased and shouldn't serve, and he or she could bring it to the attention of the court or a reporter. If the public doesn't know anything about jurors, it's also impossible to know if the scales of justice have been tilted and the outcome predetermined by the selection of people of a certain race, religion or social group. In other words, there is no way to hold jurors accountable.

Although federal law prohibits anyone, including social scientists, academics or lawyers, from forcing jurors to justify their verdicts, they retain their First Amendment right of freedom of speech and they can talk about their deliberations, if they want. That means they can talk to prosecutors and defense attorneys who may want to learn what they did wrong. I tracked jurors down after a case ended to ask them about the trial and to explain the verdict. That is becoming increasingly harder to do because judges claim they are protecting jurors' privacy by sealing records that identify them.

Once a Rarity

Until the 1990s, anonymous juries were rare, used only in cases where there was a credible threat against the safety of jurors. I covered trials of accused Mafia members in Philadelphia where judges sealed identifying information about jurors, such as their names, addresses, phone numbers and occupations, to protect them from physical harm, intimidation or bribery attempts.

There are varying degrees of secrecy surrounding anonymous juries. In some cases, lawyers for the parties are given access to jurors' personal information. Sometimes only the judge knows the jurors' names and backgrounds. Anonymous juries were selected in the trials of the survivors of the Branch Davidian cult siege and fire in Waco, Texas; "Unabomber" Ted Kaczynski, who ultimately pleaded guilty to killing and maiming several people with mail bombs; and the 1993 World Trade Center bombers.

Those situations involved violent crimes, but the identities of jurors also have been sealed in other, more traditional white-collar corruption cases, such as the perjury trial of Oliver North, a former White House official accused of lying about the illegal diversion of federal money to the Contras in Nicaragua during the Reagan administration. In Louisiana, anonymous juries also were used in two corruption trials of four-time governor Edwin Edwards.

As news organizations cut staffing and budgets in recent years, judges aren't being challenged as much as they once were. It is a dangerous development, considering how admirably reporters have performed their watchdog role. Reporters for the *Miami Herald* revealed that jurors had been bribed in drug cartel cases, and journalists at the *Chicago Tribune* found out that two jurors had lied about past convictions in the corruption trial of former Illinois governor George Ryan. Reporters cannot ensure that the courts are operating fairly if they are locked out of the courtroom during jury selection or they are denied access to jurors' names.

In 2001, four *Philadelphia Inquirer* reporters were held in contempt of court after they revealed that the foreman in the murder trial of Rabbi Fred Neulander didn't live in the New Jersey county where the trial took place, as required by law, but was staying with a friend in Philadelphia. In 2004, a New Jersey appeals court overturned the contempt findings against the reporters.

Some judges will use their power and status to urge jurors to refuse to talk to reporters after the trial is over. Generally, judges can tell them not to discuss their fellow jurors' views during deliberations, but they cannot forbid jurors from exercising their free-speech rights to talk about their part in the process.

Picking a Fight

As a reporter, if you want to oppose a judge's order to seal jurors' names or other identifying information, you may file a motion to intervene in the case. There are two goals: First, you want the judge to allow you to object to what's happened. Second, you want the court to reconsider the order to seal information. You also will need to request an expedited appeal of the trial judge's order; if you don't, the trial may end and the issue will become moot, or irrelevant, before an appellate court considers it.

What should you do if your news organization refuses to fight? If you work in a small community, you or someone else at your news organization might recognize some of the jurors. Go to the courtroom and look at them.

You also can try to get the list of names from another source in the court system, but you need to understand the risk. If a court employee provides the list in exchange for your promise to protect his or her identity, you must be prepared to withstand the anger of a judge who undoubtedly will want to know your source's name and likely will hold you in contempt of court if you refuse.

If a judge decides to keep the jurors' names secret, but allows jury selection to be conducted in open court, reporters should make sure they attend every session and pay close attention. Under questioning by the attorneys and judge, prospective jurors reveal a great deal about themselves, including information that may help a reporter ask the right questions after the verdict is reached.

Can you photograph jurors outside the courthouse? The answer is maybe, maybe not. In his decorum orders, Judge W. Terry Ruckriegle restricted photographers covering Kobe Bryant's rape trial in Colorado to specific areas inside and outside the courthouse. He also ensured that jurors wore badges that clearly identified them, and he banned the news media from taking their photographs. Was that legal? No media organization challenged it, so we don't know.

The reality is that the news media cannot afford to question every move made by a judge. A legal challenge can drag on for months, if not years, and few news organizations can afford to cover the cost. You cannot fight every battle. You must choose wisely.

Keeping Them Honest

The presence of a reporter in a courtroom can enhance the performance of all of the players in a case, especially by discouraging judges from acting like playground bullies. One day, a lawyer I knew stopped by the *Daily News* office in the pressroom in the federal courthouse in Philadelphia and asked a favor. He said he wasn't trying to spin me into writing a story about a case he knew was not newsworthy. He wanted me to sit in the courtroom—in view of a cranky senior judge—long enough for a plaintiff to finish testifying about what happened when a tractor-trailer pinned her car to a median barrier on a highway.

During the morning session, the lawyer said, the judge interrupted direct examination of the woman by berating her with questions that made her look as if she were a hysterical female who didn't know how to drive. After lunch, I went to the courtroom and took a seat in the front row. The judge didn't ask a question, and the woman made it through her testimony. Openness protects the legal process by also providing proof that judges acted honestly and treated participants with respect.

A reporter also has a duty to make judges think twice before they impose secrecy in a case. How does a reporter keep a judge from sealing a case? How do you know it's about to happen? Federal and state judges are supposed to give notice before sealing an entire case. The problem is the notice may be a cryptic reference on the court record, so brief that you might miss it if you blink. Make frequent passes through the clerk's office to check the traps for newly filed documents to increase your chances of spotting such notice. If you miss the initial reference to sealing and you learn about the case later, it gets harder to argue that it should remain on the public docket, especially if you don't know what it's about. Take it one step at a time. Try to get your news organization to file a motion that asks the court to keep the existence of the case public for now. Then later, if you learn more about it, you can fight to unseal the entire case file or, in the alternative, specific documents.

If you are in a courtroom and a judge orders it closed, you must get your objection on the record. To do so, you should:

- Stand and politely ask to be recognized;
- When the judge acknowledges you, make your objection to the closure;
- Ask the court to recess long enough for you to get an attorney to the courthouse to argue on your behalf.

If the judge denies your request, leave the courtroom and call your editor.

You also must leave the courtroom if the judge refuses to allow you to speak. Once you are outside the courtroom, write a note to the judge. Outline your objection to secrecy and ask for a recess to allow you time to get an attorney to the courthouse. Give the note to a bailiff or the judge's secretary. Why do this? If you fail to get your objection noted on the record, in the hearing transcript, it'll be harder for your news organization to file an appeal with the judge or a higher court. Call your editor immediately and tell him what's happened. You want to stop the train if you can.

If you find out about a secret proceeding after it's over, consult your editor. If she tells you to move forward, try to determine who sought the closure and on what grounds. You need to know whether it's a civil or criminal case and whether it's in the pretrial, trial or appellate phase. Your lawyer also will want to know whether the judge held a hearing to determine whether to close the proceeding and if the court made any findings on the record to justify the secrecy. If so, you'll need to get your hands on those filings.

Judges will hold secret hearings, but journalists can do what they do best: Check with sources, find out what happened and report it to the public.

No Such Thing as a Free Lunch

Lying, stealing or paying for information is not acceptable.

I never lied to get information. I never stole a document. I never paid anyone for an interview. Ever.

I felt uncomfortable buying lunch for cops and court officials. When I worked for the *Washington Post*, one of my editors chastised me for not taking advantage of the paper's generous expense account. I remember having dinner periodically with a lawyer who was a source in Washington, but we'd take turns picking up the tab. I also recall treating a couple of FBI agents to lunch to celebrate their retirements, and never having to talk to me again.

As the line between journalism and entertainment has disappeared, newsmakers—from jurors to parents of missing children—are getting paid for their stories. TV networks pay "licensing" fees for family photos or videos, or they sometimes pick up the tab for people to take their kids to Disney World in exchange for interviews. Some jurors are savvy enough to dispatch "representatives" who negotiate payments from the networks, as reportedly occurred in the Casey Anthony murder case in 2011.

Reporters and editors working for the *News of the World* in London lost the public's trust and their jobs when media mogul Rupert Murdoch's son closed the paper in 2011 during a scandal over allegations that reporters paid cops for information and hacked into voicemails of crime victims and celebrities. The paper's reporters and editors also were accused of deleting voicemails on a cell phone belonging to a missing girl to make room for new messages. It was a callous effort to obtain inside information that gave false hope to her frantic family that she was still alive.

Paying for information is bad enough. Stealing it is worse.

· Chapter ·

The Challenge of Terrorism:
Civilian or Military Justice?

■ ■ ■

> War breeds atrocities....Unfortunately, such despicable acts have a dangerous tendency to call forth primitive impulses of vengeance and retaliation among the victimized peoples....If we are ever to develop an orderly international community based upon a recognition of human dignity it is of the utmost importance that the necessary punishment of those guilty of atrocities be as free as possible from the ugly stigma of revenge and vindictiveness. Justice must be tempered by compassion rather than by vengeance.
>
> —*Justice Frank Murphy, dissenting opinion, Application of Yamashita (1946)*

President George W. Bush was condemned at home and abroad for creating a separate court system for trials by military commission of suspected terrorists captured after al-Qaeda attacked the United States on September 11, 2001. Hundreds of men taken into custody in Afghanistan and throughout the world were held at a U.S. Navy base at Guantanamo Bay, Cuba, the overwhelming majority without charges for several years. In an unprecedented step, the U.S. Supreme Court intervened before a single military commission trial could occur for the few who had been accused of crimes. In four cases, the nation's high court chastised the Bush administration over the legality of the detentions and separate judicial system it had created for terrorism suspects.

During a war, which system of justice is better—trials in military or civilian courts? Are terrorists nothing more than criminals, no different than Mafia hit men, and should they be treated the same as any other accused murderer? Should they face trials in America's civilian courts? Or should they face trials before military tribunals on charges that they violated the laws of war? Should they receive the panoply of rights for which the United States is known throughout the world? Or should they be denied access to the rights they mocked and the ideals they despised and face trials in partial or complete secrecy?

Before 9/11, few Americans probably knew that civilians and members of the military are subjected to separate systems of justice, or thought little, if at all, about whether rights provided to defendants in both arenas should be suspended during a crisis. There are no easy answers to those questions and they divide Americans. In this chapter, we will discuss why it is important for reporters to act as watchdogs in a crisis, challenging policymakers and ordinary citizens to think critically about the consequences of how the United States behaves, particularly when Americans are afraid.

"I am from al-Qaeda"

"Stop!" yelled Army Colonel Peter Brownback, a military commission's presiding officer, during a hearing in a Guantanamo Bay courtroom in August 2004. Defendant Ali Hamza Ahmad Sulayman Al Bahlul was cut off in mid-sentence: "I am from al-Qaeda," he was saying, "and the relationship between me and September …" The colonel followed his instincts, believing the unsworn statement was inadmissible as evidence, but he was wrong, as a military prosecutor promptly told him. Under the Pentagon's military commission rules, the defendant's confession was admissible and could be used against him. This newly constructed judicial system was a throwback to a time when soldiers and sailors had few rights, and its rules were as foreign to Colonel Brownback, a veteran military judge, as they must have seemed to the defendant.

Al Bahlul's strategy in the military court mimicked the approach taken two years earlier by Zacarias Moussaoui in federal court in Alexandria, Virginia. Like Moussaoui, Al Bahlul rejected court-appointed counsel and asked to act as his own attorney. In doing so, both admitted terrorists alarmed the administration and elected officials. I was present in both courtrooms in Cuba and in Virginia and witnessed the defendants' antics, which shouldn't have shocked anyone. They weren't the first defendants in history to demonstrate an uncanny grasp of the American legal system, or to try to use that insight to challenge and subvert the authority of civilian or military courts. Yet critics of civilian trials for terrorism suspects point to Moussaoui and Al Bahlul as the poster boys for the need for trials by tribunals on military bases, where it is easier to impose tight security and secrecy than in a civilian courtroom in New York, Washington or another American city.

No criminal trial is easy. Who, by the way, said it should be? Taking away someone's freedom, even for a day, should be difficult. But terrorism cases are in a category of their own because they test the core values of American justice more than murders, rapes and robberies that are resolved every day in courts across the nation. Should an accused terrorist be given access to classified or secret evidence against him? Can a suspected terrorist hire a lawyer of his choice? Should a terrorism suspect be permitted to call witnesses he wants? Should a terrorism defendant be allowed to appeal all the way to the U.S. Supreme Court? And if he's acquitted, should the United States be permitted to ignore the verdict and continue to hold him indefinitely because of the perceived danger he poses to Americans at home and abroad?

In 1946, Justice Frank Murphy worried about how fear and anger affect victors in war when they decide punishment for their vanquished opponents. *Yamashita* was a World War II case involving a high-ranking Japanese officer who was convicted for allowing his subordinates to run wild in the Philippines, raping and murdering people. Unlike other countries, Justice Murphy wrote, the United States has a reputation for its commitment to justice. "[W]e are not free to give effect to our emotions in reckless disregard of the rights of others," he wrote. "We live under the Constitution, which is the embodiment of all the high hopes and aspirations of the new world. And it is applicable in both war and peace. We must act accordingly."

History Repeats Itself—Repeatedly

Solutions to these dilemmas have confounded the nation's military officers, judges and policymakers since the American Revolution, when British Major John Andre, who headed England's spy network in America, was caught, dressed in civilian clothes, as he crossed battle lines in 1780 to meet with the famous American traitor Benedict Arnold. General George Washington convened a trial, and Andre was convicted and hanged.

The U.S. Supreme Court confronted its first case on the use of a military tribunal when Clement Vallandigham was convicted and imprisoned for saying the Civil War was "wicked, cruel and unnecessary." In 1864, the justices cited procedural reasons in refusing to hear the appeal filed by Vallandigham, who argued that the military tribunal had no jurisdiction over him as a private citizen.

Two years later, the high court had a change of heart, ruling in *Ex parte Milligan* that use of a military tribunal was improper in the trial of an Indiana man who was convicted and sentenced to hang because of his membership in a group that advocated the overthrow of the government. "The Constitution of the United States is a law for rulers and people, equally in war and in peace, and covers with the shield of its protection all classes of men, at all times, and under all circumstances," the Court said. But that didn't stop the subsequent trial by military tribunal of the people accused of conspiring to assassinate President Abraham Lincoln and other top government officials.

During World War II, the issue resurfaced when eight Nazi saboteurs disembarked from two German submarines off Long Island and a beach in Florida, buried their uniforms, changed into civilian clothes and set off to sabotage American war industries and facilities. They didn't get far. They were captured and later prosecuted by a military commission convened by President Franklin D. Roosevelt in Washington. All eight were convicted, and six were sent to the electric chair five days after they were sentenced to death. In *Ex parte Quirin* in 1942, the Supreme Court upheld the use of a military tribunal in cases against "unlawful belligerents," such as the Nazi saboteurs.

In 1950, the Supreme Court again upheld the use of military commissions in *Johnson v. Eisentrager,* a case brought by a group of Germans who were captured in China and convicted by military tribunal during World War II. The justices decided that American courts are not open to nonresident aliens during wartime, and they may face trials by military tribunals. The Bush administration relied heavily on the *Eisentrager* decision to argue that hundreds of terrorism suspects captured after 9/11 and held at Guantanamo Bay had no rights of access to American courts to file *habeas corpus* petitions to challenge the legality of their detentions, specifically whether they were properly designated and detained as "enemy combatants."

The term was controversial among legal and military scholars at home and abroad, who questioned its validity and use to justify the post–9/11 detentions. White House and Pentagon officials defined an enemy combatant as someone who did not wear a uniform or insignia, didn't fight on behalf of a country, and did not play by the accepted rules of war as outlined by the Geneva Conventions, a series of international standards of behavior and treatment of prisoners that were adopted by nations in the aftermath of the atrocities committed by Germany and Japan during World War II.

Equally controversial was where the administration decided to hold the detainees—on a once-sleepy Navy base that the United States leases in a bizarre landlord-tenant arrangement with Cuba's communist government.

Across the Sea

In a one-two punch delivered on June 28, 2004, the U.S. Supreme Court stunned the Bush administration by opening the doors of federal courthouses to detainees held at Guantanamo Bay and to U.S. citizens held as enemy combatants on American soil. Four British and Australian citizens captured by the U.S. military in Pakistan and Afghanistan sought access to federal judges to determine whether their detentions were unconstitutional because they were held indefinitely without charges. Many detainees denied Vice President Dick Cheney's description of them as "the worst of the worst," and instead claimed that they were in the wrong place at the wrong time, scooped up in a dragnet set up by opportunistic tribal leaders in Afghanistan who collected large cash "bounties" offered by the U.S. military for Arabs and other Middle Easterners.

The Bush administration argued that the federal courts had no jurisdiction because the captives were not American citizens and were held in territory over which the United States lacked sovereignty. In 1903, the United States signed an indefinite lease with Cuba for the base at Guantanamo Bay. Writing for a 6-to-3 majority in *Rasul v. Bush*, Justice John Paul Stevens said U.S. control over the base is sufficient, Cuba's role as the ultimate sovereign is irrelevant, and the ability to seek *habeas corpus* review is not dependent on American citizenship.

That same day, Justice Sandra Day O'Connor said in *Hamdi v. Rumsfeld* that the separation-of-powers doctrine did not require federal judges to be so deferential to the president that they could not hear challenges by U.S. citizens to detentions. "We have long since made clear that a state of war is not a blank check for the President when it comes to the rights of the Nation's citizens," she wrote. A federal public defender in northern Virginia had forced the issue by filing suit on behalf of Yaser Hamdi, a U.S. citizen captured while fighting for the Taliban in Afghanistan in 2001, and challenging the constitutionality of the government's decision to bar Hamdi's access to a lawyer or a trial while he was held in a Navy brig on a South Carolina base.

During the oral argument in *Hamdi* on April 28, 2004, several justices expressed reservations about the Bush administration's refusal to put a time limit on the length of detentions of captives, particularly American citizens, in a war, the so-called War on Terrorism, that had no end in sight. Justice Stevens engaged in a short but portentous exchange with Solicitor General Paul Clement about methods used in interrogations. Clement asserted that "the last thing you want to do is torture somebody" because "you would really wonder about the reliability of the information you were getting" from a detainee. In a matter of days, the Abu Ghraib prison scandal broke, documented by graphic photographs, taken by American military police officers of their treatment of detainees in Iraq who were stripped, forced while naked to participate in "dog piles," and sexually humiliated. A group of several low-level Army reservists faced courts-martial for their treatment of Iraqi detainees and were sent to prison.

As a reporter for *USA Today*, I visited Camp Delta, the detainee prison at Guantanamo Bay, on the two-year anniversary of the 9/11 attacks and attended a ceremony honoring the people who died in New York, Washington and Pennsylvania. There, I met Army Major General Geoffrey Miller, commander of detainee operations, who had just returned from Iraq, where we learned later he had given tips to military officials at Abu Ghraib on how to get the most information out of interrogations. What we didn't know was that questionable techniques were used at Guantanamo Bay and transported by General Miller to Iraq. A couple of years later, government documents revealed that FBI agents went nose-to-nose with General Miller—around the time of my visit—as they urged him to stop using harsh interrogation tactics, such as handcuffing detainees in pretzel-like stress positions or placing them naked in rooms with freezing temperatures for long periods of time.

Stories often develop incrementally. Eventually all of the pieces come together and you'll be able to do a story that gives readers and viewers a more complete picture of what government officials are doing, or not doing.

The Long Arm of (Civilian) Law

On November 8, 2004, I was in the courtroom at Guantanamo Bay, listening to Lieutenant Commander Charles Swift, a Navy defense attorney, as he wrapped up pretrial arguments on behalf of Salim Ahmed Hamdan, a Yemeni who served as a chauffeur for al-Qaeda leader Osama bin Laden. A bailiff handed a note to Colonel Peter Brownback, the presiding officer, who called a recess and immediately left the room. He returned a few minutes later to announce, "We are going to have an indefinite recess." Reporters and spectators in the courtroom exchanged confused looks and asked each other what could have possibly happened—yet again—to derail the Bush administration's attempts to launch military commission trials against suspected terrorists.

Colonel Brownback had learned that a federal judge in Washington had ruled that the Bush administration was wrong when it said hundreds of men captured in Afghanistan were not entitled to prisoner-of-war protections provided under international law. Responding as he did, the colonel displayed the U.S. military's unquestioning deference to civilian authorities and law.

Eventually the chauffeur's case also made its way to the U.S. Supreme Court. Justice Stevens, writing for the majority in *Hamdan v. Rumsfeld*, said President Bush's military commissions violated Common Article 3 of the Geneva Conventions, which guarantees "minimum" protections for detainees and prohibits use of trials that are inferior to "a regularly constituted court affording all the judicial guarantees which are recognized as indispensible by civilized peoples." Justice Stevens said the Bush administration's procedures should have mirrored rules for military commissions established under the Uniform Code of Military Justice, the American military's criminal code, and should have mimicked those of courts-martial unless that was not possible. President Bush also should have asked Congress for permission if he didn't want to follow the UCMJ, Justice Stevens wrote.

In June 2008, the Supreme Court again rebuffed the Bush administration and Congress, which, in response to the high court's previous decisions, had stripped the federal courts of jurisdiction to hear petitions filed by detainees seeking to challenge their designations as enemy combatants. Justice Anthony Kennedy, writing for a 5-to-4 majority in *Boumediene v. Bush*, said that an alternative review process created by the Detainee Treatment Act fell far short of the quality of review provided by a court in dealing with a *habeas corpus* petition. Chief among his concerns: Detainees were not permitted to present evidence that might exonerate them.

I vividly recall a night in the Caribbean in late August 2004, when I was among several reporters and human rights activists who chatted as we drank beer outside our quarters on the Navy base, where a pretrial hearing was under way for Australian detainee David Hicks. The human rights activists, all lawyers, opposed the Bush administration's military commissions because of what they thought were fatal flaws in the lack of protections for defendants' rights. But that night, they said they expected the Supreme Court to behave as the high court had during World War II by allowing the administration to conduct at least one trial by commission before agreeing to review the procedures for violations of U.S. or international law. Most reporters agreed.

We were wrong. The justices weighed in before a single commission trial could be held, opting to keep tabs in real time on the president's use of his commander-in-chief powers to wage the legal side of war. The Supreme Court's actions in *Rasul*, *Hamdi*, *Hamdan* and *Boumediene* were extraordinary not only because the justices rebuked President Bush for his controversial assertion of broad executive power. The decisions also showed that the Court wasn't buying the administration's "trust us" approach to fighting terrorism. The Supreme Court said it wasn't going to wait around to see what happened and hope for the best. For reporters, the Guantanamo Bay cases provide two lessons: First, speculation about how the Supreme Court will or won't behave is often off the mark. Second, fear can eat away at civil liberties. If the nation's leaders are afraid, or prey on the people's fears, journalists need to put those worries into context historically and make sense of the current state of affairs.

Discipline v. Justice

From the nation's founding until 1950, American soldiers and sailors had few rights in a disciplinary system that permitted floggings, hard labor and executions. Few changes occurred until World War I when three levels of courts-martial were created. Public outrage led to revolutionary changes in military justice after two million courts-martial—nearly one for every eight Americans—were conducted during World War II, when more than 100 servicemen were executed and 45,000 were imprisoned.

Congress responded to the outcry by enacting the Uniform Code of Military Justice and applied its provisions to all military personnel worldwide. Today, military courts follow the Manual for Courts-Martial, which outlines how legal proceedings are supposed to be conducted in all five branches of the military—the Army, Air Force, Navy, Marine Corps and the Coast Guard. All of the branches except the Coast Guard are part of the Department of Defense. The Coast Guard is part of the Department of Homeland Security. Reporters who are assigned to cover a court-martial should obtain a copy of the manual and become familiar with its provisions.

After I volunteered to take responsibility for *USA Today*'s coverage of the military commissions at Guantanamo Bay, one of the first steps I took was to buy a copy of the Manual for Courts-Martial. I compared the manual to its civilian counterpart, the Federal Criminal Code and Rules, to identify differences, focusing on how each handled classified evidence. I also reached out to current and former military lawyers, some in private practice and others in law schools, who helped me understand the distinctions between a court-martial and a civilian trial. To fully understand military justice, I needed to see a court-martial in action, and I arranged to watch a trial on the U.S. Navy base in Quantico, Virginia, for a serviceman who was accused of dealing drugs.

The most confusing part of the military justice system is its insular nature and the influence—potentially good and bad—that commanding officers have over virtually every phase of an investigation and prosecution. Commanding officers can start and stop an investigation, initiate or dismiss criminal charges, and select the pool of people from which jurors (called members) are ultimately chosen. To curtail possible command abuses, servicemen and women receive additional rights that are not available in the civilian courts. When a member of a service branch is accused of an offense, the person's commanding officer launches an investigation. If the charge is complicated or serious, civilian or military law enforcement agencies will investigate. Military law enforcement agencies include: the Army's Criminal Investigation Command; the Naval Criminal Investigative Service; the Air Force Office of Special Investigations; and the Coast Guard Investigative Service.

Reporters assigned to cover an investigation by one of those agencies should try to develop contacts and sources, exactly as you would in the FBI or local police department.

Learn the Lingo

Like its civilian counterpart, the military justice beat has its own language. Reporters need to learn the lingo and how military courts operate. You will know what to ask, and when, once you have identified the pressure points in civilian or military trials, the key moments when each of the players must make important decisions that determine a case's direction.

After an investigation is completed, the commanding officer may do nothing, he may take administrative action against the service member, he may "prefer" charges or he may ask a higher-ranking officer to prefer the charges. Preferring charges means that the charges are read to the accused service member off a charge sheet, which is similar to an indictment in that it lists the allegations. The accused service member signs the charge sheet under oath in front of a commissioned officer. A commissioned officer received his rank via a government document, or commission. Noncommissioned officers, considered the backbone of the military, are enlisted men and women who earned their ranks through promotions. Enlisted servicemen and women joined the military voluntarily and perform various jobs as part of their duties.

After criminal charges are preferred, they are then referred, or sent, to one of three courts-martial, depending on the seriousness of the offenses. They are:

- *Summary Court-Martial*, which handles minor charges against enlisted service members, unless the defendant objects and asks that the case be referred to another level of court-martial.
- *Special Court-Martial*, which hears offenses that would be defined as misdemeanors in civilian courts.
- *General Court-Martial*, which is where the most serious offenses are considered. Before a general court-martial is convened, a pretrial proceeding, known as an Article 32 hearing, is held. The Article 32 hearing is similar to convening a grand jury to hear testimony in the civilian justice system in that it is held to determine whether there is enough evidence to support the charges. But targets of Article 32 hearings receive rights that are absent in a grand jury investigation: Servicemen and women and their counsel may participate in the hearing, questioning witnesses and making arguments—often in public. Subjects of a secret civilian grand jury investigation cannot. At an Article 32 hearing's conclusion, the investigating officer makes a recommendation to a convening authority to form a court-martial or dismiss the charges. Verdicts in general courts-martial need to be unanimous only in capital, or death penalty, cases. The members can impose any sentence, including death, authorized under the Manual for Courts-Martial.

A service member who is convicted by a special or general court-martial can appeal to his branch's Court of Criminal Appeals. If a death sentence was imposed, the appeal is automatic and mandatory. If the conviction is affirmed, the defendant may appeal to the Court of Appeals for the Armed Forces in Washington and then to the U.S. Supreme Court. Both of those courts may refuse to consider the appeal.

Each branch of the military has a Judge Advocate General, or JAG, a senior legal officer who advises the service's secretary. Military lawyers, called judge advocates or the JAG Corps, serve as prosecutors and defense attorneys who are assigned to prosecute or represent servicemen and women who face courts-martial. A judge advocate may become a military judge if the top JAG in his service branch certifies that he or she is qualified.

Like their civilian counterparts, each military branch divides its court system into geographic divisions, or circuits, that oversee specific bases and command centers. Courts-martial can be convened anywhere in the world, on a ship at sea, on the battlefield or on a military base, which is a point of pride with the service branches. It is a source of frustration for reporters who cannot board a ship, walk onto a battlefield or drop in at the local military base without permission.

If a Tree Falls in the Forest

In the civilian system, reporters can wander over to the courthouse, chat up clerks, check dockets, get up to speed on pending matters and spot new cases. Not so with the military justice system. Military bases don't have clerks' offices or courthouses except in unusual situations, such as Guantanamo Bay, where a courtroom was built.

Civilian clerks' offices follow long-standing practices and policies in maintaining court files and making them available to the public. In contrast, military case dockets and files are made available at the whim of commanders, some of whom fail to appreciate that the public should know whether servicemen and women are treated fairly when they get into trouble. There are indications that the military branches are becoming increasingly aware of the possibilities of online docketing and posting of court records, but the policies for making information public in a timely and complete way vary from commander to commander.

As in the civilian courts, reporters covering military proceedings have a qualified First Amendment right of access. And, as in the civilian system, military judges need to justify in writing their reasons for closing all or part of proceedings. An entire military trial has never been closed, according to the Reporters Committee for Freedom of the Press. The Court of Appeals for the Armed Forces has repeatedly ruled that judges and officers cannot use broad excuses to shut out reporters, such as concerns that a case's details are too embarrassing for the service and the service member, there might be a security threat, or providing press access is difficult and it's easier to operate in secrecy.

Some, but certainly not all members of the military fail to appreciate that a court-martial makes news at the moment it's held, not six months from now. To be fair, there are civilian judges at the federal and state levels who don't understand the news-is-now concept either. Reporters covering military justice always must be prepared to object if they are shut out of a proceeding. If that happens, the reporter's pitch is similar to what you would say in civilian court: "Please don't kick me out. But if you're going to, please take a recess to give me time to get a lawyer here to argue on my behalf before you move forward with the hearing."

The reporter who covers military justice also must cultivate sources and educate commanders about the rights of the press to attend and report on criminal cases. As a reporter seeking access to a military base and court-martial documents, you need to start with the public affairs officer, alerting him or her that you're interested in a particular case and want to know about any and all developments. To cultivate additional sources, which you must, you need to be diligent and methodical about reaching out to military prosecutors and defense attorneys, as well as civilian lawyers and police officers who may be involved on the periphery or have knowledge about a case.

Discovery, the exchange of evidence between the prosecution and defense, also occurs in a court-martial, providing backdoor access to court records. I capitalized on the discovery process to gather information I needed to write a front-page story for *USA Today* in May 2004 that said military intelligence officials had hindered efforts to determine who was to blame for orchestrating abuse of detainees at the Abu Ghraib prison in Iraq. The records revealed that CIA officers and independent contract interrogators had obscured their identities by signing the prison's visitor logs as Special Agent John Doe and James Bond.

Keeping Secrets Secret

Long before the 9/11 attacks, some defendants charged with espionage or other serious offenses engaged in graymail, a play on the word blackmail, by forcing government officials to drop charges, or reveal their most-guarded secrets. In 1980, Congress passed the Classified Information Procedures Act. The CIPA created a process for civilian judges, prosecutors and defense attorneys to sanitize classified information into summaries that could be presented to juries in open court.

If you cover federal court, you likely will encounter a case where the CIPA comes into play. In my career, I saw judges who used the law as Congress intended and others who used it as an excuse to perpetuate secrecy. Chief U.S. District Judge Royce Lamberth in Washington told me many times that there's always a way to craft a public summary of government stealth. Yes, it's hard work, he'd say, but it can be done if the judge takes charge, rolls up his or her sleeves, and forces the lawyers to work together to figure it out.

In 1989, Independent Counsel Lawrence Walsh faced more than one opponent in court as he tried to prosecute Lieutenant Colonel Oliver North, the former National Security Council staffer at the center of the Reagan administration's efforts to exchange arms with the Nicaraguan Contras for release of the Americans who were taken hostage in Iran in 1979. The U.S. intelligence community and the White House opposed much, if not all, of Walsh's case because they feared it would reveal too many of the nation's secrets and require testimony from the president and vice president in open court. North and his lawyers insisted on use of classified government secrets in front of a jury, betting prosecutors would back down and dismiss charges to avoid the risk of exposing U.S. intelligence sources and methods. Prosecutors pressed forward, but North and his attorneys played their cards perfectly. A federal appeals court later reversed North's conviction on three felonies.

The fear generated by the 9/11 attacks also prompted the Bush administration to turn its back on a special secret court that had been established in the late 1970s in response to President Richard Nixon's abuses of power. The Foreign Intelligence Surveillance Court was created to oversee searches and eavesdropping on agents of foreign nations who were operating on U.S. soil. The chief justice of the United States appoints federal judges to sit on the secret court, which acts as a check on the FBI and other agencies in investigations of foreign and domestic spies. President George W. Bush bypassed the special court when he instructed the National Security Agency to eavesdrop on American citizens' overseas communications without seeking court approval to conduct wiretaps and other surveillance. The *New York Times* won a Pulitzer Prize in 2006 for revealing the existence of the spy program.

Why does any of this matter? The government's desire to keep its secrets secret clashes with two fundamental principles of American law. The Sixth Amendment says, "In all criminal prosecutions, the accused shall enjoy the right...to be confronted with the witnesses against him; to have compulsory process for obtaining witnesses in his favor." The first part is known as the confrontation clause, and it is designed to ensure defendants receive a fair trial by giving them the opportunity to challenge the people and paper that prosecutors are using to prove their guilt. The second part gives defendants the right to present information that might exonerate them of wrongdoing.

Dirty Laundry

The government classifies its most sensitive secrets based on official assumptions about the risks if they were revealed. The "Top Secret" label means that unauthorized disclosure of the information reasonably could be expected to cause *exceptionally grave damage* to national security. The unauthorized disclosure of "Secret" information reasonably could be expected to cause *serious damage*, while revealing "Confidential" matters reasonably could be expected to *damage* national security.

Through the CIPA procedures, trial judges in criminal cases rule on questions of admissibility of evidence involving classified information before it is introduced in open court by either side. In its case, the government can use redactions, or blacked out documents, summaries and stipulations, agreements between both sides, in place of classified evidence, if the federal judge presiding over the case is convinced the substitutions are adequate for use at trial. The law also requires defendants to give notice if they want to use classified evidence at trial. The government can insist that the defense use substitutions, such as redacted documents, summaries or stipulations about what the real evidence would show. Judges are permitted to review classified information *in camera*, or in chambers alone, to determine whether the evidence is worthy of protection from disclosure in open court.

A showdown between the attorney general and the trial judge can occur if the judge disapproves of the government's suggested substitutions and decides to allow the defense to use the classified information in its original form. If the attorney general files an *ex parte* affidavit, for the judge's eyes only, outlining the reasons for the Justice Department's opposition to an evidentiary ruling, a formal process kicks in to gear that gives the judge an opportunity to impose sanctions on the government. The sanctions range from striking, or excluding some testimony or exhibits, to dismissal of some or all of the charges in the indictment.

In civil lawsuits, the government can play its ace, the state secrets privilege, a judge-created evidentiary rule that allows federal agencies to ignore court-ordered disclosure of information in civil litigation. The privilege trumps the right that plaintiffs have to "every man's evidence," the opportunity to gather and present testimony and documents to prove their allegations. The U.S. Supreme Court established the parameters of the state secrets privilege in a 1953 decision in a lawsuit filed by the widows of three civilians who died aboard a military plane that crashed while they were testing secret equipment.

In *Reynolds v. United States*, the Court established a two-part process that judges must follow before allowing a plaintiff to use classified evidence to prove his case. First, the head of the government agency asserting secrecy must file a formal claim of the privilege to protect state secrets. Second, the judge must independently determine whether the privilege claim is appropriate, but he must do so without looking at the material the privilege is supposed to protect. The Court declined to allow judges to inspect the information at issue, saying, "too much judicial inquiry into the claim of privilege would force disclosure of the thing the privilege was meant to protect, while a complete abandonment of judicial control would lead to intolerable abuses." The Court said judges should uphold the privilege if they are satisfied that there is a reasonable danger that disclosure would expose military matters that, in the interest of national security, should not be revealed. Once judges find the privilege is valid, they cannot examine the material in question.

William G. Weaver and Robert M. Pallitto wrote in a 2005 article in the *Political Science Quarterly* that from 1953 to 1976 the government invoked the privilege only four times. From 1977 to 2001, the professors found, the government used the privilege 51 times to derail lawsuits. The Bush and Obama administrations have invoked the privilege to nullify lawsuits against the government over renditions, the CIA's practice of taking terrorism suspects into custody abroad and transporting them to another country where they were interrogated under legal rules that provide less stringent rights than those in the United States.

All I Want for Christmas

After the 9/11 attacks, Congress passed the USA PATRIOT Act (Uniting and Strengthening America by Providing Appropriate Tools Required to Intercept and Obstruct Terrorism) without holding a single hearing. The legislation eliminated a long-standing barrier and allowed the CIA and FBI to share criminal and intelligence information. The Act also contained grants of powers that federal law enforcement officials had sought from Congress for years in a governmental version of a Christmas wish list. After 9/11, Congress gave the FBI practically anything it wanted, expanding the government's use of surveillance tools to spy on Americans.

The FBI also dramatically increased its use of national security letters, a type of administrative subpoena, to demand and obtain information from businesses and individuals, without judicial oversight. The Justice Department's inspector general rebuked the FBI for its use of nearly 200,000 of those demands for information between 2003 and 2006. The inspector general also criticized the FBI for its use of exigent letters, emergency requests for records that were supposed to be followed up with formal subpoenas but weren't because it turned out there was no real crisis.

In 9/11's aftermath, the Justice Department also exploited the material witness statute, a little-known provision of criminal law that prosecutors used to ask judges to imprison dozens of people to ensure that they provided information government agents thought they possessed. The statute was designed to keep witnesses from fleeing before they provide key evidence in criminal cases. In one notable example, the tactic backfired and cost taxpayers $2 million: The FBI held the wrong man based on a flawed analysis of a fingerprint found on a plastic bag that contained detonator caps discovered at the scene of the 2004 terrorist bombings in Madrid.

To monitor the government's performance in a crisis, reporters should focus on who is being locked up, which legal tool is being used to justify detentions—and why—and how top officials, from the president down to FBI agents, are behaving.

I also strongly suggest that all reporters—especially those who are too young to remember 9/11 and its aftermath—read the *Final Report of the National Commission on Terrorist Attacks Upon the United States*. The report, available online and in paperback, tells the story of how several federal agencies, mainly the FBI and CIA, failed to detect and stop a ragamuffin group of anti-American fighters trained in Afghanistan from pulling off such a shocking attack.

History often comes back and bites people who know nothing of it—and that includes reporters.

· Chapter ·

The Last Word:
The U.S. Supreme Court

■ ■ ■

The U.S. Supreme Court decides issues that define the American way of life in all of its complexities, spanning issues as diverse as abortion, civil rights, gun control and gay rights. Like the nation, the high court is polarized, which means its decisions often are fractured and fail to provide clear guidance on the law, which is needed by the nation's police, prosecutors, judges and jurors.

The Constitution itself is brief, comprised of about 4,500 words, and there are 27 amendments. In some parts, it is specific; while in other places, it's vague, leaving future generations to solve political and social conundrums beyond the imaginings of the founding fathers. In this chapter, we will talk about two concepts that permeate the Constitution: the separation and limitation of powers. The founding fathers realized that might not be enough to prevent one branch from dominating the others, and they created a network of checks and balances that require government officials to work together and share power.

"Ambition must be made to counteract ambition," as James Madison put it in *The Federalist Papers*, No. 51. Congress and the president must work together because they need each other to pass laws: The president has the power to veto a piece of legislation, and Congress can vote to override his rejection. The president negotiates treaties and appoints judges and other high-ranking government officials, but he needs the Senate's approval. The president is responsible for enforcing the laws, but Congress, with its power over the nation's budget, decides the funding of departments responsible for keeping order. As the sole interpreters of the Constitution and federal laws, the courts keep tabs on Congress's legislative work and the president's policies. But Congress decides the types of cases the lower courts will hear.

The people also have power. The Constitution limits the federal government to exercise only its enumerated powers, which means authority that is specifically delegated to it. If legislative rights are not granted to Congress, they generally are reserved for the states. But the Fourteenth Amendment, ratified in 1868, prohibits states from depriving any person the equal protection of the law. The Supreme Court has made most of the Bill of Rights' provisions applicable to the states, giving the federal government sweeping power over state laws and policies, particularly in the area of crime and justice.

Seizing the Moment

The Supreme Court derives its power from *Marbury v. Madison*, an 1803 case in which Chief Justice John Marshall, the only American depicted on the north and south walls of the high court's chamber, asserted the Supreme Court alone may declare acts of Congress as unconstitutional. "It is emphatically the province of the judicial department to say what the law is," he wrote. In doing so, Chief Justice Marshall created a system of judicial review and made it possible for the then-obscure third branch to become a powerful player in government.

In 1810, the Court declared in *Fletcher v. Peck* that it could void state laws as unconstitutional. Nine years later, in *McCulloch v. Maryland*, the Court established the supremacy of the federal government. Today the Supreme Court issues rulings that presidents, Congress and the people may criticize but largely obey without the necessity of force.

Why is judicial review so important? The Supreme Court stands as the last line of defense in protecting the rights of the minority against the heavy hand of the majority. It also serves as a check on the politically motivated branches that can be swayed by the passions of a mob. In times of crisis, the high court is supposed to act as a stabilizer and a neutral arbiter, motivated by the words "Equal Justice Under Law" chiseled above the main entrance to the classical Corinthian Supreme Court building.

If you take the time to read and understand the Supreme Court's greatest crime-and-justice hits—including *Brady, Jencks, Strickland, Batson, Gregg, Furman, Gideon, Miranda, Terry, Mapp* and *Booker*—you will learn how the nation's criminal justice system developed and why. If you take the time to understand key concepts in the law—such as equal protection and due process—you'll turn out sophisticated stories that inform and challenge your readers or viewers to think about the meaning of justice.

The Real Deal

The Constitution does not say exactly how many justices should serve on the Court. President George Washington appointed six justices in 1789. The Judiciary Act of 1869 set the number at nine—a chief justice plus eight associate justices—and it has stayed that way ever since. The Constitution says the Supreme Court handles "cases and controversies," which means the justices do not provide presidents, Congress or anyone else with advisory opinions. When the Court issues an opinion, it resolves a real case; it is not a hypothetical exercise.

In the past 30 years, the Supreme Court has become more selective about the cases and issues it considers, accepting 75 to 80 a term. Each year, the Court receives about 10,000 appeals, known as *writs of certiorari*. The writs, nicknamed cert petitions, lay out the legal issues in a way that is designed to entice the justices into accepting a case for review. How can each of the nine justices read 10,000 petitions? How can a reporter assigned to cover the Supreme Court read that many? It's possible. When I worked for the Associated Press, two of us skimmed every petition, looking for newsworthy cases we thought the Court might accept for review.

Most of the justices don't spend their summers doing what we did, but rely instead on their law clerks to screen the petitions. Several law clerks form a cert pool, reviewing the petitions and writing memos for the justices about the issues raised in each case. Critics of this practice worry that a small group of inexperienced law school graduates has the power to decide which cases the Court hears each term.

The Court adheres to the Rule of Four, granting a *writ of certiorari* if four justices vote in favor of accepting a case. If the court grants cert, the parties file another round of briefs on the merits to go into more detail on the legal issues. Public interest groups, labor unions and business associations often ask the Court for permission to intervene in a case as *amicus curiae*, or a friend of the court, and file a brief outlining their concerns and legal positions. Amicus briefs can be newsworthy and helpful to a reporter by explaining the broader political and social ramifications of a case.

When covering a Supreme Court case, reporters focus on the key issue, which is usually summarized in the front of the briefs on a page that explains the question or questions posed by the case. By focusing on the question at issue, a reporter can zoom in on what matters and avoid getting bogged down in extraneous details. The strategy doesn't always work: The Court may not answer the question because it wants to avoid a legal issue that is too political, or one that isn't fully developed.

For a reporter who covers the legal system, there is nothing else like a Supreme Court argument. Football players and coaches often say speed is the biggest difference between games in college and the National Football League. The same can be said about the Supreme Court, which begins each term, or annual session, on the first Monday in October and usually concludes by the end of the following June. In the trial courts, one judge interacts with a prosecutor and defense attorney. In the appeals courts, the arguments speed up a bit as three judges question lawyers for each of the parties. At the Supreme Court, nine justices grill the lawyers, often interrupting, as each party takes a turn in the line of fire.

The Rhythm of the Court

The term is divided into sittings and recesses that alternate at about two-week intervals. A sitting is when the justices hear arguments in cases and deliver opinions. During a recess, justices consider the business of the court and write opinions. Arguments usually are held in the mornings, beginning at 10 a.m. on the dot. There usually are no public sessions on Thursdays and Fridays. On Fridays during and before argument weeks, the justices meet to discuss cases that have already been argued and to review new cert petitions, which are filed year-round.

On Monday mornings before arguments, the Court will issue an orders list, a public report on the cases it has accepted or rejected, as well as action taken on applications, which are requests for emergency, or immediate, responses. Usually the Court does not explain its reasons for denying a cert petition. Sometimes, individual justices feel so strongly that they will write an opinion. When that happens, it often makes news. Applications usually are routine, seeking extensions of time to file briefs. Some are true emergencies, such as a late-night motion for a stay to stop an inmate's execution or a request for a restraining order to halt government or private action. An application often tries to buy time while the Court considers whether to accept a cert petition filed by the same parties. The chief justice assigns each of the justices to cover specific federal circuits and applications filed from those areas. There are no oral arguments, and the matters are resolved on paper, or increasingly, by electronic filings. A justice doesn't need to be in the building, as long as he or she has access to a phone or email.

Decision days typically are Tuesdays and Wednesdays. Opinions are released on those mornings and also on the third Monday of a sitting, when the Court takes the bench but there are no arguments scheduled. The chief justice will introduce the justice who wrote the majority opinion in a particular case. That justice will read a summary of the decision. Justices who dissented also may read brief summaries of their opinions.

By May and early June, the Court usually has heard arguments in all of the cases under consideration and takes the bench only to announce orders and opinions. The Court's rulings are final and become known as precedent, the practice of honoring past rulings to ensure continuity and stability in the law. Precedents can be overruled if a majority of justices believes a case was wrongly decided. Often precedents stand for decades, but sometimes they last only a term or two.

Five justices must vote to grant a stay of execution. If a justice rejects an application, the petitioner technically can try another justice of his choice, and on and on until he has tried all nine. Usually the second justice to receive the application will refer it to the entire court to thwart such a shopping spree. If a justice grants an application, he or she may write an opinion explaining the length of the stay, which usually lasts until the cert petition is considered. If the justice who oversees a particular circuit writes the opinion alone, it is called an in-chambers opinion. Once the Court acts on an application, it's over and the parties cannot try again unless they return raising a different legal issue.

Of all of the institutions in Washington, the Supreme Court is one of the few that can keep a secret. The outcomes of cases remain a mystery until the Court announces them. Like everything else with the Court, there is protocol in how decisions are dispensed to the news media. Shortly before 10 a.m. on decision days, reporters crowd into the first-floor office of the Court's public information officer. There, reporters and the Court's employees listen intently to a speaker through which audio from the courtroom on a floor above can be heard. When the chief justice calls on a justice to deliver his or her summary of the majority opinion, the Court's employees hand out paper copies of the decision, its concurrences and dissents, if any. Some reporters display sharp elbows as they rush to grab the opinion to gain a second or two of an advantage on their competition to begin reading to figure out the bottom line. If you are covering a decision alone, you probably won't want to sit in the courtroom to listen to the announcement, especially if you need to file a story quickly. You can skim through a paper copy faster than a justice takes to read the summary from the bench.

Right and Wrong

When the justices are bitterly divided in their rulings, the chances for reporter error skyrocket. Reporters were under enormous pressure to provide a fast explanation of the Court's decision in *Bush v. Gore*, which halted Florida's recount of votes in the 2000 presidential battle between Republican George W. Bush and former Vice President Al Gore. NBC's Pete Williams and Dan Abrams went live on the air, trying to read and make sense of a complicated decision with multiple dissents, as the wicked winter wind whipped the pages of the decision they held in their hands. The Associated Press held off for at least an hour before reporting the final outcome to give its reporters time to read the decision and make sense of it. I was working at *USA Today* helping Supreme Court reporter Joan Biskupic line up reaction from lawyers around the country. We had time to read the decision before going to print, and we took full advantage of it to avoid making an embarrassing mistake.

In a rush to be first with the news, CNN and Fox News reported incorrectly on June 28, 2012, that the Court had struck down a provision of the controversial health care law that required Americans to buy insurance. In a 5-to-4 decision in *National Federation of Independent Business et al. v. Sebelius,* the Court ruled that the individual mandate could not be sustained by Congress's power to regulate commerce but upheld the law under its authority to tax. CNN's error was splashed across TV screens ("Individual Mandate Struck Down") for several minutes before its reporters realized the Court had accepted a back-up argument made by the Obama administration. The Huffington Post, NPR and The Fix, a *Washington Post* blog, re-tweeted CNN's error, sending misinformation around the world on Twitter and confusing millions of people about the case's outcome. I was simultaneously watching CNN and monitoring a live feed on SCOTUSblog.com, a highly respected site that covers Supreme Court cases. SCOTUSblog's correspondent Lyle Denniston and its lawyers got it right at 10:08 a.m., a minute after posting that they had the decision in hand and at the same time CNN and Fox News got it wrong. How could this happen? Arguments before the Supreme Court are nuanced, with multiple layers, and lawyers often cite several options in the Constitution for the justices to fall back on to justify ruling one way or another. In the health care case, the solicitor general gave the justices three possibilities. Reporters must keep in mind all of the options when reading a final decision by the Court. If you look for the Court's response to only one of a party's arguments, as CNN did, you'll increase your chances of being wrong.

Veteran Supreme Court reporter Tony Mauro of the *National Law Journal* offered the following tips for reading an opinion in the digital age:

- The first rule in writing about a Supreme Court opinion on deadline is: Take the time to actually read it.
- If you must feed a blog, scan the syllabus (at the front of the opinion) and the opinion itself briefly, paying the closest attention to the bottom line: Was the lower court opinion overturned or affirmed?
- Read the dissent first because it will often summarize what the majority did more concisely than the syllabus and it will expose the issues on which the Court is fractured or divided. By working backwards, you often can make more sense of the majority opinion and concurrences.
- Carve out time to close the door and read the opinion, start to finish, and don't forget the footnotes. Some of the best quotes are in the footnotes.
- As you read concurrences, keep track of the parts that those justices agree with the majority, and the parts they don't. By doing so you can tally the votes.
- Provide your readers with the end result high up in your story.
- Explain the legal reasoning. You owe it to your readers to tell them why the Court reached that conclusion.

Dressed for Success

Every part of a Supreme Court argument is choreographed to adhere to traditions that are treasured by the justices, which means they aren't likely to be abandoned anytime soon.

There are no jurors or witnesses. There are only the justices, seated at a winged-shaped, mahogany bench according to seniority. The chief justice takes the middle chair. The senior justice is seated to the chief's right and the next senior justice is seated at the chief's left. The seating assignments continue to alternate right and left by seniority.

The justices used to wear powder wigs and robes with red facing. Today they wear black robes. Former Chief Justice William Rehnquist caused a stir when he placed gold bars on his robe. The current chief, John G. Roberts Jr., wears a solid black robe.

Attorneys appearing before the Court used to wear gray morning clothes, formal attire with tails. Now, only the representative of the solicitor general, the federal government's lawyer, dons a morning coat with tails. Quill pens are still placed at both counsel tables, providing lawyers with souvenirs of their appearances before the nation's highest court.

The lawyers for each side receive 30 minutes to make their points about the law as the lower courts applied it; the petitioner, or appellant, can reserve a few minutes for rebuttal, receiving the last word for the party that initiated the appeal. The Court uses a light system: When it turns amber, the lawyer knows he has about five minutes left. When it turns red, his time is up. Former Chief Justice Rehnquist would cut a lawyer off in mid-sentence when the light turned red.

Once the arguments are concluded, the chief justice says, "The case is submitted."

Political Questions and Answers

As the guardian of the Constitution, the Court mediates disputes between the national government and the states, resolves conflicts between the president and Congress and the president and the courts, and it ensures that officials in all three branches honor the separation of powers doctrine by staying in their lanes of authority and not interfering with the prerogatives of the others.

It is up to the Court to decide if and when it should back off, such as when a political question is raised in a case. In those instances, the power to resolve the issue belongs to one or both of the other branches, and the Court is supposed to step aside to allow the president and Congress to figure it out on their own. Sometimes the Court can use this as an excuse to avoid tackling a difficult legal issue. The justices also might sidestep a controversy by deciding that an issue isn't ripe, or ready for consideration, or if the question raised is moot, meaning it's no longer a big deal that needs to be resolved.

National emergencies—armed or economic—pose the greatest risk to democracy by threatening to throw off-kilter the delicate balance among the three branches of government. During a war or economic troubles, reporters must monitor how the president, Congress and the courts are using their powers. Is the president taking over responsibilities that Congress usually carries out? Are judges acting too deferential, accepting without question the president's legal justification for whatever he wants to do?

Why shouldn't we trust our leaders, you might ask. Don't they have our best interests at heart, especially in a crisis? Power is seductive and it affects even the best-intentioned people, making them more secretive, especially in their desire to hide their mistakes or abuses of authority. It's human nature. If you want to be a reporter, you need to understand that elected officials have strengths and weaknesses.

The Limits of Power

Throughout history, presidents have clashed with the Supreme Court by invoking their war powers, derived from their duties as commander-in-chief, and executive privilege, their authority to keep matters secret that involve national security or foreign policy. If a president invokes his war powers, as President George W. Bush did to justify detaining terrorism suspects without charges, or executive privilege, as President Bill Clinton did during the Monica Lewinsky sex scandal, reporters probably will hear two words, *Youngstown* and *Nixon*, shorthand references to two significant cases in Supreme Court history.

In 1952, the Supreme Court ruled in *Youngstown Sheet & Tube v. Sawyer* that President Harry Truman exceeded his authority by seizing control of the nation's steel mills when faced with a possible strike by workers. Truman said he was justified because the military needed steel to fight the Korean War. Justice Robert Jackson said the president's powers are at their greatest strength when he acts with the express or implied approval of Congress. If he acts with the express or implied disapproval of Congress, his powers are at their lowest strength, Justice Jackson wrote.

The nation faced its most dangerous constitutional crisis in 1974 when President Richard Nixon refused to turn over tape recordings of Oval Office conversations sought by prosecutors during the investigation into the burglary of the Democratic Party's headquarters at the Watergate hotel and apartment complex in Washington. A grand jury had been convened and returned indictments against several Nixon aides, when another White House assistant shocked the political establishment by blurting out during a congressional hearing that the president routinely taped conversations in the Oval Office. Special prosecutor Leon Jaworski, in a savvy tactical move, made sure the justices had individual copies of all of the secret grand jury materials, which made clear that President Nixon was an unindicted co-conspirator in the Watergate burglary. In a unanimous opinion, Chief Justice Warren Burger said the needs of the criminal justice system and the importance of fair trials trumped President Nixon's interest in keeping the materials secret because of executive privilege.

When addressing the rights of the people, the Supreme Court focuses primarily on three areas of constitutional law: equal protection; due process; and the First Amendment, with its five crucial safeguards against a tyrannical government.

The Constitution includes several protections for individuals by prohibiting Congress from suspending the *writ of habeas corpus*, also known as the Great Writ, from enacting bills of attainder, and from passing *ex post facto* laws. The *writ of habeas corpus* prevents government from jailing people without giving a reason, or filing charges. The prohibition on bills of attainder keeps government officials from singling out and sending a particular person to prison. Banning *ex post facto* laws prevents people from being punished for committing acts that were once legal but have since become illegal.

If you spend any time in the Supreme Court's chambers, you also are likely to hear mention of the Constitution's Commerce Clause, which empowers Congress to regulate the exchange of goods and services with foreign nations, among the states and with Indian tribes. Congress has used its authority over interstate commerce as a police power to regulate virtually every aspect of the American economy and its underbelly, including gangsters collecting debts and restaurants that refuse service based on race. In the 2012 health care case, the Court's rejection of the use of Congress's power to regulate commerce could have significant repercussions in resolving future controversies.

"An evil eye and unequal hand"

When a law is passed, it may sound perfectly reasonable. But the key to determining whether a statute is "equal" under the law is figuring out how officials apply it to various groups in a community. If one group gets a break and another doesn't, the law is likely a violation of the Fourteenth Amendment's equal protection clause. The amendment, ratified in the aftermath of the Civil War, caused a massive change in constitutional law, when the Court broadened its interpretation to include an examination of how local, state and federal officials implemented an approved piece of legislation.

In 1886, the Court found that San Francisco officials committed illegal discrimination when they waived a city ordinance requiring that laundries must be housed in brick buildings for all businesses—except those run by Chinese immigrants. In *Yick Wo v. Hopkins*, Justice Stanley Matthews wrote: "Though the law itself be fair on its face and impartial in appearance, yet, if it is applied and administered by public authority with an evil eye and an unequal hand, so as practically to make unjust and illegal discriminations between persons in similar circumstances, material to their rights, the denial of equal justice is still within the prohibitions of the Constitution."

Scholars say the Court nearly destroyed the equal protection clause in two famous sets of cases: the *Civil Rights Cases* of 1883 said the federal government could do nothing about private discrimination, and *Plessy v. Ferguson* in 1896 upheld "separate but equal" treatment and facilities for people of races other than white.

In the 1930s and 1940s, the Court began easing up on its restrictive interpretation of the equal protection clause, but in a case in 1944, the justices sanctioned one of the most controversial acts of discrimination in the nation's history. In *Korematsu v. United States*, the Court upheld a military order that banished people of Japanese ancestry from the West Coast to internment camps in the California deserts during World War II. *Korematsu* also introduced the idea that judges should view with immediate suspicion legal restrictions based on race and should employ the most rigid form of judicial scrutiny in evaluating their legality.

To determine whether governmental actions violate a fundamental interest, or right, judges employ a strict scrutiny test to determine whether the equal protection clause is violated by the creation of a suspect class, a group of people who are singled out because of race or ethnicity. Courts will use strict scrutiny, the highest form of review, to strike down laws unless they serve a substantial and compelling government interest and are necessary to achieve lawmakers' purposes.

Laws that restrict rights based on gender must withstand intermediate scrutiny, or heightened examination. Legislation will fail the test unless it serves important governmental objectives and is substantially related to achieving those goals. All other laws are evaluated with the test at the low end of the scale: Judges will uphold a law unless it lacks a rational basis, or its means are not rationally related to its purpose.

It is important for reporters to pay attention to the test a judge decides to use to evaluate laws designed to restrict the rights of women to obtain abortions, of gays to marry and of city residents to own guns. Virtually all laws could pass the rational basis test, while some statutes would flunk the strict scrutiny exam.

The Essence of Liberty

"Due process" is another phrase reporters will hear repeatedly in state and federal courtrooms. The words are found in the Fifth and Fourteenth amendments. The Supreme Court has used what is known as procedural due process to develop a large body of law dealing with protections for criminal defendants facing trial in state and federal courts.

Another type, known as substantive due process, provides mainly for protection of privacy, one of the most controversial aspects of American law today. At its core, substantive due process addresses whether government has a good enough reason to interfere with a person's liberty. The analysis is not easy: What is liberty? What constitutes a substantive interest? What is substantive?

In *Dred Scott v. Sandford*, one of the most reviled decisions in Supreme Court history, the justices used the due process clause of the Fifth Amendment to rule that a slave could not become free simply by traveling to a territory where slavery was outlawed. The Court said Congress could not deprive the slave owner of a property right to his slave without due process of law.

Over the next four decades, the Court struck down numerous state and federal laws by using a confusing theory of economic due process. In another constitutional law embarrassment, the Court ruled in 1905 that New York could not regulate the hours worked by bakers. In *Lochner v. New York*, the Court said employers and their employees must be free to enter into contracts of their choosing.

When the Court turned its attention to noneconomic due process, the justices transported the law and the country into the highly contentious realm of privacy by using the term "fundamental rights." The Court said these rights are part of the recipe, even if they aren't listed as ingredients in the Constitution. In 1965, the Court heard a case that challenged a ban on contraceptives that was designed to prevent adultery. In *Griswold v. Connecticut*, the Court found that the right to privacy is rooted in the Constitution and can be found in nearly all of the Bill of Rights.

Griswold's legal reasoning led to the decision in *Roe v. Wade*, one of the most criticized and polarizing cases in history. In 1973, Justice Harry Blackmun, a former lawyer for the Mayo Clinic in Minnesota, wrote in the majority opinion that a woman has a right to choose whether to have an abortion because of the right to privacy protected by liberty under due process. Conservatives say the Court created a right out of thin air. *Roe's* defenders say the Court was correct in finding that government cannot interfere with a woman's deeply personal and private right to decide whether to have a child.

Despite the culture wars over abortion, gay rights, gun control and other polarizing issues of our time, the right to privacy resonates with many Americans, especially in the Internet age, as people worry about identity theft, data mining and the utilization of other methods of tracking their personal interests on the World Wide Web.

"Freedom for the thought that we hate"

Former *New York Times* reporter Anthony Lewis used those words as the title for his 2007 book on the First Amendment. In it, Lewis chronicled the development of free-speech law, writing about judges who found it was not always easy to protect unpopular speech by disfavored groups during times of crisis, especially when public officials engaged in fear-mongering and disinformation, often about groups that posed little, if any, legitimate threat.

In 1798, Congress passed the Alien and Sedition Acts that gave President John Adams sweeping powers to deport aliens and prosecute anyone who criticized him, Congress or the government generally. The Acts eventually were denounced and ruined Adams's chances for re-election, but not until more than a dozen newspaper editors, mostly supporters of Adams's archrival Thomas Jefferson, were jailed.

Fear of anarchists led Congress to pass the Espionage and Sedition Acts of 1917 and 1918. It happened again when fear of communism prompted Congress to enact the Smith Act in 1940. And fear of Islamic extremists and terrorism led to passage of the USA PATRIOT Act in 2001.

In times of crisis, reporters should be on the lookout for efforts by government leaders to capitalize on the public's fear and convince people to give up some of their most precious rights in exchange for a promise of security.

Shouting "Fire" in a Crowded Theater

Next to the Vietnam conflict, World War I was the most controversial war in U.S. history. An anarchist had killed President William McKinley. The economy was a mess. Poison gas was being used in battles fought across Europe when socialist Charles Schenck sent leaflets to American draftees blaming the war on Wall Street and urging them to resist military service.

In response to such protests, Congress passed the Espionage and Sedition Acts to prohibit interference with military recruitment and ban disloyal or abusive criticism of the U.S. government, its flag or the uniforms of the Army and Navy. In 1919, Supreme Court Justice Oliver Wendell Holmes wrote the majority opinion in *Schenck v. United States* that upheld the constitutionality of the acts, using the famous words that have been repeated throughout history to justify government restrictions on speech: In a crowded theater you cannot shout, "Fire!"

In 1940, Americans again were consumed with fear, this time of communism. Congress passed the Smith Act, the nation's second peacetime sedition law, making it a crime to advocate or conspire to overthrow the U.S. government.

The Supreme Court upheld the constitutionality of the Smith Act in 1951, by which time many of the nation's top communists were convicted and sent to prison. By 1957, the American people had calmed down, and so had the Supreme Court. In *Yates v. United States,* the Court raised the bar of proof for Smith Act prosecutions, requiring evidence that "actual action" was taken in seeking the overthrow of the government. The higher burden of proof made prosecutions more difficult, and the number of criminal cases dwindled.

What about hate speech? Can a member of one religion attack others for their beliefs? Can the Ku Klux Klan urge violence against the government? Hate speech includes words that are written or spoken to attack race, ethnicity, gender or sexual orientation. There is considerable debate about whether hate speech has any socially redeemable value, but the Supreme Court gradually has provided protection under the First Amendment, even if hateful words cause harm.

As with other areas of the law, it took time for the Court to reach such a point. In 1942, the Court was confronted with *Chaplinsky v. New Hampshire*, a case in which a Jehovah's Witness attracted a hostile crowd as he stood on a street attacking other religions as "rackets." The Court introduced the concept of unprotected speech by ruling that government could ban "fighting words" that created a "clear and present danger" of violence. The very utterance of fighting words was believed to tend to incite an immediate violent response. Today the fighting words doctrine has all but disappeared.

A Reality Check

In many of the speech cases throughout history, the people who were prosecuted over what they said and believed were often rag-tag groups of agitators who failed to attract huge numbers of followers.

In 1969, the Court established a test for judges to use to evaluate the seriousness of the danger posed by provocative speech and whether a government response was appropriate. In *Brandenburg v. Ohio*, a Ku Klux Klan leader was convicted of violating a state law that banned the advocacy of violence to accomplish political reform. He suggested in a speech that violence could occur unless the president and Congress ceased in their suppression of the white race. The only people who showed up to hear the speech were a reporter and a photographer he had alerted ahead of time.

The Court set out a series of questions for judges to consider in reviewing a government restriction on speech:

- Did the speaker actually intend for his words to incite lawless or illegal action?
- Was the threat imminent?
- Was the action a crime?
- Was the action likely to occur and not merely speculation?

In other words, the Court told judges to conduct a reality check: If no one is listening, or responding, why should government care?

Symbolic speech is another popular form of protest. In 1968, the Court said in *United States v. O'Brien* that a young man who burned his draft card in protest over the Vietnam War could be prosecuted under a federal law that banned the destruction of the cards because they contained important identifying information that the government needed.

But government officials cannot restrict symbolic speech—such as wearing t-shirts with political messages or burning the American flag—without a significant governmental interest, and the restrictions cannot be any greater than necessary to achieve that goal.

What, Where and When

Government officials can pass rules and regulations to impose time, place and manner restrictions on public demonstrations. They can pass ordinances, for example, requiring that permits be obtained in advance of marches, parades or other events on public streets. They also can restrict access to airports, prisons, shopping malls, parks and other locations, but they cannot manipulate the language in ordinances or licensing requirements to preclude certain disfavored groups from taking their unpopular messages to the streets.

In 1977, the Court said the town of Skokie, Illinois, violated the First Amendment when it required licenses for public demonstrations and passed an ordinance that banned protesters from wearing military-style outfits. Skokie officials passed the ordinance to block members of the Nazi party from marching in their mostly Jewish town.

The first question a judge is supposed to ask is where does the speaker want to speak? In other words, what is the forum, or venue, in which the speech will take place?

Next, the judge must figure out if the venue is a public forum. There are four types of forums: A traditional public forum is a park, city street, or plaza in front of City Hall. A designated public forum is a city-owned auditorium, fairground, or a community meeting hall. Not all types of public property fit the definition of a public forum; prisons and military bases are exceptions because people cannot come and go as they please. Private property, owned by businesses or individuals, is usually not a public forum; privately owned shopping malls could be, if they are treated like city streets.

If the forum is public, a judge must ascertain whether government restrictions on speech are content neutral, meaning the rule is applied evenly regardless of what is said and who says it. The restriction must provide an alternative means of a forum and cannot be a complete ban on a specific kind of communication.

The government also must have a substantial interest to justify the restraint on speech, such as banning loudspeakers at night when most people sleep. The regulation also must be narrowly tailored, meaning it does not restrain expression beyond what the ban initially addressed. For example, a ban on free papers could prevent political candidates from getting their message out in the form of pamphlets or other printed brochures.

For journalists, the First Amendment is the glue that holds the Constitution together. Remove any of its freedoms—of religion, of speech, of the press, to petition and to assembly—and the American government would collapse like a house of cards.

Break a Leg

After reading this book, I hope you have a deeper understanding of the power and reach of the American legal system, and that you are prepared to take on the responsibility of assessing whether the authority to enforce and interpret the nation's laws is used or misused, and who benefits and who doesn't.

I also hope you have as much fun as a reporter as I did.

Glossary

■ ■ ■

A

Acquittal: A verdict after a trial finding a defendant in a criminal case has not been proven guilty beyond a reasonable doubt.

Actus reus: Means "guilty act," a wrongful deed that supports proof that a criminal act occurred.

Additur: An increase by a judge in the damages awarded by a jury, usually with the defendant's consent, that avoids a new trial because of inadequate damages.

Adjudication: The legal resolution of a dispute or judgment.

Admonition: A warning, usually from a judge, to jurors and lawyers, regarding their oaths to be fair and their duties as officers of the court.

Adversarial system: The legal method used in the United States and other countries to search for the truth by giving opposing parties the opportunity to contest evidence offered by each before a neutral judge or jury.

Affiant: A person who signs an affidavit.

Affidavit: A voluntary, written statement of facts that is sworn under oath.

Affirm/Affirmed: Confirm a ruling that has been appealed.

Alford plea: A plea that a defendant makes without admitting guilt.

Allegation: A statement in a lawsuit, indictment or other document that a party says it expects to prove.

Allocution: A trial judge's verbal exchange with a convicted defendant, in which he or she is given a chance to speak before a sentence is imposed.

Alternative dispute resolution (ADR): Settling a dispute without a trial, typically through mediation or arbitration.

Amicus curiae: Means "friend of the court," a person or group not party to a legal dispute that asks the court, or is asked by the court, to weigh in on an issue because of special interest or expertise.

Anonymous jury: A jury with members whose names and other identifying information are sealed, or secret.

Answer: A response to a question, pleading or discovery request for information.

Appeal: A losing party's request that a higher court review a ruling or judgment.

Appellant: The party that appeals a lower court ruling, usually seeking reversal. Also known as petitioner.

Appellee: The party against whom an appeal is taken. Also known as the respondent.

Arbitration: A form of alternative dispute resolution in which all sides in a case agree to abide by the decision of a neutral third party.

Argumentative: Typically used by lawyers to describe objections to the other side's questions because they state inferences and conclusions.

Arraignment: In a criminal case, a defendant is brought before a judge to hear the charges against him or her and enter a plea, usually of not guilty.

Arrest: Taking or keeping a person in custody by legal authority.

Assistance of counsel: Representation by a lawyer, particularly in a criminal case.

Authentication: To prove that something, such as a document, is genuine so it can be admitted into evidence.

Award: A final decision, by an arbitrator or by a jury in assessing damages.

B

Bail: Money or property used to secure a defendant's release from custody pending future court appearances.

Bailiff: A court officer who keeps order when court is in session.

Bail revocation: A court's cancellation of bail granted to a defendant.

Bench: The elevated area occupied by a judge in a courtroom.

Bench ruling: An oral ruling by a judge from the bench.

Bench trial: A trial by judge, not jury, usually at a defendant's request.

Beyond a reasonable doubt: The highest standard of proof in the law, a burden resting on prosecutors, that a jury finds as close to a 100-percent certainty as possible that a defendant is guilty in a criminal case.

Bill of particulars: A formal statement that provides details of claims or charges brought by a plaintiff in a civil lawsuit or a prosecutor in a criminal case, usually in response to a defendant's request for specifics.

Bill of Rights: First 10 amendments to the U.S. Constitution.

Bind or Bound over: Hold a person for trial, if a judicial officer finds probable cause to believe that a crime was committed and the accused committed it.

Bond: A written promise to pay money or do something; a bail bond is a promise given to the court by a bond company to guarantee a defendant will appear at future hearings.

Booking: The process undertaken by police after an arrest to photograph, fingerprint and check a suspect for outstanding warrants.

Brief: A written statement, or document, that outlines a party's legal position and arguments.

Burden of proof: A party's duty to prove disputed assertions, allegations or charges.

C

Calendar: A court's list of civil and criminal cases; also known as docket.

Capias: Means, "that you take." Any writ, or court order, that requires an officer to take a person into custody.

Capital crime: A crime punishable by death.

Cause of action: Facts that give rise to a lawsuit; also used to describe the lawsuit.

Certiorari: Means "to be more fully informed." An extraordinary writ, or an order, that an appellate court issues directing a lower court to deliver the record in a case for review. The U.S. Supreme Court uses certiorari for most of the cases it decides to review.

Chain of custody: A process used by police to record the history of movements of a piece of evidence from the time it was seized to its use in court.

Challenge for cause: A party's request that a judge disqualify a potential juror or entire jury panel because of bias or prejudice.

Chambers: A judge's private office. If a hearing takes place in chambers, it is held outside the presence of the jury, the public and the press.

Change of venue: The transfer of a case from one location to another court in the same judicial system to minimize the effects of perceived prejudicial publicity or for the convenience of the judge, parties or witnesses.

Charge: A formal accusation.

Charge to the jury: The judge's instructions on the law and how to apply it to the facts of a case given shortly before deliberations begin.

Circumstantial evidence: The most common form of evidence in criminal cases, it suggests something by implication. It is indirect, in contrast to eyewitness testimony, which is direct evidence.

Civil actions: Non-criminal cases in which a person or business sues another over a dispute.

Class action: A lawsuit in which the court authorizes a person or a small group to sue on behalf of several others with similar interests.

Clear and convincing evidence: A mid-level standard of proof commonly used in civil lawsuits that means that the thing to be proved is highly probable.

Clemency: An act of mercy or leniency by the president or a governor to pardon a convicted criminal or commute, or reduce, a sentence.

Common law: The body of law created by judges' decisions, rather than statutes or constitutions.

Community policing: A neighborhood-oriented law-enforcement technique in which police officers develop relationships with residents to detect and thwart criminal activity.

Commutation: Reducing a sentence, from death to life in prison, for example.

Compensatory damages: Usually money awarded by a jury to make an injured person whole again to compensate for actual losses.

Competency: A criminal defendant's ability to understand proceedings, make decisions and consult with his or her attorney in a trial.

Complainant: The party who brings a legal action against another.

Complaint: The legal document that begins a lawsuit; another word for lawsuit.

Concurrence: An agreement or vote cast by a judge who agrees with the decision of the majority.

Concurrent sentence: Punishment for more than one conviction that is to be served at the same time.

Confrontation Clause: The Sixth Amendment provision that generally guarantees a criminal defendant's right to confront accusers and to cross-examine them.

Consecutive sentence: Punishment for more than one conviction served one after another.

Contempt of court: A finding by a judge against a party for defying a court order.

Continuance: A postponement of a court proceeding to a future date.

Conviction: The act or process of judicially finding someone guilty.

Corpus delicti: Means "body of the crime." It is the objective proof that a crime was committed and often refers to the victim.

Count: A separate or distinct accusation in an indictment or a lawsuit.

Counterclaim: A claim made by a defendant against a plaintiff in a lawsuit.

Court-martial: A military court convened to try a member of the armed services.

Court of general jurisdiction: A court with unlimited or nearly unlimited trial jurisdiction in civil and criminal cases, typically to handle felonies and lawsuits seeking large damages.

Court of limited jurisdiction: A court with jurisdiction over certain types of cases involving minor crimes and civil disputes.

Cross-claim: A claim by a co-defendant or co-plaintiffs against each other in a lawsuit.

D

Damages: Money awarded by a judge or jury to a person injured by the unlawful act or negligence of another.

Death row: The area of a prison housing inmates who have been sentenced to death.

Decorum order: An order used by a judge to control access that reporters and photographers have to participants in a trial.

Default judgment: A judgment against a defendant who has failed to respond to a lawsuit's claims.

Defendant: A person sued in a lawsuit or accused in a criminal case.

Defense: A defendant's response to charges or accusations.

Deliberations: The process by which a judge or jury carefully considers evidence and arguments before making a decision.

Demurrer: A motion to dismiss a civil case because the facts alleged in a complaint, although true, are insufficient to state a claim.

Deposition: A witness's sworn, out-of-court testimony that is reduced to writing for use in discovery and questioning during trial.

Directed verdict: An instruction by a judge to the jury to return a specific verdict, or a situation where the judge takes the decision away from the jury and rules that the prosecution has not proven its case. A judge cannot order a jury to convict a defendant in a criminal case.

Direct evidence: Proof by witnesses who saw acts or heard words spoken regarding an issue in a case.

Direct examination: The first round of questioning of witnesses by the lawyers who called them to testify.

Discovery: The pre-trial process in which both sides exchange information that relates to the case.

Dismissal: Termination of a legal action without additional hearings or a trial.

Dissenting opinion: A written opinion by a judge or judges who disagree with the majority.

Docket: A formal record of a case that lists all filings and actions.

Double Jeopardy Clause: The Fifth Amendment provision that bars a person from being tried twice for the same crime.

Due process: The process of conducting legal proceedings according to rules and principles that are designed to protect rights.

E

Elements of a crime: Parts of a crime that a prosecutor must prove, usually showing that a crime was committed, the defendant intended it to happen and a timely connection between the two.

En banc: The full court, with all judges present.

Establishment Clause: The First Amendment provision that prohibits government from establishing an official religion.

Et al.: Means "and other persons."

Exculpate: To free from blame. Exculpatory evidence tends to show that a defendant did not commit a crime.

Executive privilege: Based on the Constitution's separation of powers doctrine, it exempts the executive branch from disclosing matters of national security or foreign policy.

Ex parte: A meeting between a judge and one of the parties without notice to the other.

Ex post facto: Means "after the fact." The Constitution prohibits enactment of laws that punish retroactively.

Expunge: To erase or destroy.

Extradite: To deliver a suspect from one jurisdiction to another.

F

Family Court: A court that handles criminal cases against juveniles, divorces, child custody battles and allegations that children have been abused or neglected.

Felony: A serious crime punishable by more than a year in prison, or by death.

Felony murder: A death resulting from the commission of a crime or attempted commission of a crime.

Finding of fact: A determination by a judge or jury that a fact is supported by evidence.

First appearance: Often called initial appearance before a judicial officer of a person under arrest.

G

Gag order: A judge's order that prohibits the public discussion of a case's facts by lawyers, witnesses, parties and reporters.

Garnish: To attach property to satisfy a debt.

Good time: A reduction in a sentence for a prisoner as a reward for good behavior.

Grand jury: A panel of up to 23 citizens who hear evidence presented by a prosecutor in secret and decide whether to issue an indictment.

Graymail: A criminal defendant's threat to reveal classified information during a trial in trying to force the government to drop the charges.

H

Habeas corpus: Means "you have the body." A writ used to bring a person before a court to ensure his imprisonment or detention is legal.

Harmless error: A mistake during a trial that was not serious enough to affect the outcome and prejudice the rights of the losing party.

Hearsay: Evidence that a witness does not know personally but has heard someone else say.

Homicide: The killing of one person by another.

Hostile witness: A witness whose testimony is unfavorable to the party who called him or her to the stand.

Hung jury: A jury that cannot reach a consensus on a verdict.

I

Immunity: A grant by a court that allows a person to provide evidence of a crime but avoid prosecution for his or her wrongdoing.

Impeaching a witness: Discrediting a witness by attacking his or her credibility.

Inadmissible: Evidence that is not allowed or worthy of consideration by a judge or a jury.

In camera: To review information inside a judge's chambers, or in private.

Inculpate: To implicate in wrongdoing.

Indeterminate sentencing: The practice of imposing a range of years for a sentence, not a specific time.

Indictment: Formal written accusation of a crime made by a grand jury.

Information: A formal charge made by a prosecutor in states that do not use grand juries. In federal courts, a prosecutor needs a defendant's consent to bring charges this way.

Injunction: A court order that prohibits action.

Interlocutory appeal: A challenge to a judge's ruling on some issues raised in a case.

Interrogatory: A written question submitted by one party to another.

J

Jail: A detention facility operated by a local government, usually a county, to house people awaiting trial or criminal defendants who have been convicted of misdemeanors.

Judgment: A court's final determination in a lawsuit.

Judicial review: A court's power to review the actions of the other branches of government.

Jurisdiction: A court's authority to decide a case.

Jury: A group of people selected and sworn to determine the facts in the trial of a case and return a verdict, also known as a petit jury.

Jury nullification: A jury's deliberate refusal to apply the law.

L

Leading question: A question framed in such a way as to suggest an answer.

Liable: Legally obligated or accountable.

Lien: A legal claim against another person's property as security for a debt.

Limine: A motion requesting that a court exclude evidence that might prejudice the jury.

Litigant: A party in a lawsuit.

M

Magistrate: A local judicial officer who exercises some but not all of a judge's powers.

Malice: The intent, without justification, to commit a wrongful act.

Mandamus: A writ issued by a court ordering a public official to perform an act.

Mandate: An order from an appellate court that directs a lower court to take certain action.

Mediation: A method of non-binding dispute resolution between parties.

Mens rea: A defendant's guilty state of mind that a prosecutor must prove to secure a conviction.

Misdemeanor: A less serious crime punishable by a fine or brief confinement in a local jail.

Mistrial: A trial that a judge ends before a verdict because of a procedural error or a jury's inability to reach a consensus.

Mitigating circumstances: Evidence that tends to explain but not excuse criminal behavior.

Moot: An issue that is no longer important because it's been resolved.

Motion: A request that a judge make a specific ruling or order.

Murder: The killing of a person with malice aforethought.

N

Negligence: Failure to exercise a standard of care that a reasonable person would have in a similar situation.

No bill: A grand jury's notation that there was insufficient evidence to indict.

Nolle prosequi: A prosecutor's decision to abandon a criminal case.

Nolo contendere: Means "I do not wish to contend." A defendant enters a plea of no contest to the charges. In some jurisdictions, its effect is the same as a guilty plea.

O

Objection: A formal statement in opposition to something that has happened or is about to happen in court.

Opinion: A court's written explanation of its decision.

Overrule: To rule against.

Overt act: An action, however innocent, done in furtherance of a conspiracy.

Own recognizance (OR): When a defendant is released from custody without payment of bail or posting of bond but with a promise to return for future court appearances.

P

Pardon: An official nullification or prevention of prosecution, punishment or legal consequences of a crime.

Parole: The supervised release of a prisoner before the full sentence is served.

Penitentiary: A correctional facility of long-term confinement, also known as prison.

Peremptory challenge: Used during jury selection by lawyers to reject a prospective juror without providing a reason.

Perjury: The criminal offense of giving false testimony under oath.

Petitioner: A person or entity filing a legal action, particularly an appeal.

Plaintiff: A person or an entity that files a lawsuit.

Precedent: A previously decided case that guides decisions in the future.

Preponderance of the evidence: The standard of proof in most civil cases, it means the stronger evidence, however slight the advantage.

Prima facie case: Producing enough evidence to rule in a party's favor.

Prior restraint: A governmental restriction on speech or publication before its expression.

Probable cause: A reasonable belief that a crime was committed and a suspect committed it.

Probation: A sentence that does not include incarceration but rather release into the community for a period of time, usually under supervised conditions.

Pro se: A person who represents him- or herself in a court proceeding.

Protective order: A restriction placed on what information lawyers can and cannot disclose.

Punitive damages: An award designed to punish a defendant for acting with malice, recklessness or deceit.

Q

Quash: To void a summons or subpoena.

R

Reasonable doubt: The doubt that keeps a person from being firmly convinced of a defendant's guilt.

Reasonable person: A phrase used for a person who acts sensibly.

Rebuttal: The time given to a prosecutor or plaintiff to counter evidence presented by a defendant.

Reckless disregard: A person's conscious indifference to consequences of actions.

Redaction: The practice of blacking out or excising portions of documents, often because of concerns about national security.

Redirect examination: A second round of questioning, after cross-examination, by the lawyer who called the witness to the stand.

Rejoinder: A defendant's response to a plaintiff's reply.

Remand: Sending a case back for further action, typically from an appellate court to a trial court.

Remittitur: A reduction of a jury award by a judge that requires a plaintiff to accept less in exchange for not having to retry the case.

Respondent: The party against whom an appeal is taken.

Restitution: Compensation for loss.

Return: A police officer's inventory of items seized during execution of a search warrant.

Reversible error: A mistake in a trial that is prejudicial or harmful that justifies reversing the judgment of a lower court.

S

Seal: To keep secret and deny public access to documents or court proceedings.

Search warrant: A judicial officer's written order authorizing police to search a specific area for certain items in a definite time frame.

Sequester: To segregate or isolate witnesses or jurors during a trial.

Service: The formal delivery of a pleading or lawsuit.

Settlement: An agreement that ends a lawsuit or legal dispute.

Severance: The separation of claims or defendants by a judge to handle them individually.

Shield law: A statute that provides journalists with the privilege of not revealing the identities of confidential sources. A rape shield law provides legal protection for victims of sexual assault.

Sidebar conference: A meeting among the lawyers and judge at the side of the bench.

Sitting: A court session, especially an appellate court.

Standing: A party's right to make a legal claim or seek judicial enforcement of a right or duty.

Stare decisis: Means "to stand by things decided." Refers to the doctrine of precedent, which requires courts to follow previous decisions when the same points are raised in a case.

Statute of limitations: A law that bars claims after a specific period of time.

Statutory construction: The interpretation of a statute or law.

Statutory law: The body of law derived from legislation, rather than constitutions or judicial decisions.

Stay: A temporary halt in a case or enforcement of a judgment.

Stipulation: An agreement between parties in a case regarding a relevant point.

Stop and frisk: A warrantless stop and search by a police officer that results in a brief detention, questioning and search for a weapon of a person suspected of engaging in criminal activity.

Strike: To remove a prospective juror from a panel by a peremptory challenge or challenge for cause.

Subpoena or subpoena duces tecum: A court order compelling a person to testify or provide physical evidence.

Summary judgment: An order by a judge deciding a case in favor of one side on the basis of pleadings before a trial, determining there is no factual dispute that a jury need decide.

Summons: A notice to a defendant that he or she has been sued and is required to answer a lawsuit or an appeal in court.

Suppress: To forbid the use of evidence at trial because it is improper or was illegally obtained.

Sustain: To uphold or rule in favor.

T

Temporary restraining order (TRO): A court order preserving the status quo until a litigant's request for a permanent injunction can be considered.

Third party: A person who is not a party to a lawsuit but is somehow implicated.

Three strikes law: A statute that carries enhanced penalties, such as life in prison, for repeat offenders. About half of the states have such laws.

Tort: A civil wrong for which a remedy may be obtained.

Trial de novo: A new trial.

True bill: A grand jury's notation that a criminal charge should go before a jury for trial.

U

Unconstitutional: A finding that a law is contrary to or in conflict with a constitution, usually the U.S. Constitution.

Under submission: Being considered by a court.

United States attorney: A lawyer appointed by the president to represent the U.S. government in civil and criminal cases in a federal judicial district.

V

Vacate: To nullify or set aside.

Venire: A panel of people selected for jury duty.

Venue: The proper place for a lawsuit to proceed because of a connection between a place and allegations in the case.

Verdict: A jury's finding or decision about a case's facts.

Voir dire: Means "to speak the truth." It is the questioning of prospective jurors by a judge and lawyers to decide whether they are suitable to serve on a jury.

W

Waiver: The voluntary relinquishment of a right. In legal fights over the identities of journalists' sources, judges pressure reporters to ask their sources to release them from promises of confidentiality.

Warrant: A court order directing or authorizing law-enforcement officers to make an arrest or conduct a search.

Whistleblower: Someone who reports wrongdoing by a business or government agency.

Wiretapping: Electronic eavesdropping by police under a court order to listen to private conversations.

With prejudice: To dismiss a case and bar the issues from being brought again.

Without prejudice: To dismiss a case but allow issues to be filed again.

Witness: Someone who gives testimony about what he or she saw, heard or experienced.

Writ: A court's written order directing a person to do something.

Wrongful death lawsuit: A suit brought on behalf of someone who died that seeks damages from a person or an entity that is accused of causing the death.

Bibliography

■ ■ ■

Chapter 1

Chiasson, L. (1997). *The press on trial: Crimes and trials as media events*. Westport, CT: Greenwood.

Kovach, B., & Rosenstiel, T. (2001). *The elements of journalism: What newspeople should know and the public should expect*. New York: Crown.

Locy, T. (1990, June 3). Inquiry questioned in unexplained death. *Boston Globe*, p. 1.

Locy, T. (1991, April 7-10). Bungling the basics. *Boston Globe*, p. 1.

Powell v. Alabama. (1932). *The Oyez Project at IIT Chicago-Kent College of Law: A Multimedia Archive of the Supreme Court of the United States.* Available at http://www.oyez.org/cases/1901-1939/1932/1932_98

Richmond Newspapers, Inc. v. Virginia. (1980). *Legal Information Institute.* Available at http://www.law.cornell.edu/supct/html/historics/USSC_CR_0448_0555_ZS.html

Sheppard v. Maxwell. (1966). *The Oyez Project at IIT Chicago-Kent College of Law: A Multimedia Archive of the Supreme Court of the United States.* Available at http://www.oyez.org/cases/1960-1969/1965/1965_490

State v. Sheppard, 165 Ohio St. 293 (1956). *Leagle.* Available at http://www.leagle.com/xmlResult.aspx?xmldoc=1956458 165OhioSt293_1397.xml&docbase=CSLWAR1-1950-1985

Chapter 2

Alexander, M. (2010). *The new Jim Crow: Mass incarceration in the age of colorblindness*. New York: New Press.

Chiasson, L. (1997). *The press on trial: Crimes and trials as media events*. Westport, CT: Greenwood.

Florida v. Bostick. (1991). *The Oyez Project at IIT Chicago-Kent College of Law: A Multimedia Archive of the Supreme Court of the United States.* Available at http://www.oyez.org/cases/1990-1999/1990/1990_89_1717

Fulwider, J. (2001, October 18). O'Connor lectures lawyers, recollects for students in Lincoln. *Nebraska State Paper.* Available at http://nebraska.statepaper.com/vnews/display.v/ART/2001/10/18/3bcf6460c1279

Gideon v. Wainwright. (1963). *The Oyez Project at IIT Chicago-Kent College of Law: A Multimedia Archive of the Supreme Court of the United States.* http://www.oyez.org/cases/1960-1969/1962/1962_155/

Hamilton, A. (1788). The Federalist #78: The judiciary department. *Independent Journal.* Available at http://www.constitution.org/fed/federa78.htm

Lafler v. Cooper. (2012). Supreme Court of the United States. Available at www.supremecourt.gov/opinions/11pdf/10-209.pdf

Locy, T. (2002, March 28). Lindh charges reflect U.S. hard line. *USA Today.* Available at http://www.usatoday.com/news/nation/2002/03/28/lindh-charges.htm

McCleskey v. Kemp. (1987). *The Oyez Project at IIT Chicago-Kent College of Law: A Multimedia Archive of the Supreme Court of the United States.* Available at http://www.oyez.org/cases/1980-1989/1986/1986_84_6811

Miranda v. Arizona. (1966). *The Oyez Project at IIT Chicago-Kent College of Law: A Multimedia Archive of the Supreme Court of the United States.* Available at http://www.oyez.org/cases/1960-1969/1965/1965_759/

Missouri v. Frye. (2012). Supreme Court of the United States. Available at www.supremecourt.gov/opinions/11pdf/10-444.pdf

Montross Jr., W. R., & Mulvaney, P. (2009). Virtue or Vice: Who will report on the failings of the American criminal justice system? *Stanford Law Review, 61*(6), 1429–1462.

New York Times. (2003, August 12). Justice Kennedy speaks out. *New York Times.* Available at http://www.nytimes.com/2003/08/12/opinion/justice-kennedy-speaks-out.html

Purkett v. Elem, 514 U.S. 765 (1995). *Legal Information Institute.* Available at http://www.law.cornell.edu/supct/html/94-802.ZPC.html

Stevens, J. P. (2005, August 6). Address to the American Bar Association, Thurgood Marshall Awards Dinner, Chicago, Ill. Available at http://www.supremecourt.gov/publicinfo/speeches/viewspeeches.aspx?Filename=sp_08-06-05.html

Stuntz, W. J. (2011). *The collapse of American criminal justice.* Cambridge, Mass.: Belknap Press of Harvard University Press.

United States v. Armstrong. (1996) *The Oyez Project at IIT Chicago-Kent College of Law: A Multimedia Archive of the Supreme Court of the United States.* Available at http://www.oyez.org/cases/1990-1999/1995/1995_95_157

Whren v. United States. (1996). *The Oyez Project at IIT Chicago-Kent College of Law: A Multimedia Archive of the Supreme Court of the United States.* Available at http://www.oyez.org/cases/1990-1999/1995/1995_95_5841

Chapter 3

Miranda v. Arizona. (1966). *The Oyez Project at IIT Chicago-Kent College of Law: A Multimedia Archive of the Supreme Court of the United States.* Available at http://www.oyez.org/cases/1960-1969/1965/1965_759/

Nebraska Press Assoc. v. Stuart. (1976). *The Oyez Project at IIT Chicago-Kent College of Law: A Multimedia Archive of the Supreme Court of the United States.* Available at http://www.oyez.org/cases/1970-1979/1975/1975_75_817

Chapter 4

Kovach, B., & Rosenstiel, T. (2001). *The elements of journalism: What newspeople should know and the public should expect.* New York: Crown.

Miranda v. Arizona. (1966). *The Oyez Project at IIT Chicago-Kent College of Law: A Multimedia Archive of the Supreme Court of the United States.* Available at http://www.oyez.org/cases/1960-1969/1965/1965_759/

Chapter 5

Argersinger v. Hamlin. (1972). *The Oyez Project at IIT Chicago-Kent College of Law: A Multimedia Archive of the Supreme Court of the United States.* Available at http://www.oyez.org/cases/1970-1979/1971/1971_70_5015

Baze and Bowling v. Rees. (2008). *The Oyez Project at IIT Chicago-Kent College of Law: A Multimedia Archive of the Supreme Court of the United States.* Available at http://www.oyez.org/cases/2000-2009/2007/2007_07_5439

Berghuis v. Thompkins. (2010). *The Oyez Project at IIT Chicago-Kent College of Law: A Multimedia Archive of the Supreme Court of the United States.* Available at http://www.oyez.org/cases/2000-2009/2009/2009_08_1470

Berkemer v. Mccarty. (1984). *The Oyez Project at IIT Chicago-Kent College of Law: A Multimedia Archive of the Supreme Court of the United States.* Available at http://www.oyez.org/cases/1980-1989/1983/1983_83_710

Brewer v. Williams. (1977). *The Oyez Project at IIT Chicago-Kent College of Law: A Multimedia Archive of the Supreme Court of the United States.* Available at http://www.oyez.org/cases/1970-1979/1976/1976_74_1263

Brigham City, Utah v. Stuart. (2006). *The Oyez Project at IIT Chicago-Kent College of Law: A Multimedia Archive of the Supreme Court of the United States.* Available at http://www.oyez.org/cases/2000-2009/2005/2005_05_502

Brown v. Mississippi, 297 U.S. 278 (1936). *Justia U.S. Supreme Court Center.* Available at http://supreme.justia.com/cases/federal/us/297/278/case.html

California v. Acevedo. (1991). *The Oyez Project at IIT Chicago-Kent College of Law: A Multimedia Archive of the Supreme Court of the United States.* Available at http://www.oyez.org/cases/1990-1999/1990/1990_89_1690

Caplin & Drysdale, Chartered v. United States. (1989). *The Oyez Project at IIT Chicago-Kent College of Law: A Multimedia Archive of the Supreme Court of the United States.* Available at http://www.oyez.org/cases/1980-1989/1988/1988_87_1729

Chimel v. California. (1969). *The Oyez Project at IIT Chicago-Kent College of Law: A Multimedia Archive of the Supreme Court of the United States.* Available at http://www.oyez.org/cases/1960-1969/1968/1968_770

Colorado v. Connelly. (1986). *The Oyez Project at IIT Chicago-Kent College of Law: A Multimedia Archive of the Supreme Court of the United States.* Available at http://www.oyez.org/cases/1980-1989/1986/1986_85_660

Dickerson v. United States. (2000). *The Oyez Project at IIT Chicago-Kent College of Law: A Multimedia Archive of the Supreme Court of the United States.* Available at http://www.oyez.org/cases/1990-1999/1999/1999_99_5525

Edwards v. Arizona, 451 U.S. 477 (1981). *Justia U.S. Supreme Court Center.* Available at http://supreme.justia.com/cases/federal/us/451/477/

Faretta v. California. (1975). *FindLaw: Cases and Codes.* Available at http://caselaw.lp.findlaw.com/scripts/getcase.pl?court=us&vol=422&invol=806

Ford v. Wainwright. (1986). *The Oyez Project at IIT Chicago-Kent College of Law: A Multimedia Archive of the Supreme Court of the United States.* Available at http://www.oyez.org/cases/1980-1989/1985/1985_85_5542

Furman v. Georgia. (1972). *The Oyez Project at IIT Chicago-Kent College of Law: A Multimedia Archive of the Supreme Court of the United States.* Available at http://www.oyez.org/cases/1970-1979/1971/1971_69_5003

Gideon v. Wainwright. (1963). *The Oyez Project at IIT Chicago-Kent College of Law: A Multimedia Archive of the Supreme Court of the United States.* Available at http://www.oyez.org/cases/1960-1969/1962/1962_155

Gregg v. Georgia. (1976). *The Oyez Project at IIT Chicago-Kent College of Law: A Multimedia Archive of the Supreme Court of the United States.* Available at http://www.oyez.org/cases/1970-1979/1975/1975_74_6257

Haynes v. Washington. (1963). *The Oyez Project at IIT Chicago-Kent College of Law: A Multimedia Archive of the Supreme Court of the United States.* Available at http://holmes.oyez.org/cases/1960-1969/1962/1962_147

Herring v. United States. (2009). *The Oyez Project at IIT Chicago-Kent College of Law: A Multimedia Archive of the Supreme Court of the United States.* Available at http://www.oyez.org/cases/2000-2009/2008/2008_07_513

Hudson v. Michigan. (2006). *The Oyez Project at IIT Chicago-Kent College of Law: A Multimedia Archive of the Supreme Court of the United States.* Available at http://www.oyez.org/cases/2000-2009/2005/2005_04_1360

Katz v. United States. (1967). *The Oyez Project at IIT Chicago-Kent College of Law: A Multimedia Archive of the Supreme Court of the United States.* Available at http://www.oyez.org/cases/1960-1969/1967/1967_35

Lisenba v. California, 314 U.S. 219 (1941). *Justia U.S. Supreme Court Center.* Available at http://supreme.justia.com/cases/federal/us/314/219/case.html

Mapp v. Ohio. (1961). *The Oyez Project at IIT Chicago-Kent College of Law: A Multimedia Archive of the Supreme Court of the United States.* Available at http://www.oyez.org/cases/1960-1969/1960/1960_236

Michigan v. Moseley, 423 U.S. 96 (1975). *Justia U.S. Supreme Court Center.* Available at http://supreme.justia.com/cases/federal/us/423/96/case.html

Miranda v. Arizona. (1966). *The Oyez Project at IIT Chicago-Kent College of Law: A Multimedia Archive of the Supreme Court of the United States.* Available at http://www.oyez.org/cases/1960-1969/1965/1965_759/

Moran, D. A. (2006). The end of the exclusionary rule among other things: The Roberts court takes on the Fourth Amendment. *Cato Supreme Court Review, 2005–2006.* Washington, D.C.: Cato Institute. Available at http://www.cato.org/pubs/scr/issue.php?year=2006

Nardone v. United States, 308 U.S. 338 (1939). *Justia U.S. Supreme Court Center.* Available at http://supreme.justia.com/cases/federal/us/308/338/case.html

New York v. Belton. (1981). *The Oyez Project at IIT Chicago-Kent College of Law: A Multimedia Archive of the Supreme Court of the United States.* Available at http://www.oyez.org/cases/1980-1989/1980/1980_80_328

Oregon v. Bradshaw. (1983). *The Oyez Project at IIT Chicago-Kent College of Law: A Multimedia Archive of the Supreme Court of the United States.* Available at http://www.oyez.org/cases/1980-1989/1982/1982_81_1857

Oregon v. Mathiason. (1977). *The Oyez Project at IIT Chicago-Kent College of Law: A Multimedia Archive of the Supreme Court of the United States.* Available at http://www.oyez.org/cases/1970-1979/1977/1977_76_201

Powell v. Alabama. (1932). *The Oyez Project at IIT Chicago-Kent College of Law: A Multimedia Archive of the Supreme Court of the United States.* Available at http://www.oyez.org/cases/1901-1939/1932/1932_98

Spano v. New York, 360 U.S. 315 (1959). *Justia U.S. Supreme Court Center.* Available at http://supreme.justia.com/cases/federal/us/360/315/case.html

Stansbury v. California, 511 U.S. 318 (1994). *Legal Information Institute.* Available at http://www.law.cornell.edu/supct/html/93-5770.ZPC.html

Strickland v. Washington. (1984). *The Oyez Project at IIT Chicago-Kent College of Law: A Multimedia Archive of the Supreme Court of the United States.* Available at http://www.oyez.org/cases/1980-1989/1983/1983_82_1554

Terry v. Ohio. (1968). *The Oyez Project at IIT Chicago-Kent College of Law: A Multimedia Archive of the Supreme Court of the United States.* Available at http://www.oyez.org/cases/1960-1969/1967/1967_67

United States v. Gonzalez-Lopez. (2006). *The Oyez Project at IIT Chicago-Kent College of Law: A Multimedia Archive of the Supreme Court of the United States.* Available at http://www.oyez.org/cases/2000-2009/2005/2005_05_352

United States v. Jones. (2012). *The Oyez Project at IIT Chicago-Kent College of Law: A Multimedia Archive of the Supreme Court of the United States.* Available at http://www.oyez.org/cases/2010-2019/2011/2011_10_1259

Warden v. Hayden. (1967). *Legal Information Institute.* Available at http://www.law.cornell.edu/supct/html/historics/USSC_CR_0387_0294_ZS.html

Chapter 6

Bernstein, C., & Woodward, B. (1974). *All the president's men.* New York: Simon & Schuster.

Branzburg v. Hayes. (1972). *The Oyez Project at IIT Chicago-Kent College of Law: A Multimedia Archive of the Supreme Court of the United States.* Available at http://www.oyez.org/cases/1970-1979/1971/1971_70_85

Chapter 7

Brady v. Maryland. (1963). *The Oyez Project at IIT Chicago-Kent College of Law: A Multimedia Archive of the Supreme Court of the United States.* Available at http://www.oyez.org/cases/1960-1969/1962/1962_490

Chandler v. Florida. (1981). *The Oyez Project at IIT Chicago-Kent College of Law: A Multimedia Archive of the Supreme Court of the United States.* Available at http://www.oyez.org/cases/1980-1989/1980/1980_79_1260

Estes v. Texas. (1965). *The Oyez Project at IIT Chicago-Kent College of Law: A Multimedia Archive of the Supreme Court of the United States.* Available at http://holmes.oyez.org/cases/1960-1969/1964/1964_256

Jencks v. United States, 353 U.S. 657 (1957). *Justia U.S. Supreme Court Center.* Available at http://supreme.justia.com/cases/federal/us/353/657/

Radio Television Digital News Association (RTDNA). (n.d.). Freedom of Information. Cameras in the court: A state-by-state guide. Available at http://www.rtdna.org/pages/media_items/cameras-in-the-court-a-state-by-state-guide55.php

Reporters Committee for Freedom of the Press. (n.d.). *Secret justice: access to juror questionnaires.* Available at http://www.rcfp.org/secret-justice-access-juror-questionnaires

Sheppard v. Maxwell. (1966). *The Oyez Project at IIT Chicago-Kent College of Law: A Multimedia Archive of the Supreme Court of the United States.* Available at http://holmes.oyez.org/cases/1960-1969/1965/1965_490

Stuntz, W. J. (2011). *The collapse of American criminal justice.* Cambridge, Mass.: Belknap Press of Harvard University Press.

Chapter 8

Blakely v. Washington. (2004). *The Oyez Project at IIT Chicago-Kent College of Law: A Multimedia Archive of the Supreme Court of the United States.* Available at http://www.oyez.org/cases/2000-2009/2003/2003_02_1632/

Bronner, E. (2012, July 2). Poor land in jail as companies add huge fees for probation. *New York Times.* Available at http://www.nytimes.com/2012/07/03/us/probation-fees-multiply-as-companies-profit.html?ref=ethanbronner

Chanenson, S. L., & Berman, D. A. (2007, June). Federal cocaine sentencing in transition. *Federal Sentencing Reporter*, *19*(5), 291–296.

Haque, F. (2010, November 5). DOJ official: Fraud sentencing guidelines need an update. *Main Justice: Politics, Policy and the Law*. Available at http://www.mainjustice.com/2010/11/05/doj-official-fraud-sentencing-guidelines-need-an-update/

Locy, T. (1998, Oct. 1). A crime with little punishment; many embezzlers avoid jail, but few repay what they stole. *Washington Post*. Page 1.

Maclean, P. A. (2008, December 1). Circuit split deepens over jury bias issue. *Law.com: Legal News, Technology, In-House Counsel, & Small Firms Legal Resources*. Available at http://www.law.com/jsp/law/LawArticleFriendly.jsp?id=1202426262024&slreturn=1

Markowitz, A. (2001). Jury secrecy during deliberations. *Yale Law Journal*, *110*(8), 1493–1530.

Pell v. Procunier. (1974). The Oyez Project at IIT Chicago-Kent College of Law: A Multimedia Archive of the Supreme Court of the United States. Available at http://www.oyez.org/cases/1970-1979/1973/1973_73_918

Pew Center on the States. (2008). One in 100: Behind bars in America 2008. Pew Center on the States, Research and State Policy Initiatives. Available at http://www.pewtrusts.org/uploadedFiles/wwwpewtrustsorg/Reports/sentencing_and_corrections/one_in_100.pdf

Ruprecht, C. H. (1997). Are verdicts, too, like sausages? Lifting the cloak of jury secrecy. *University of Pennsylvania Law Review*, *146*(1), 217–267.

Stuntz, W. J. (2011). *The collapse of American criminal justice*. Cambridge, Mass.: Belknap Press of Harvard University Press.

Tanner v. United States. (1987). The Oyez Project at IIT Chicago-Kent College of Law: A Multimedia Archive of the Supreme Court of the United States. Available at http://www.oyez.org/cases/1980-1989/1986/1986_86_177/

Turner v. Louisiana. (1965). The Oyez Project at IIT Chicago-Kent College of Law: A Multimedia Archive of the Supreme Court of the United States. Available at http://www.oyez.org/cases/1960-1969/1964/1964_53

United States v. O'Brien. (1968). The Oyez Project at IIT Chicago-Kent College of Law: A Multimedia Archive of the Supreme Court of the United States. Available at http://www.oyez.org/cases/1960-1969/1967/1967_232

Chapter 9

Blackstone, W. (1979). *Commentaries on the laws of England*. Chicago, Ill.: University of Chicago Press.

BMW v. Gore (1995). The Oyez Project at IIT Chicago-Kent College of Law: A Multimedia Archive of the Supreme Court of the United States. Available at http://www.oyez.org/cases/1990-1999/1995/1995_94_896

Cipollone v. Liggett Group, 505 U.S. 504 (1992). *LII: Legal Information Institute*. Available at http://www.law.cornell.edu/supct/html/90-1038.ZS.html

Cooper Industries v. Leatherman Tool Grp. (2001). The Oyez Project at IIT Chicago-Kent College of Law: A Multimedia Archive of the Supreme Court of the United States. Available at http://www.oyez.org/cases/2000-2009/2000/2000_99_2035

Galligan Jr., T. C. (2005). U.S. Supreme Court tort reform: Limiting state power to articulate and develop its own tort law—defamation, preemption and punitive damages. *Bepress Legal Series*, *74*(702), 1189–1274. Available at http://law.bepress.com/expresso/eps/702/

Honda Motor Co. v. Oberg, 512 U.S. 415 (1994). *LII: Legal Information Institute*. Available at http://www.law.cornell.edu/supct/html/93-644.ZS.html

State Farm Mutual Auto Ins. Co. v. Campbell. (2003). The Oyez Project at IIT Chicago-Kent College of Law: A Multimedia Archive of the Supreme Court of the United States. Available at http://www.oyez.org/cases/2000-2009/2002/2002_01_1289

Chapter 10

Bourgeois v. Peters, 02-16886 - U.S. 11th Circuit Case Summary. (2004). *FindLaw Caselaw*. Available at http://caselaw.findlaw.com/summary/opinion/us-11th-circuit/2004/10/15/126193.html

Locy, T. (2004, Nov. 3). Detainees' cases show another side of Gitmo. *USA Today*. Available at http://www.usatoday.com/news/nation/2004-11-03-gitmo-detainees_x.htm

Nebraska Press Association v. Stuart. (1976.) *The Oyez Project at IIT Chicago-Kent College of Law: A Multimedia Archive of the Supreme Court of the United States*. Available at http://www.oyez.org/cases/1970-1979/1975/1975_75_817

Press-Enterprise Co. v. Superior Court. (1986). *The Oyez Project at IIT Chicago-Kent College of Law: A Multimedia Archive of the Supreme Court of the United States*. Available at http://www.oyez.org/cases/1980-1989/1985/1985_84_1560

Press-Enterprise Co. v. Superior Court of California. (1984). *The Oyez Project at IIT Chicago-Kent College of Law: A Multimedia Archive of the Supreme Court of the United States*. Available at http://www.oyez.org/cases/1980-1989/1983/1983_82_556

Reporters Committee for Freedom of the Press. (n.d.). *Secret justice: Anonymous juries*. Available at http://www.rcfp.org/secret-justice-anonymous-juries/survey-law

Richard Scrushy: Prelude to trial. (n.d.). *Report from Birmingham*. Available at http://www.scrushy-report.com/rsprelude.html

Richmond Newspapers, Inc. v. Virginia. (1980). *LII: Legal Information Institute*. Available at http://www.law.cornell.edu/supct/html/historics/USSC_CR_0448_0555_ZS.html

Chapter 11

Bassiouni, M. C. (2004). Terrorism: The persistent dilemma of legitimacy. *Case Western Reserve Journal of International Law, 36*(2 & 3), 299–306.

Boumediene v. Bush. (2008). *The Oyez Project at IIT Chicago-Kent College of Law: A Multimedia Archive of the Supreme Court of the United States*. Available at http://www.oyez.org/cases/2000-2009/2007/2007_06_1195

Ex parte Milligan. (1866). *The Oyez Project at IIT Chicago-Kent College of Law: A Multimedia Archive of the Supreme Court of the United States*. Available at http://www.oyez.org/cases/1851-1900/1865/1865_0

Ex parte Quirin. (1942). *The Oyez Project at IIT Chicago-Kent College of Law: A Multimedia Archive of the Supreme Court of the United States*. Available at http://www.oyez.org/cases/1940-1949/1941/1941_1_ORIG

Ex parte Vallandigham. (1864). *The Oyez Project at IIT Chicago-Kent College of Law: A Multimedia Archive of the Supreme Court of the United States*. Available at http://www.oyez.org/cases/1851-1900/1863/1863_2/

Fine, G. (2003, June). DOJ/OIG Special Reports. *The September 11 detainees: A review of the treatment of aliens held on immigration charges in connection with the investigation of the September 11 attacks*. Available at http://www.justice.gov/ oig/special/0306/index.htm

Hamdan v. Rumsfeld. (2006). *The Oyez Project at IIT Chicago-Kent College of Law: A Multimedia Archive of the Supreme Court of the United States*. Available at http://www.oyez.org/cases/2000-2009/2005/2005_05_184

Hamdi v. Rumsfeld. (2004). *The Oyez Project at IIT Chicago-Kent College of Law: A Multimedia Archive of the Supreme Court of the United States*. Available at http://www.oyez.org/cases/2000-2009/2003/2003_03_6696

In re Yamashita, 327 U.S. 1 (1946). *Justia U.S. Supreme Court Center*. Available at http://supreme.justia.com/cases/federal/us/327/1/case.html

Johnson v. Eisentrager, 339 U.S. 763 (1950). *Justia U.S. Supreme Court Center*. Available at http://supreme.justia.com/cases/federal/us/339/763/

Liu, E. C. (2009, May 28). The State Secrets Privilege and other limits on litigation involving classified information. *Open CRS*. Available at http://opencrs.com/document/R40603/

Locy, T. (2004, May 27). Interrogators hid identities. *USA Today*. Available at http://www.usatoday.com/news/world/iraq/2004-05-27-cover-abuse_x.htm

McCarthy, A. C. (2004). Terrorism on trial: The trials of al Qaeda. *Case Western Reserve Journal of International Law, 36*(2 & 3), 513–527.

People v. Defore. (1926). Criminal procedures: Cases, statutes and executive materials, Wake Forest University. Available at http://www.wfu.edu/~wrightrf/Aspen-Students/additionalreading_ch06-1.htm

Rasul v. Bush. (2004). *The Oyez Project at IIT Chicago-Kent College of Law: A Multimedia Archive of the Supreme Court of the United States*. Available at http://www.oyez.org/cases/2000-2009/2003/2003_03_334/

Reporters Committee for Freedom of the Press. (n.d.). *A reporter's guide to military justice*. Available at http://www.rcfp.org/reporters-guide-military-justice

Reynolds v. United States. (1953). *The Oyez Project at IIT Chicago-Kent College of Law: A Multimedia Archive of the Supreme Court of the United States.* Available at http://www.oyez.org/cases/1950-1959/1952/1952_21/

Tenet v. Doe. (2005). *The Oyez Project at IIT Chicago-Kent College of Law: A Multimedia Archive of the Supreme Court of the United States.* Available at http://www.oyez.org/cases/2000-2009/2004/2004_03_1395

Totten v. United States, 92 U.S. 105 (1875). *Justia U.S. Supreme Court Center.* Available at http://supreme.justia.com/cases/federal/us/92/105/

Weaver, W. G., & Pallitto, R. M. (2005). State secrets and executive power. *Political Science Quarterly,* 120(1), 85–112.

Chapter 12

Batson v. Kentucky. (1986). *The Oyez Project at IIT Chicago-Kent College of Law: A Multimedia Archive of the Supreme Court of the United States.* Available at http://www.oyez.org/cases/1980-1989/1985/1985_84_6263/

Bowers v. Hardwick. (1986). *The Oyez Project at IIT Chicago-Kent College of Law: A Multimedia Archive of the Supreme Court of the United States.* Available at http://www.oyez.org/cases/1980-1989/1985/1985_85_140

Brady v. Maryland. (1963). *The Oyez Project at IIT Chicago-Kent College of Law: A Multimedia Archive of the Supreme Court of the United States.* Available at http://www.oyez.org/cases/1960-1969/1962/1962_490

Brandenburg v. Ohio. (1969). *The Oyez Project at IIT Chicago-Kent College of Law: A Multimedia Archive of the Supreme Court of the United States.* Available at http://www.oyez.org/cases/1960-1969/1968/1968_492

Brown v. Board of Education (I). (1954). *The Oyez Project at IIT Chicago-Kent College of Law: A Multimedia Archive of the Supreme Court of the United States.* Available at http://www.oyez.org/cases/1950-1959/1952/1952_1/

Chaplinsky v. State of New Hampshire. (1942). *The Oyez Project at IIT Chicago-Kent College of Law: A Multimedia Archive of the Supreme Court of the United States.* Available at http://www.oyez.org/cases/1940-1949/1941/1941_255

Civil Rights Cases. (1883). *The Oyez Project at IIT Chicago-Kent College of Law: A Multimedia Archive of the Supreme Court of the United States.* Available at http://www.oyez.org/cases/1851-1900/1882/1882_2

Dennis v. United States. (1951). *The Oyez Project at IIT Chicago-Kent College of Law: A Multimedia Archive of the Supreme Court of the United States.* Available at http://www.oyez.org/cases/1950-1959/1950/1950_336

Dred Scott v. Sandford. (1857). *The Oyez Project at IIT Chicago-Kent College of Law: A Multimedia Archive of the Supreme Court of the United States.* Available at http://www.oyez.org/cases/1851-1900/1856/1856_0/

Fletcher v. Peck. (1810). *The Oyez Project at IIT Chicago-Kent College of Law: A Multimedia Archive of the Supreme Court of the United States.* Available at http://www.oyez.org/cases/1792-1850/1810/1810_0/

Furman v. Georgia. (1972). *The Oyez Project at IIT Chicago-Kent College of Law: A Multimedia Archive of the Supreme Court of the United States.* Available at http://www.oyez.org/cases/1970-1979/1971/1971_69_5003

Gideon v. Wainwright. (1963). *The Oyez Project at IIT Chicago-Kent College of Law: A Multimedia Archive of the Supreme Court of the United States.* http://www.oyez.org/cases/1960-1969/1962/1962_155/

Gregg v. Georgia. (1976). *The Oyez Project at IIT Chicago-Kent College of Law: A Multimedia Archive of the Supreme Court of the United States.* Available at http://www.oyez.org/cases/1970-1979/1975/1975_74_6257

Griswold v. Connecticut. (1965). *The Oyez Project at IIT Chicago-Kent College of Law: A Multimedia Archive of the Supreme Court of the United States.* Available at http://www.oyez.org/cases/1960-1969/1964/1964_496

International Society for Krishna Consciousness v. Lee. (1993). *FindLaw: Cases and Codes.* Available at http://caselaw.lp.findlaw.com/scripts/getcase.pl?navby=search&court=US&case=/us/505/672.html

Jencks v. United States, 353 U.S. 657 (1957). *Justia U.S. Supreme Court Center.* Available at http://supreme.justia.com/cases/federal/us/353/657/

Korematsu v. United States. (1944). *The Oyez Project at IIT Chicago-Kent College of Law: A Multimedia Archive of the Supreme Court of the United States.* Available at http://www.oyez.org/cases/1940-1949/1944/1944_22

Lawrence and Garner v. Texas. (2003). *The Oyez Project at IIT Chicago-Kent College of Law: A Multimedia Archive of the Supreme Court of the United States.* Available at http://www.oyez.org/cases/2000-2009/2002/2002_02_102

Lewis, A. (2007). *Freedom for the thought that we hate: A biography of the First Amendment.* New York: Basic Books.

Lochner v. New York. (1905). *The Oyez Project at IIT Chicago-Kent College of Law: A Multimedia Archive of the Supreme Court of the United States.* Available at http://www.oyez.org/cases/1901-1939/1904/1904_292

Lovell v. City of Griffin, 303 U.S. 444 (1938). *Justia U.S. Supreme Court Center.* Available at http://supreme.justia.com/cases/federal/us/303/444/case.html

Madison, J. (1788). The Federalist #51: The structure of the government must furnish the proper checks and balances between the different departments. *Independent Journal.* Available at http://www.constitution.org/fed/federa51.htm

Mapp v. Ohio. (1961). *The Oyez Project at IIT Chicago-Kent College of Law: A Multimedia Archive of the Supreme Court of the United States.* Available at http://www.oyez.org/cases/1960-1969/1960/1960_236

Marbury v. Madison. (1803). *The Oyez Project at IIT Chicago-Kent College of Law: A Multimedia Archive of the Supreme Court of the United States.* Available at http://www.oyez.org/cases/1792-1850/1803/1803_0/

McCulloch v. Maryland. (1819). *The Oyez Project at IIT Chicago-Kent College of Law: A Multimedia Archive of the Supreme Court of the United States.* Available at http://www.oyez.org/cases/1792-1850/1819/1819_0/

Miranda v. Arizona. (1966). *The Oyez Project at IIT Chicago-Kent College of Law: A Multimedia Archive of the Supreme Court of the United States.* Available at http://www.oyez.org/cases/1960-1969/1965/1965_759/

National Federation of Independent Business et al. v. Sebelius. (2012). Supreme Court of the United States. Available at http://www.supremecourt.gov/opinions/11pdf/11-393c3a2.pdf

National Socialist Party of America v. Village of Skokie. (1977). *FindLaw: Cases and Codes.* Available at http://caselaw.lp.findlaw.com/cgi-bin/getcase.pl?court=us&vol=432&invol=43

Plessy v. Ferguson. (1896). *The Oyez Project at IIT Chicago-Kent College of Law: A Multimedia Archive of the Supreme Court of the United States.* Available at http://www.oyez.org/cases/1851-1900/1895/1895_210

Roe v. Wade. (1973). *LII: Legal Information Institute.* Available at http://www.law.cornell.edu/supct/html/historics/USSC_CR_0410_0113_ZS.html

Romer v. Evans. (1996). *The Oyez Project at IIT Chicago-Kent College of Law: A Multimedia Archive of the Supreme Court of the United States.* Available at http://www.oyez.org/cases/1990-1999/1995/1995_94_1039

Schenck v. United States. (1919). *The Oyez Project at IIT Chicago-Kent College of Law: A Multimedia Archive of the Supreme Court of the United States.* Available at http://www.oyez.org/cases/1901-1939/1918/1918_437

Strickland v. Washington. (1984). *The Oyez Project at IIT Chicago-Kent College of Law: A Multimedia Archive of the Supreme Court of the United States.* Available at http://www.oyez.org/cases/1980-1989/1983/1983_82_1554

Terry v. Ohio. (1968). *The Oyez Project at IIT Chicago-Kent College of Law: A Multimedia Archive of the Supreme Court of the United States.* Available at http://www.oyez.org/cases/1960-1969/1967/1967_67

United States v. Booker. (2005). *The Oyez Project at IIT Chicago-Kent College of Law: A Multimedia Archive of the Supreme Court of the United States.* Available at http://www.oyez.org/cases/2000-2009/2004/2004_04_104/

United States v. O'Brien. (1968). *The Oyez Project at IIT Chicago-Kent College of Law: A Multimedia Archive of the Supreme Court of the United States.* Available at http://www.oyez.org/cases/1960-1969/1967/1967_232

Yates v. United States. (1957). *The Oyez Project at IIT Chicago-Kent College of Law: A Multimedia Archive of the Supreme Court of the United States.* Available at http://www.oyez.org/cases/1950-1959/1956/1956_6

Yick Wo v. Hopkins. (1886). *The Oyez Project at IIT Chicago-Kent College of Law: A Multimedia Archive of the Supreme Court of the United States.* Available at http://www.oyez.org/cases/1851-1900/1886/1886_0

Youngstown Sheet & Tube Co. v. Sawyer. (1952). *The Oyez Project at IIT Chicago-Kent College of Law: A Multimedia Archive of the Supreme Court of the United States.* Available at http://www.oyez.org/cases/1950-1959/1951/1951_744

Index